WRITING OF THE FORMLESS

Sara Guyer and Brian McGrath, series editors

Lit Z embraces models of criticism uncontained by conventional notions of history, periodicity, and culture, and committed to the work of reading. Books in the series may seem untimely, anachronistic, or out of touch with contemporary trends because they have arrived too early or too late. Lit Z creates a space for books that exceed and challenge the tendencies of our field and in doing so reflect on the concerns of literary studies here and abroad.

At least since Friedrich Schlegel, thinking that affirms literature's own untimeliness has been named romanticism. Recalling this history, Lit Z exemplifies the survival of romanticism as a mode of contemporary criticism, as well as forms of contemporary criticism that demonstrate the unfulfilled possibilities of romanticism. Whether or not they focus on the romantic period, books in this series epitomize romanticism as a way of thinking that compels another relation to the present. Lit Z is the first book series to take seriously this capacious sense of romanticism.

In 1977, Paul de Man and Geoffrey Hartman, two scholars of romanticism, team-taught a course called Literature Z that aimed to make an intervention into the fundamentals of literary study. Hartman and de Man invited students to read a series of increasingly difficult texts and through attention to language and rhetoric compelled them to encounter "the bewildering variety of ways such texts could be read." The series' conceptual resonances with that class register the importance of recollection, reinvention, and reading to contemporary criticism. Its books explore the creative potential of reading's untimeliness and history's enigmatic force.

WRITING OF THE FORMLESS

José Lezama Lima and the End of Time

—+—

Jaime Rodríguez Matos

Fordham University Press

New York   2017

THIS BOOK IS MADE POSSIBLE BY A COLLABORATIVE GRANT
FROM THE ANDREW W. MELLON FOUNDATION.

Library of Congress Cataloging-in-Publication Data available online at catalog.loc.gov.

Printed in the United States of America

19 18 17   5 4 3 2 1

First edition

for María Dolores, Marcos, and Julia

Contents

What is there and not there, what appears and disappears, needs a place of protection out beyond the Pillars of Hercules.

—José Lezama Lima, "Confluencias"

Introduction

The dislocation of form and content: I take my epigraph from a piece
in which Brett Levinson reviews the state of the Latinamericanist field
in recent years. He emphasizes the extent to which scholarship on Latin
America has been fundamentally defined by the need to point to or show
phenomena that are most essentially characterized by the lack of graspable
form, or formlessness, if by form we understand Western schemata meant
to determine universally what is and is not thinkable, and more generally,
what can and should be and what falls beneath the dignity of Being. In
reference to the subaltern, he explains in more detail what is at issue in the
dislocation of form and content that the epigraph thematizes. The subaltern
space/time is often represented "as a grumble, murmur, or shout that, not
unlike [the sublime . . .], refuses submission to the Symbolic Order" (70).
Understood as any discourse that speaks for or in the name of Latin America—in the same sense that Orientalism produced "knowledge" of the
Orient for the West—the paradox of Latinamericanism is that its "object"
is defined as an excessive *figure*.

The persistence of this paradox is remarkable, for it can be tracked
through the various historical turns in academic paradigms. Allow me to
illustrate this point by way of a brief description of the shift from the literary and philological methodology that defined the field until the 1990s to
the model of cultural, historical, and political interpretation that ensued. If
the fiction of Vargas Llosa, Cortázar, Borges, García Márquez, and Lezama
Lima, among others, was mediated by the high-aesthetic framework, those
authors were nevertheless posited as the transgression of the western fron-
tier of understandability, as the murmur from the other's mouth itself.

As a category of world literature, Latin America's "Boom" has been the writing of the formless from its inception. To take but two examples of the same critical move regarding the work of Lezama Lima: in the famous collection *Latin America in Its Literature* we are told that "in the hands of Lezama Lima, the novel loses its ground [se desfonda] . . . and after its very slow fall, it begins to move underneath the formless and nameless cover of a collective beast" (Alegría 247).[1] And Emir Rodríguez Monegal, one of the most important voices in the canonization of the Boom as a whole, called Lezama's *Paradiso* "a moment of complete poetic freedom" and attributed this to the fact that, as a book, it was "without measure and formless" (134; desmesurado e informe). The absolute freedom and the collective beast involved in these two descriptions are an index of the political import of the literature in question.

Were we to take the reemergence of the category of the sublime in the second half of the twentieth century, when it became necessary in order to make sense of the art forms that emerge in that period, we would think that the literary production of the marginal world of societies in development and dependency were by this very condition the vanguard of post-modern art.[2] Within Latinamericanism, the postmodern debate was also, and in an important sense, the framework through which the question of postcoloniality and subalternism first came to the fore (Beverley, Oviedo, and Aronna). Yet, by the mid-1990s, the question of the postmodern was immensely more complicated. Not only had the facile distinction between center and periphery lost ground as a tool for understanding the reality of capitalism, but also the term "postmodernity" itself had undergone a shift from a celebratory and transgressive name for things in the world to a periodizing category with which to read contemporary global history. The shift was not only a conceptual one; it was intricately connected with the crisis of Marxism and of the Left in more general terms. To simplify matters, once the monolithic subject of history assumed by the Marxist legacy was untenable, it became imperative to identify lesser-formed and more "sublime" figures that would take on the work of political trans-formation. With this, the people, as a sign of minor and heterogeneous identitarian subject positions, came to be opposed to the People, under-stood as the homogeneous and ideologically conservative answer to the proletariat. Without the worker and without the monolingual and cultur-ally homogeneous image of the national body politic, the political field opened toward a diverse group of subjects that did not necessarily cohere or form a seamless whole. Ernesto Laclau, the Argentine political theorist whose work on hegemony came to be of immense value at this juncture (precisely because it offered a way of making sense of that heterogeneity within the confines of a clearly graspable political agency), would come to give this multiplicity the name of "the people" (cf. *On Populist Reason*).

Even as today we see some of the critics who most ardently argued the case of subalternism declaring its end (e.g., Beverley, *Latinamericanism*), what I would argue is that Levinson's piece, which dates from 2007, was prescient in detecting the return of the people as the true target of much of what seemed to be the most radical political theory Latinamericanism had produced until that point in its history. For it is this category of the people, now as a heterogeneous and multiple force represented by the nation-state, that makes "postsubalternism" possible today (cf. Beverley, *Latinamericanism* 58–59). It is as if the crisis of Marxism, and of the Left on a global scale, led directly to the founding question of a revolutionary modernity that was supposedly a thing of the past: how to represent the people as the embodiment of the principle of sovereignty once the unitary and universal body of the king, which incarnated it, was no longer available for the task? Levinson sums up the issue with remarkable clarity:

> The people, in this view, is the historical nineteenth-century marker neither
> of progress nor of underdevelopment but of the state's undeviating, thereby
> ahistorical, essence. . . . [A] subalternist reinvention of the people would . . .
> "seek to articulate the people as historical bloc. . . . the people (and so,
> too, the nation) is itself internally assured, heterogeneous, multiple. The
> people-multitude or people-as-many would be the egalitarian imaginary
> inherent in multicultural heterogeneity" [Beverley]. . . . Latin American
> subaltern studies, we can therefore argue, does not offer a "study of actual
> subalterns" because its task is to invent a "people" who would effect within
> globalization what the Latin American "people" of the nineteenth century
> could not. The oppressed . . . and the people would operate as agents of the
> most sublime irruption . . . , to wit, revolution. As it turns out, the signifier
> without signified . . . is the unidentified din of a people-to-come, agents of a
> soon-to-be-true global revolt. ("Globalizing Paradigms" 71)

For my own purposes, what I want to underscore is that even if subalternism, along with other forms of Latinamericanism of the same historical moment, can manage to avoid the task of producing a political subject (in the classical sense that orthodox Marxism gave to the term), it nevertheless becomes entangled in the wider problem of how to represent such a heterogeneity: this is a problem that, paradoxically, is not endemic to its "field" of study. The moment the discourse on/of/from Latin America proposes to think through this notion of the people, the question it broaches is linked to the modern problematic of how to represent something that cannot take on any one particular objective form. However much Latinamericanism rejects or avoids dealing with the absence of its object of knowledge, which cannot for that very reason be located, once this notion of the people comes to the foreground, it is also entangled in a very long and very modern problematic vis-à-vis what Eric Santner has called the excarnated principle of sovereignty in the era of revolutions (92). It becomes impossible to avoid thinking the interrelations between the arts, politics, theology, and philosophy—all of which are regions that much of the same modern tradition that is at stake here, up to and including Latinamericanism, wants to see as autonomous spheres.

It is not uncommon to understand the advent of modern(ist) art in tandem with the political shift from the king to the people as the "body" that incarnates the principle of sovereignty. The central event in this regard is the French Revolution. The question is how to represent the general will without turning its incarnation into yet another representation of the monarch. In a recent book on precisely these questions, Eric Santner explains: "The task was to put forth a body that would . . . incarnate the now empty place of the king . . . [,] to incarnate in some ostensibly new way the excarnated principle of sovereignty" (92). Santner is in part recasting the views of T. J. Clark, who in his *Farewell to the History of an Idea* makes the point that the task in question is formally impossible: the "body" that had to be represented could not take on the form of an empirical or actually existing object without, at the same time, investing it with an aura that the new principle of sovereignty was meant to interrupt. The impasse had the effect of illuminating the role of representation as a technology of power. From that premise, Santner takes the following leap: "The history of European art from this point on was in some sense dedicated to the task of *figuring out abstraction*, this eventful opening onto the nonfigurative" (94).

In this reading, the history of abstraction is tied to the need to give form to something that is present only as a void. This emptiness is not only the void that is left with the closure of one mode of politics and the tentative beginnings of a different order. It is also the presentation of the absent foundations of politics as such, the paradoxical appearance of the lack at the heart of historical change, the absent foundation of history as a whole. If there were no such lack, change would be impossible, as it would mean that a particular historical configuration has a point that sutures it to a stable, eternal, and atemporal ontological bedrock. Thus, it is important to note that when Santner makes the point about abstraction, we are not broaching the question of the possibility of an event but the rather more complicated issue of the substitution of one precarious and contingent foundation by another.

This problem is tackled by adopting Clark's conclusions regarding one of the first major paintings of that moment of transition: Jacques-Louis David's *Death of Marat* (1793). In this work, according to Clark and Santner, the upper half, which is a dark representation of empty or negative space, is assumed by the two critics to stand in for the impossibility of representing the people. This void suddenly has the paradoxical charge of a positive and even oppressive objectivity—it is not the people but the impossibility of its representation, an impossibility that exposes painting to itself as mere technique. The upper half of David's painting is also, and above all, a representation of painting as a way of achieving effects with color and composition (Santner 93).

Though I have some objections, which I will outline in what follows, I find Santner's demarche illuminating on a number of points. By opening the question of the body that incarnates the principle of sovereignty to the larger problem of its artistic representability, he is able to establish very useful links across a number of theoretical questions, all of which are intricately linked historically but often treated as separate problems for separate academic disciplines. He shows to what extent the question of the desire to name the unnameable, to represent the unrepresentable—all of which could easily be relegated to a question of romantic or modernist aesthetics—is, in fact, a more complex field of tensions linking politics and aesthetics with the hope of resolving the deadlocks of modernity as a whole. He also points out to what extent psychoanalysis has a bearing on this problem, and precisely as a framework with which to explain the emergence of a regulative formational pressure that is no longer politically exerted from without but is instead at the very heart of the political subject. This is his entry into the debate on biopolitics: that moment when "the bodies of the citizens of modern nation-states take on a surplus element, one that . . . introduces into immanence an excess it cannot fully close in upon" (98). Biopolitics, for Santner, works in the same way as the upper half of David's *Death of Marat*. That "dense painterly agitation" indicates to what extent every citizen answers to a substance that is his or her own responsibility, "not as the supernatural aura surrounding a few crowned heads . . . but rather under a series of new and in some sense more 'democratic' names" (99). And further: "Modernist artists stand under the compulsion to respond to the ever-ramifying biopolitical pressures generated by the displacement of the king—and the practices of picture-making sponsored, in some fashion by the political theology of his representative corporality—by the 'people' in the wake of the French Revolution" (103).

Whether it is Marx's fetish character of the commodity, in the technical sense of its theological niceties, the emergence of pure abstraction, or the rise of fiction increasingly concerned with monsters, the undead, and the revenant—what is at issue is the possibility of imagining the invisible and ectoplasmic nature of this substance that inhabits the subject of modernity. And, for Santner, phantasmagoria and biopolitics are two different sides of the same modern event: the moment when the flesh of the sovereign is no longer located in the king but is, paradoxically, both excarnated and made to appear in the (nonexistent and unrepresentable) "body" of the people (100).

Thus, another important point to make regarding Santner's argument is that he is interested in producing a new way of reading modernism that is not simply against the grain—which would only be an academic occlusion of what is actually at stake here—but is a way of thinking through the status of the sovereign and its principle in all its historical complexity. This is the reason why Santner points out that Bataille's writings on formlessness cannot be separated from his concerns regarding a sovereignty that was more sovereign than the sovereignty of the master itself, which is to say a sovereignty that was no longer simply a retelling of the master-slave dialectic as imagined by Hegel (and which Bataille, in turn, saw as the essential pattern at the heart of Marxism). Bataille's project, centered around the journal *Acéphale*, can then be read as a further and more radical step in the "drama of sovereignty" in biopolitical times (104). Lacan's relationship with Bataille is significant in this regard, for it is the discourse of the analyst itself that comes closest to the debasement that is at issue in Bataille's *informe*.[3] But that is as far as the link between Bataille and Lacan can go, at least according to Santner.

The disagreement is most evident when it comes to the kind of (non) inscription within the symbolic order that Bataille's "scatological" conception of materialism seems to espouse. Against the desire for liberation through an "ecstatic passage beyond the symbolic order" (107), what Santner is interested in pointing out is that it is the very formless and debased matter of the subject, his or her own flesh, that harbors the symbolic, imaginary, and real aspects of sovereignty today (140). But this is to underscore that (despite the passage through the scatological discourse of the analyst, despite the focus on the formless mass where sovereignty is located) what is at issue in his reading is to delimit this kind of base materialism, which is always on the lookout and ready to decapitate anything that resembles the head of the sovereign. Base materialism, horizontality, entropy, pulse, and the formless as such "can never give rise to a renewed and reconfigured engagement with the forms and locations of normative pressure that define the symbolic order of modern societies" (138). The implications of this limitation are extreme; for what is thus sacrificed is nothing less than the ability to engage with the actual historicity of modern art in all its manifestations and, perhaps more important, the ability to identify the political theology that is further strengthened in the process, even as it is exactly the theologico-political that the partisans of the formless want to depose.[4]

It is difficult to leave unremarked the ambiguous position in which this leaves Santner. On the one hand, the new sovereign principle is itself formless, ectoplasmic, lacking a concrete body except the body of each and every subject in all the heterogeneity and multiplicity this entails; on the other, this formlessness as such cannot engage in a politically productive manner with the symbolic order of modern societies. The formless as transgression only manages to decapitate the sovereign, and since the sovereign is the head on that body itself, this amounts to something like a suicide. Hence the need to allude to a different stratum of the political, one in which it is not the formless that operates but the symbolic order that takes advantage of that failed transgression/suicide. It is as if formlessness was only for the people, while somewhere, some *thing*, beyond and above the people, manages to escape the reach of that excessive substance that haunts the plane of immanence. The biopolitical ghostly substance of sovereignty is put forth in tandem with an equally excessive and unfigurable outside that is immune to it. This would no longer be a question of a nontranscendental excess within immanence. Rather, it would entail the reinscription of a dictatorial sovereign as the mark of the symbolic order of modernity itself. What is at issue here, I would like to suggest, is not so much a more complicated image of modernity but a limitation regarding the engagement with the formless—and the question leads straight to the founding moment of psychoanalysis itself. I delve further into this not with the aim of circumscribing my argument to a differend with psychoanalysis (for I find the later elucidation on the *sinthome* to be of great import for my general take on these issues), but because it will offer a way into the question of antifoundationalism.

In his own considerations on Bataille's *informe*, Georges Didi-Huberman, who is oddly absent from Santner's analysis, has pointed out that the identification of flesh and the formless is at the center of an early Lacan for whom "the foundation of things" is the "flesh one never sees"; the "flesh inasmuch as it is suffering, is formless, inasmuch as its form in itself is something which provokes anxiety"—the closest and most intimate is also the furthest and strangest: "You are this, which is so far from you, this which is the most *informe*" (Lacan 154–55, translation modified). The topic under discussion is Freud's interpretation of the dream of Irma's injection, and the emergence of anxiety.[5] Lacan underscores this foundational quality when he has Freud ask: "How well-founded is my therapy of neurosis?" (157). The foundation is certainly achieved: the dream is a search for the signification of the dream, a quest for "signification as such" (160). And the answer finally comes: "There is no other word of the dream than the very nature of the symbolic" (160). The symbolic appears as the general zone where subjectivity comes to be: "As soon as true speech emerges, mediating, it turns them into two very different subjects from what they were prior to speech. This means that they only start being constituted as subjects of speech once speech exists, and there is no before" (160).

Yet, there is a before, and Lacan himself points it out. It is not the *informe*, for it never appears as such in the texts in question, which are too obsessively concerned with the possibility of finding a secure ground for psychoanalysis. What provokes anxiety is rather the form of the formless—it is this form and not the formless itself which first gives something to be interpreted. It is as if the representational void of the formless were more terrifying than the actual images with which it is represented. In its place, the abyss is covered over with images: Irma's mouth covered in a whitish membrane, the dirty injection of trimethylamine, and so forth.[6] In Freud's words, the abyss is still represented, as it is the issue of a woman who "opened her mouth properly" that proves to be "unplumbable—a navel . . . that is [the dream's] point of contact with the unknown," the point where "the dream-wish grows up, like a mushroom out of its mycelium" (Freud 143, 564). Freud and Lacan come to the conclusion that this was the foundation, the secure ground for their endeavors; there is a meaning—and it is from here that the enterprise departs. Nevertheless, it is, at the same time, a dream that is haunted by the decay and disintegration of that foundation, by the fact that a decision was made to avoid the groundless as the first "sense" of psychoanalysis.[7]

What "explains everything," according to Lacan, is the injection of trimethylamine:

> The dream does not only owe its meaning to Freud's research on the meaning of dreams. If he can continue to ask himself the question, it is because he asks himself if all of this communicates with Fliess, in whose elucidations trimethylamine plays a role in connection with the decomposition prod-

ucts of sexual substances. Indeed—I've made inquiries—trimethylamine is a decomposition product of sperm, and it gives it its ammoniacal smell when it's left to decompose in the air. The dream, which culminated a first time . . . with the horrific image I mentioned [Irma's open mouth], culminates a second time at the end with a formula [the chemical composition of trimethylamine] . . . on the wall, beyond what we cannot but identify as speech. (158)

Irma is injected not with semen but with that which in semen causes it to decompose when exposed to air. The decay at the heart of the foundation is already inscribed in the very element that represents the symbolic order for Lacan (the chemical formula for trimethylamine). Thus, the symbolic is marked from its first psychoanalytical instance as a contingent and impermanent ground. The fact that this scene was displaced by Santner (in his book it appears in a previous chapter and not in his engagement with the formless as a cypher for the people after the French Revolution) should give an indication of the complexity behind the decision to see the unrepresentability of the people, the principle of sovereignty, in the representation of negative space in David's painting. For there also, what is at stake is a way of avoiding the radical antifoundationalism that the Revolution exposes and displaces as soon as it comes to power. In both cases, in the foundation of psychoanalysis and in the events that follow the revolutionary sequence, what we see is the need to abstain from taking the abyss as the first evidence of a new configuration of thought. The consequences are significant.

In covering over the void in order to establish the new contingent foundation, the already decomposing foundation, that element that Santner claims exceeds the immanence of the revolutionary field (whether psychoanalytical or revolutionary) begins to look less like the interiorization of the sovereign principle as biopolitics and more like the command to care for an order that emerges in full awareness of its finitude: newly born, it is already decaying. The issue is not so much the shift of the sovereign principle from one body to another but, rather, the breaking down of sovereignty itself. And this breakdown is such that its effects are retroactive: what is exposed is that sovereignty was always a decrepit and decaying mass even prior to the revolution—sovereignty itself was always fundamentally formless. What is made impossible with this always already formless sovereign principle was supposed to be the movement upward, away from the muddy earth and into the atemporal realm of the eternal: such was the story that modernity told itself about the mythical emergence of sovereignty.[8] And the people, however heterogeneous and multiple, is one more image in the arsenal of images meant to cover over that gap in the foundation. Compared to the abyss, even the formless collective beast (like Irma's mouth) will prove less horrifying. Bataille's formless is a way of pointing out that there is the possibility, perhaps, of a politicity that sees in that movement toward the suprapolitical realm of the Idea the negation of politics as such—the possibility, that is, of a politicity of the infra, a sovereignty minimally different from the sovereign master-slave, one that is subjected to no-thing and that subjects no one to care for its senile and decrepit image of eternal glory.

Perhaps the most surprising aspect of recent writings on the idea of the formless, or the *informe*, is the predictably academic gesture of beginning with a definition. The procedure is a familiar one: the critic cites Bataille's entry on "informe" and moves on to a close reading of all its key elements.[9] Despite all the efforts one can make to emphasize the ironic and antidefinitional character of the text, when read in isolation or without regard for the rest of Bataille's oeuvre, it proves impossible to marshal that notion as anything but what it was meant to destabilize. The fact itself is proof of the efficacy of forms, of the predisposition to think only in terms of the formal stability that Bataille was questioning. For this reason, I find it more expedient in these introductory pages to begin explaining what I understand by my title not through a direct leap into the most familiar name associated with the formless, but with one of his most careful commentators. A gliding toward the secondary that already should be understood as part of the dislocating operation of the *informe*. This book takes as a point of departure the following description Jacques Derrida made of the writing of Georges Bataille, perhaps the single most important point of reference when it comes to the *informe* as an operative concept in contemporary debates on everything from abstract art to sovereignty in the era of biopolitics, moving through the history of psychoanalysis and the reception and critique of Marxism:

> *This* . . . writing will be called *writing* because it *exceeds* the *logos* (of meaning, lordship, presence, etc.). Within this writing—the one sought by Bataille— the *same* concepts, apparently unchanged in themselves, will be subject to a mutation of meaning, or rather will be struck by (even though they are apparently indifferent) the loss of sense toward which they slide, thereby ruining themselves immeasurably. . . . Bataille's writing . . . does not tolerate the distinction of form and content. Which makes it writing, and a requisite of sovereignty. (Derrida, *Writing and Difference* 267, italics in original)[10]

What is at issue here concerns Bataille's complicated relation to Hegel's thought. On the one hand, it is impossible to take Bataille, or Hegel, seriously and pluck out notions and concepts in order to apply them to objects of knowledge (in part because what is in question is the status of any such object in the first place); on the other hand, however, and here Bataille is no longer Hegelian, it would also be impossible to contextualize a notion like the formless by locating and making explicit the system where it would finally make sense (cf. Derrida, *Writing and Difference* 272–73, 253).[11] Thus, a first clarification: by writing what is meant here is precisely that kind of composition that unsettles the harmonious relation between something like form and something like content. But as such, this is not enough. As became clear from the opening remarks in relation to Levinson's text, it could be argued that Latin America as an object of study, in the most traditional academic sense of that term, is nothing but such a dislocation. Writing is what emerges when something that cannot be reduced to the ideality of a stable architectonics of things and their proper places makes its way into a textual apparatus. Yet the crux of the matter is not only that meaning is not conveyed in ways that are themselves formal—what is most important in this context is the inherent decomposition already at work in the architectonics of a text, the decay that has already begun to deform all the forms of thought and practice even before they are fully and finally constructed. "Form and time have an uneasy relationship," writes Lucia Allais, commenting directly on the materiality of buildings. Not only does form tend to deteriorate on every temporal level, but also the emergence of the formless and of decay makes it impossible to fix in time "the relationship between form and surface" (Allais 3, 27). The logocentric gaze that searches for the sovereign leap out of the muddy depths of the temporal is a move that takes for granted that form is our specific link to the eternal, the atemporal. And when this ideology is forced to defend itself in the final analysis by stating that, at least "for us," there is nothing that does not have a form, what needs to be pointed out is that it is form itself that is always constantly unforming, shifting, sliding toward something other, and thus that it is time itself that makes it impossible to fix in time, with precision, our trusting impression that everything has a form. The *informe*, then, would be a way of restating the "concept" of form, but within a minimal difference that already unworks and ruins its place within the logocentric system of fixed places.

Bataille wrote that, faced with the abyss, there are those who draw back and those who say it is nothing. There are also, we can add—but this addendum is already at work in Bataille—those who wish to be almost scientific about the void. It is in that sense that Bataille proposes a program of scientific research concerned with the void that is at stake in the "sovereign" moment. "The study I envision," he explains, is no doubt . . . a study in the sense of scientific research, but in that case this research appears as contradictory to the sovereign moment itself. . . . The sovereign is in the domain of silence, and if we talk about it we incriminate the silence that constitutes it. It is always a comedy, a practical joke. . . . On the level of the sovereign moment, language troubles everything it touches. . . . Insofar as we seek something, whatever this might be, we do not live sovereignly, we subordinate the present moment to a future moment, which will follow it. Perhaps we will attain the sovereign moment as a result of our effort, and it is possible in fact that an effort is necessary, but between the time of our effort and sovereign time, there is obligatorily a fissure, and we can even say an abyss. (*The Unfinished* 126)

Could this serve as the basis for a project that accepts the abyss as the first evidence, without images or stories to cover over its gaping mouth? Doubtless it is still too radical a mission statement for the thought allowed by academic disciplines. It is precisely to this radicalness that Didi-Huberman objects, both in Bataille and in Derrida's reading of Bataille. For Didi-Huberman, Derrida's engagement with the question of form is too drastic in its ontological reach. For it is nothing less than the sense of being that has been limited by the imposition of form (Derrida, *Margins* 187, 188). Didi-Huberman's claim is that such a statement assumes it is necessary to tackle the purely philosophical meditation, concerned with the possibility of a phenomenology of language, in order to think through modern art (*Ce que nous* 159). He goes on to claim a more modest position: "What is at issue for us is not exactly the sense of being, nor the status of language in general . . . but the status of a black cube, of a sculpture, in general. Of a *form*, to sum up" (160). The concern is with the specificity of artistic form. The search, in his opinion, should be for an opening that is at once dialectical, conceptual, and practical (160). The issue, which he sees reproduced in Denis Hollier's *La prise de la concorde,* centers on the question of transgression. According to Hollier: "[Bataille] is always tempted to interrupt a form. Form is the temptation of discourse. It is in taking on form that discourse develops, to then be fixed and become recognizable. . . . [Bataille] knew how to oppose the violence of a desire to the temptation of form" (qtd. in Didi-Huberman, *La ressemblance* 19n4). It is this notion of transgression that Didi-Huberman assumes is not legitimate to adopt when considering the field of the visual arts (19).

The operation carried out in these remarks deserves closer scrutiny, for what it proposes is to limit not only Derrida's thought to a localized philosophical and phenomenological disciplinary question but also, and less openly so, the reach of Bataille's *informe* vis-à-vis the history of phi-losophy, the anti-idealism and strange materialism that is at stake precisely as a philosophical intervention. Though not commenting directly on the relationship between Derrida and Didi-Huberman, Matteo Spandoni has touched on the fundamental difference at issue: for Didi-Huberman, the problem is never to put in question the founding cause, or foundation. It is not a question of an an-archic[12] thought but of finding the principle of continuous revolt: "The *informe* . . . is not an anarchic principle for consciousness; the difficulty of this reflection is precisely that of analyzing the *informe* as a condition of possibility for aesthetic experience. Bataille's *informe* is a principle that attempts to take the crisis of sense upon itself, not through a negation of form, but through the construction of hetero-geneous hermeneutic spaces" (D'Ammando and Spadoni 291, cf. 283). The reconfiguration does not only touch on the concept of space. It is also an intervention on the temporal plane. And it is here that the real limitation of this kind of reading of the *informe* is exposed, not only in terms of the temporal concept that it underwrites but also in terms of its search of a hermeneutic delimitation of the notion to the field of the arts and visuality that seeks to safeguard ultimate foundations in every way. Temporally, what obtains is the return of the repressed and an opening toward the stratified and sedimented temporalities of the subject. It is an opening that discovers that time is not one but many, and that this is so through the symptomatology of the subject (D'Ammando and Spadoni 294–95). This is the materialism that Didi-Huberman is interested in emphasizing when it comes to a Lacanian and Freudian intersection with Bataille's thought.[13]

The perceived radicalism of this multiplication of temporalities brings him in line with another major work on the *informe*: Yve-Alain Bois and Rosalind Krauss's *Formless: A User's Guide*, published in 1996—one year after the appearance of Didi-Huberman's *La ressemblance informe*. Together, these two books give form to the real entrance of the concept within con-temporary debates on modernism and art. And despite their disagreements, they are similar in the way that they delimit the question at hand to a disciplinary problem concerning the field of the visual and the destiny of images, and in the importance both studies place on the temporal as a way of translating Bataille's notion into the context of the 1990s. Bois and Krauss introduce the notion of "pulse" as an attack on "the modernist exclusion of temporality from the visual field" (32). In the throb of Mar-cel Duchamp's *Rotoreliefs* (1935), "the rotating discs . . . [open] the very concept of visual autonomy—of a form . . . owing nothing to time—to the invasion of a sense of dense, corporeal pleasure . . . because the pulse itself . . . associates it with the density of nervous tissue, with its temporality of feedback. . . . [W]ithout this temporal wave, no experience at all, visual or otherwise, could happen" (135). This opening to the temporal, as a condition of possibility for experience and its representation in the work of art, achieves something paradoxical. Yes, it cancels out the possibility of claiming autonomy for artistic praxis, but it also cancels out its specificity by bringing it in line with a much wider project also related to the possibility of representing the unrepresentability of the temporalities of modernity—a project that Frederic Jameson has identified as coming to fruition for the first time with the emergence of the modern novel (*Valences* 498). The same could be said for Didi-Huberman's sedimented temporal layers of the image. And the issue goes to the heart of the problem of making historical time appear as such in the age of revolution. The problem is not merely phenomenological or philosophical; it is the key to achieving a subject of political transformation capable of being sovereign within the plane of absolute immanence. In short, we are back to the question of how to represent the people, in all its heterogeneity, without this image returning us to the same symbolic order that this new sovereign body was meant to topple. In that case, then, the issue with the formless, such as it came to be theorized in the 1990s, is not only that it mirrors too closely what it seeks to contest and transgress (this was Hal Foster's argument then as it is now), but that an opportunity was missed to mine the notion in its antifoundationalist import, which is to say in all its ontological implications. Its ontological implications, however, are directly tied to its implications for politics.

In the context of the 1990s, the debate on the *informe* raised a major concern regarding the (post)structuralism that framed much of *Formless: A User's Guide* and *La ressemblance informe*: whether or not "high theory" was capable of finding a sufficiently convincing way of articulating structure and history in order to think politics anew. However, in thinking politics anew what was meant was to recommence the old politics in an effective manner. For the politics at issue were clear beforehand: irrespective of the operative terms, it could have been the abject, the *informe*, horror, just as now it is a question of precarity—then and now the issue, as Helen Molesworth put it, centers on the possibility for certain works of art, and for certain subjects, to transgress and disturb the status quo (cf. Foster et al. 21). The formless as an operation that questioned the foundations of metaphysical reason was too quickly instrumentalized into a possible political program. At the very least, it was from the unquestionable horizon of the political demand that it entered a wider debate beyond the reading of modernist art.[14] And the traces of this historical context can still be read in more recent arguments that deploy the formless.[15] This is why Hal Foster was so concerned with what he saw as the emptying out of any possible subject of history and substituting it for what in his eyes seemed to be only a corpse. It is precisely here that the paradox of the formless emerges, though in a way that was perhaps impossible to perceive in the 1990s.

What I want to suggest is that the debate on the formless exposes us to the radical questioning of foundationalist or essentialist thought. The ungrounding of the thought that defines reason cannot be simply undertaken as a task that goes hand in hand with the politics of reason. If the salvific telos of Marxism, along with all progressive politics, and the subject of history that it presupposes are all incompatible with a radical deconstruction of the thought of foundations, this is not because the "politics" of such a deconstruction ends in a nihilist program that is difficult to distinguish from capitalist disorder (falsely amalgamated, then, with anarchy, formlessness, and so forth). What the deconstruction of Western metaphysics entails is a politicity that is, not surprisingly, different from the politics of the tradition in question. From the point of view of a politicity that assumes the abyss, caring for the shortcoming of the politics of the (ever-shifting) "good" amounts to a very limited and historically inaccurate understanding of what is actually at stake in the work of capitalism, sexism, racism, colonialism, neocolonialism, and all the oppressive phenomena that are often ascribed to the general logic of modernity.

In this context, it seems possible now to suggest that Derrida's "radicalism" regarding the link between the formless and the deconstruction of presence, of the temporality of the presence of the present, is far from a disciplinary consideration related only to the history of philosophy and phenomenology. In fact, what is at issue in the destruction of time as presence also has immense implications for the possibility of philosophy as academic discipline. With the slippage of the concept of time into the *informe* there opens the possibility of a temporality that is neither one nor multiple, but that is also not the end of time or a leap into eternal atemporality. The aim of that line of inquiry would be to see the formless as something other than another name for the exceptionality of the sovereign as political theology imagines this figure. Furthermore, in terms of the political implication this possibility entails, we would be broaching the question of a politicity that escapes the grasp of a politics of representation in which the Right and the Left, progressive and conservative, keep shifting with each dialectical overturning of the master-slave dialectic. At issue is the movement of the formless such that it is no longer possible to be "reassembled and represented, at a point of the canvas by the figure of the slave"; while this would make politics readable, it would also make it merely reversible—for these figures could be read "from left to right or from right to left, as a reactionary movement or as a revolutionary movement, or both at once" (Derrida, *Writing and Difference* 276). The indifference between left and right in this passage is not the result of not having determined clearly and forcefully enough a politics of redemption; rather, it stems from having incorporated that very same politics too quickly back into the logic of work and subjugation that defines the dialectical passage of the slave to the position of mastery. In this sense, a deconstruction of time does not entail only a reconfiguration of philosophical categories but also a retreat from the grand politics of liberation (which is always the politics of submission, of forced labor, of the mandate to care for the always already too decrepit foundations) and the attempt to think through a different politicity beyond the reversibility of the sovereignty of the master.

I would like to illustrate some of the consequences of this proposal by way of an example related to the issue of temporality in the context of the Cuban Revolution before and after the fall of the Soviet Union. The Cuban historian Rafael Rojas has recently attempted to outline some of the consequences of the transformation of the island as it moves toward an uncertain new era. His aim is to highlight to what extent the temporalities of the new situation make the figure of the slave or the subaltern a perpetual prisoner unable to found a new state:

> The biggest paradox of the post-messianic time [the time defined by the exhaustion, though perhaps not the persistence, of dictatorial socialist politics] resides . . . in the limited memory of the past it allows. In not recognizing that the reign of the Messiah [Castro] . . . has come to its end, past, present and future are not constituted as such and subjects fall prey to a historical disorientation. The temporality of the island begins to function . . . as a sort of carnival of the simultaneous, which makes the foundation of a new sovereign legality more difficult. As a citizen, the reader can live time any way he wants. . . . But as a subject of the State, that same citizen has no other option but to remain in his subaltern condition until a new legality and a new sovereignty are founded. (*El estante vacío* 137)

The transition, in 1992, to a post-Soviet culture is understood as the passage from the time of utopia to the time of globalized urbanity, most fundamentally characterized by the increasing illegibility and unnarratability of public space. For this transition to be possible, however, it is necessary to erect a time of utopia that is perfectly visible as a "fallacy" concerning the eternal character of the Revolution and its state, a time that is the domestication of temporality, which becomes fixed forever and erases all historical cuts (138, 136, 128). It is in its aftermath that the fluidity of globalization comes into the picture. That it is a globalized phenomenon is perhaps best illustrated by the fact that Rojas's reference on this score is the writing of the Spanish anthropologist Manuel Delgado, whose work would seem to apply equally well to Barcelona as it does to Havana, equally well, that is, to a neoliberal urban space as to a (post)socialist one. And here it is the formless that is once again at issue. This is how Delgado defines the time of globalized urbanity: "An illegible rigmarole, without meaning . . . which does not say anything, since the sum of all the voices produces a murmur, a rumor, sometimes a clamor, which is an incomprehensible sound, that is untranslatable given that it is not of the order of words, but a noise that has not been codified, similar to a loud buzzing" (Delgado 189, qtd. in Rojas, *El estante* 127). The pattern is a recognizable one: sovereignty, true liberation, the redemption of the subaltern, will only be possible with the new legal order, and for that it is necessary to sublate the formless muck that Delgado describes in this passage. Without a doubt, Rojas is not asking for a new eternal sovereign principle. For him, following Giorgio Agamben, it is the dictatorship of the sovereign, the sovereignty of utopia, that posits that leap toward the stability of the atemporal. It is odd, then, that on this issue and having cited Agamben, for whom even that messianic time is already irreducible to a duality, Rojas would suggest that the elevation of the subaltern to the freedom of the new legality would be contingent on the possibility of overcoming the formlessness of global urban time.

The political consequences of this slip back to the redemptive politics of sovereignty are of import when trying to understand not just the unprecedented transition currently under way on the island but its past as well. On the one hand, it becomes increasingly hard to avoid the question and, to some, the paradox, of a capitalist dictatorship in contemporary Cuba (a cultural context dominated by a Manichean view of politics where capitalism and communism are either absolutely evil or absolutely good). And to make sense of this scenario without falling back on facile oppositions, it is the figure of the state and of the sovereign, of any sort, that will have to be interrogated in greater detail. On the other hand, such a project will remain impossible so long as we fail to see the complexity and heterogeneity not only of the revolutionary state but also of the modern principle of sovereignty in all its political, aesthetic, religious, and philosophical ramifications. The time of the dictatorship of the utopian state can be multiple because it is One, and it can be One because it is Many. The dialectic of the one and the many is also the dialectic of modern politico-theological-aesthetico-onto-logo-centric time. To interrogate the possibility of its suspension without pleading for a leap into the eternal is not a theoretical sign of voluntarism; rather, it is the only possible way to open ourselves to the complexity of our historical being in the world.

As I think through that constellation of problems, the central character of this book will be the Cuban poet and thinker José Lezama Lima (1910–1976). I am interested in reading with Lezama, in taking his texts, and the debates to which he has given rise as well as those that his work has illuminated, as points of departure for less obvious destinations. If I venture to track the emergence of the formless in his work, it is as a way of underscoring my own search for a less formalized place of enunciation than the ones currently available within the academy, whether it is Latinamericanism, Cuban studies and historiography, or the unruly and acrimonious realm of contemporary radical theory. I understand that the shifts that this entails might prove a struggle for my reader who has more firmly planted him- or herself in any one discipline, but I believe that only by unmooring the task of thinking from these stable hubs will we be able to shake ourselves from some of the more nefarious side effects of today's academy.

Having said that, it is, nevertheless, an established figure within academic discourse that I will treat in what follows. Lezama Lima has been a central figure in academic debates ever since Julio Cortázar, among others, made him part of the Latin American Boom, particularly after the publication of *Paradiso* in 1966. Yet Lezama fits into the general parameters of the Boom only uneasily. Something that has been in evidence in the uncomfortable place he has occupied in the critical literature, where his work often stands for less than attractive positions in the field.[16] And yet this unease is justified up to a point. For Lezama entered the canon of the Boom only under the sign of the baroque, and the poet himself quickly discovered that the "baroquization" of Latin American culture in the world market was little more than a publicity campaign designed to sell a product that was far from homogeneous. The concerns that his body of writing addresses, beginning with the materiality of the writing itself, with its reluctance to be "grasped" fully, all the way up to a meditation on the place of poetry, religion, and politics in a civilizational moment that more and more seems bent on total destruction—all of this made of Lezama a figure that was never quite comfortable within the frame of the Boom, which offered at once the promise of a finally modern Latin America and its utter exoticization and commodification. Thus, it is not surprising to find Lezama at the center of the interventions that most radically sought to question the philosophical assumptions underwriting Latinamericanist discourses in the moment of globalization (e.g., Moreiras, Levinson, Chiampi, Cruz-Malavé). But it is clear today that what had been a sustained critical engagement with Lezama that sought to bring him to bear on wider debates regarding the destiny of metaphysics, Western imperial reason, and peripheral identitarian claims has abated, making way for a reorganization of Lezama studies that is wholly centered around the question of the role the poet played in the revolutionary process, before and after Fidel Castro (e.g., Díaz, Rojas).

In the 1990s, Lezama was grafted by the post-Soviet Cuban intellectual and political elites onto the main ideological current that attempted to offer an answer to the exhaustion of Marxism-Leninism. Under the aegis of *Orígenes*, the editorial project that the poet spearheaded, there emerged a Catholic, nationalist, and utopian discourse whose task was to legitimate and care for the regime in the hour of its deepest crisis. Its efficacy seemed to be exhausted by the beginning of the next decade, but its aftereffects are still very palpable (Rojas, *El estante* 142). Part of this project had to do with promoting an image of Lezama that was in glaring contradiction with the treatment of the poet, particularly during the last decade of his life, at the hands of the state during its most aggressive phase (during the 1960s and into the late 1970s). The persecution and later rehabilitation of Lezama is a story that is important to retell here, however briefly, in order for the following pages to be more intelligible for my reader.

For many of the Cuban writers who lived through the victory of Fidel Castro and the guerrilla, it was not at all difficult to align themselves with the new order. Even those who would later become the target of state persecution eagerly declared their enthusiasm for the new era that began in 1959. At the time, not all of those declarations were equally convincing. For figures like Heberto Padilla, Antón Arrufat, Virgilio Piñera, and Guillermo Cabrera Infante—all writers who would eventually be censored, ostracized, and erased from the official literary history of the island—there was no clearer example of what not to do aesthetically in revolutionary times than Lezama and the *origenistas* (see Díaz, *Los límites* 187–262). Padilla, whose own "affair" between 1968 and 1971 would become the most important turning point in the relationship between the Revolution and Latin American intellectuals at large, was nevertheless among the first to publicly denounce Lezama. In December 1959, Padilla wrote: "The poetry that has to emerge in a new country cannot repeat the old mantras from Trocadero" (qtd. in Díaz, *Los límites* 188). It was in his house on Trocadero 162 that Lezama would spend the last decade of his life. These are years still shrouded in secrecy, in part because the rehabilitation of Lezama as a revolutionary symbol entailed the destruction and erasure of documents related to his persecution. We know, for instance, that in his "rectification" speech, made in the presence of the National Union of Writers and Artists of Cuba on 23 April 1971, Padilla told the audience that all of the poet's negative judgments and critical opinions regarding the new regime had been noted and taken seriously by state security forces, which already thought of him as a counterrevolutionary (Padilla 148). Among the documents that have been forgotten or lost, there is a recently discovered program for a 1974 exhibition on "ideological diversionism," which was located in the archives of the Ministry of State Security, or STASI, in East Germany. The exhibition detailed the state's campaign against all the cultural and intellectual threats to the Revolution during the 1960s and 1970s. The pamphlet points out that some of Lezama's still unpublished and confiscated work was on display. It was an example of the "subtlest weapon wielded by the enemies of the Revolution."[17] In the program for the exhibition, we find out, for instance, that there was an entire operation built around the poet, which went under the code name "Caso 'ORBITA' undertaken against the diversionist writer José Lezama Lima." It is an indication of the fact that he was spied on, that his conversations were recorded and used as evidence against him. By the time of his death in 1976, not even Lezama's neighbors seemed to remember that he was a well-known and influential intellectual throughout Latin America and beyond.

In large part, the persecution was less interested in eradicating explicit ideological positions than the perceived sexuality of its targets. Once the Revolution began to make the case that queerness posed a threat to its progress, the fate of many of the most enthusiastic of the new revolutionary intellectuals was sealed. In this environment, a figure like Lezama, whose 1966 novel *Paradiso* was seen as scandalous for its portrayal of homosexuality, had little chance of a fate other than ostracism. And even when he was resurrected and rehabilitated as the prophet and bard of the absolute state, his homosexuality remained a taboo for the *neo-origenista* state ideologues (e.g., Lezama's devout Catholic disciples Cintio Vitier and Fina García Marruz). The effort to "exonerate" Lezama from his "ideological diversionism" resulted in a more open relationship not with the entirety of his intellectual world but with those elements in it that could be grafted onto a teleological narrative that culminated with the redemptive Revolution. This strategy implied falling silent regarding anything that would cloud the link between the poet from Trocadero and the official stance of post-Soviet revolutionary Cuba.

It is surprising, then, that the need to discredit the hagiographic interpretation of *Orígenes*, which has shaped many recent accounts on Lezama, partakes equally of this black-and-white political imaginary. It is as if the only possible question is whether Lezama is a conservative or a progressive. Duanel Díaz, a critic who has consistently discredited all revolutionary thought, goes so far as to side with the rabid enthusiasm of the early literary and intellectual adopters of the revolutionary rhetoric against Lezama; they were right at least on one point, according to Díaz: *Orígenes*, and Lezama in particular, can and should only be read as a conservative and antimodern strain in the intellectual landscape of the island (*Los límites* 193). Outside of Cuba, and from the opposite end of the ideological spectrum, things are not much different. If we take James Buckwalter-Arias's *Cuba and the New Origenismo* (2010) as a point of comparison, now from a critic earnestly attempting to shed light on the limitations of all arguments that side with the logic of the market as a corrective to the totalitarian impulse of the regime, what we find is that Lezama and his disciples, though invested in a modernist reaction against capitalist alienation, still respond to a fundamentally romantic and conservative aesthetic program that sees art as the only possible salvation.

Why this coincidence? What makes it possible for the naïve enthusiasm of the 1960s (Padilla, Cabrera Infante, Arrufat, and others), the disenchanted and rightly critical gaze of the exiled Cuban intellectual (Díaz), as well as the no-longer-so-naïve materialist reading of *Orígenes* in the 1990s (Buckwalter-Arias), to be in agreement regarding what they see as the political inadequacy of Lezama? One possible though still insufficient answer to this question could be located in the fact that perhaps one of the most characteristic developments of the Cuban Revolution has been the reduction of politics to cultural or aesthetic categories and debates. This is in part the tack that the Revolution itself took when, beginning in the 1960s, it determined that the poems and plays of writers like Arrufat, Padilla, Lezama, and others were a real and very dangerous threat to the revolutionary process—that the war against capitalism had shifted from armed struggle to the battle of ideas and ideologies. However, that the problem is more complicated can be gathered from the fact that, immediately after the Revolution coming to power, the new Jacobins saw nothing more important to discuss and critique than the legacy of *Orígenes*. As Duanel Díaz reminds us, at the time, Mirta Aguirre, a leading orthodox Marxist critic, remarked that it was simply "ridiculous" to be debating the baroque poetics of *Orígenes*, even if in order to obliterate it, when the Agrarian Reform was on the table (*Los límites* 191–92). One wonders if Aguirre is addressing only the young would-be-revolutionary poets when she remarks on the absurdity of the situation—or if her words might also pertain to the state itself. For would it not be apposite to ask, also, given that what is on the table is the emancipation of humanity, why we are wasting our time with diversions like ideological diversionism? The mixed temporalities that collided with the entrance of Fidel Castro into Havana were eventually domesticated, not by the eradication of their multiplicity but by their political instrumentalization. The time of the slave that has become the master touches everything, but so does the time of the master that keeps the slave. Lezama's politics could never enter that kingdom in part because his politics were a secret even to himself.

If there is one central proposition in the following pages, it concerns the idea that the opposition of temporal images, which always function as vectors of hegemonization (as processes that force others to fall into a time that is not one, even if endlessly professed to be so), though a strategy that today enjoys significant popularity, is doomed to reproduce exactly the same sort of logic that it attacks. My proposal centers, then, on the possibility of the end of temporalities as frames, but this is not at all the end of Time that was theorized under the heading of the end of Grand Narratives. My aim is not to pit the grand against the small, or the One against the multiple. It is rather to begin to approach a zone that lies neither in the "order" of a single time nor in the "disorder" of multiple temporal layers that coexist. This opposition, between order and disorder, is the residual effect or the symptom of the emergence of order itself. The state is the creation of disorder by the introduction of its own formal legitimization. The state is itself a temporal crossroads positing, in all the complexity involved, the dialectical sublation of a simpler time. My way out of this conundrum has been through the idea of a "time" that is *informe* or formless, only the catachrestic turning of an absence of time, that, for all that, is not possible to align with eternity or transcendence. For this reason, what follows is *not* an exploration of memory or the perception of time but, rather, an attempt to approach what "appears" only after the synthesizing frames of time and times dissipate—which is to say: a politicity that retreats, this is the hope, from all the grand politics of modernity.

I have chosen to put this concern with the dissipation of time first, but its consequences quickly and sometimes inadvertently (as I have shown in this introduction) spill over into areas that might seem unrelated at first sight. For instance, as literature has been instrumental in making time appear, and more so in the case of multiple or juxtaposed temporalities (Jameson, *Valences* 498), to claim anything regarding the dissipation of the temporal frame would also entail something about the literary, such as it has been understood since the early German romantics—which is to say, since the literary joined the struggle for the absolute liberation of human-kind. I have chosen to broach the question of this shift by means of the formless, and the problem of being (un)able to offer a proper form. In what follows I will show that the way that this problem was handed down to the twentieth century, and the way that Lezama imagines it, requires that we question the rather common idea that the presentation of the formless and the exposition of the void are accomplished facts of romanticism. However, I do not intend to move through the history of romantic literature, and this for a very precise historical consideration. The relevance of this archive today concerns the most heated debates around the reemergence of the category of the event as a vector of true revolutionary action. It is in this context that the poetic and theoretical preoccupation with the figure of a sovereign that is more sovereign than state sovereignty, which opens the way for a reincarnation of the Muses as the voice of that radically other sovereign, gains an import that goes beyond the mere tracing of literary patterns.

That Lezama is the poet of the interruption of that dictation is the reason that he can eventually break into a writing of the formless, even as this is a nonfigure that will accompany, sometimes imperceptibly, his most recalcitrant Catholic pronouncements. I do not intend to excuse him or to applaud him in this last regard. However, I do think that it is only through an honest confrontation with his Catholicism that his writing begins to speak to us beyond the limits of *Orígenes* and the putative nihilism of the generation of intellectuals that came of age in the decade prior to the Cuban Revolution. It is in this way that reading *with* Lezama becomes not only a matter of reading in the history of literature but also of deeper insights into the revolutionary process itself.

Much of that history will occupy me in the first part of the book, in which the central aim is to show the links between the mixed times of the state and those of literature and religion (very intimately woven one into the other in the case of Lezama)—while approaching a theoretical path toward the absence of time and the writing of the formless. The second part is a slow and detailed reading of key moments in Lezama's oeuvre, and the aim is to show the process leading him toward what lies beyond the pil-lars, that is, the formless. What appears there is a thought of the Revolution that would expose politics to the dissolution of its most cherished ideals of the proper, a formless and void zone that all politics carries together with its most utopian (or dystopian) desires, even if it does not like it or admit it.

The first chapter examines the traditional explanation of the teleological time of the Cuban Revolution, which is undermined not only by the revolutionary experience itself but also by the very critical conceptual apparatus that characterizes it in those terms. Furthermore, the Revolution falls into a wider Christian and modern pattern in which the liberation from the time of alienation is posited as the irruption of a circular time of salvation. Under this model, modernity is a time of multiple temporalities in which it is impossible to unite the infinite and the finite, linear and circular time. This is the focus of the second chapter, where I explore how these modern temporalities are taken over and worked out by literature, both as the fiction of politics and in the work of the poets. To this end, I analyze how the romantic tradition makes its way into the formal exposition of political texts in Cuba, and the way that the romantic literary tradition itself thought about the issues at stake. Once I establish this temporal theoretical framework, in the third chapter I focus on how Lezama Lima and Ernesto Che Guevara rely on Christian patterns that become secularized. In the process, what also appears is the specific mixture of theology and aesthetics that belies any possible notion of the politics of the Revolution as an autonomous praxis. The book's first section closes with a chapter devoted to contemporary conceptions of nihilism and politics and how they are shaped by our inattention to the unexamined mixture of modern times. Here I delve into three different types of discourse: communism (intellectuals tied to the revolutionary state apparatus in Cuba), neorepublicanism (intellectuals critical of the Revolution), and neocommunism (intellectuals who propose a recommencement of communism outside of Cuba). These discourses, all in their own specific manner, operate on the basis of a desire for the reenchantment of politics as the highest value, against which nihilism is diagnosed. I demonstrate that so long as we do not have a clear understanding of the multiplicity of the temporal experience that modernity itself offers, any proposal for a new time of absolution and reenchantment will be doomed to repeat the mistakes it means to overcome. Furthermore, I suggest that it is only by the crossing out of all temporal schemata (in the sense of all political domestication, domination, and imposition of time) that it is possible to begin to think in a different direction.

In the second part of the book, I examine Lezama's oeuvre in more detail. Though his work has achieved canonical status, it has yet to be fully discovered in terms of its philosophical implications. If I take a closer look at his work in this part of the book, it is not in order to produce a clearer picture of a single author within the Cuban context; rather, it is with the aim of illuminating the broader question of the intricate relationship between literature, religion, and politics in the wake of post-Kantian intellectual history. I trace Lezama's own self-positioning within the history of literature with the aim of tackling problems such as the fictional structure of the political, the philosophical answers to the question of the end of time, and the problem of the intersection of aesthetics and revolutionary politics since the Romantics. Part 2 is not divided into chapters. It is one long development divided into sections of various lengths. In it, I am interested in tracking the unfolding of three related lines of thought: (1) the treatment of the concept of the void, or of the aposiopetic moment, when to "say well" means to fall silent out of respect respect for the political order that underwrites the speaking situation; (2) the way that Lezama writes and imagines the history of modern aesthetics, particularly the romantic avatars that were emphasized in the first part of this book (I pay special attention to the role of the dictation of the Other in the poet's version of literary history); and (3) the way that both a reconsideration of the concept of the void, and the particular reading of history that informs Lezama's understanding of his writing, open onto an unexpected reconsideration of the formless in the poet's late texts. These are texts in which, by way of direct treatment of the problem of formlessness and temporality, Lezama suggests ways in which to think through the essential absence at the heart of all politics, and the end of temporalities as a task for literature—that is, the end of the idea that the task of literature is to offer ever-richer juxtapositions of temporalities that oppose a putative homogeneous or empty time of alienation. Beyond these columns, beyond the idealization of politics, and beyond the image of time as a synthetic operation, what remains is the possibility of thinking with the poet beyond the current apparatus of (academic-imperial) knowledge and all of its returns.

I conclude with an analysis of Jean-Luc Godard's use of Lezama's writing in his film *Notre musique* (2004), where this entire history of political struggles and philosophical debates is brought to a head in the context of contemporary global war in order to illustrate what role literature and the arts can play in it. I show to what extent Lezama's writing of the formless is already illuminating and affecting how we think about literature and politics beyond the Cuban context. In Lezama's confrontation with antirepresentational modes of expression, what emerges is the thorough dissolution of the mechanisms by which time is synthesized, without this entailing the entrance of the eternal into history, or the disappearance of history into the infinite.

Part I

"Times"

1. Toward the Absence of Time

The Problem with Teleology in Cuba

In 2007 Fidel Castro was in seclusion, and no one seemed to know much about the actual state of his health. Since July 2006 his physical condition had become a state secret. The absence of the leader coincided with the reappearance of figures who had been in positions of power during some of the Revolution's most repressive years. These were people who many thought had disappeared for good from the public sphere. Their return, in the nation's various media, gave rise to a clamorous and by now well-known exchange of e-mails, some written by victims of these henchmen.[1] The discussion centered on the possible reasons behind the unexpected resurrection of men like Luis Pavón Tamayo. Under the pseudonym of Leopoldo Ávila, Pavón Tamayo's articles for *Verde Olivo* (the magazine of the Revolutionary Armed Forces) had paved the way for the Padilla and Arrufat affairs beginning in 1968, a defining moment regarding the Revolution's repressive position on intellectual and artistic work.[2] The Padilla case marked the moment when many Latin American intellectuals began to question their loyalty to the Revolution. Thus, 2006 also marked the return of a particularly painful historical knot between the arts and the Revolution, as it was under the command of Pavón Tamayo that the ideological purges and censorship relating to the world of letters had been carried out in the past.

In their correspondence, the victims did not arrive at a definitive answer regarding the reason for this particularly sinister return. There were many opinions, but no clear image regarding the inner workings of political *jouissance* on the island. The reactions varied from the exculpatory to the paranoid. The return of the repressors seemed to catch many off guard. Antón Arrufat's reaction is significant, not only because he lived the consequences of the purges for many years but also because it thematizes the idea of return. The playwright, who later won the National Prize in literature, is the author of the until recently censured *The Seven Against Thebes*; he is emblematic of the era insofar as his officially enforced silencing later gave way to a certain state-sponsored limelight. Thus, Arrufat was living testimony to the excesses of the ideological state apparatus such as it was at its wildest moment (1967–76), as well as of the kind of "rehabilitation" that ensued, beginning in the early 1980s.[3] His rise out of oblivion coincided with the disappearance from public life of the enforcers of the Revolution's cultural policies against what had been called "ideological diversionism."[4] When the persecutors reappeared as public figures at the end of 2006, he attempted to explain the logic behind the scenes, and he thought he had the key:

> Once the rehabilitation of artists and writers that Luis Pavón Tamayo tried to annihilate forever was underway, and cultural politics entered into its revolutionary rectification phase, once the victims of the *pavonato* were recognized and valued as creators, old [Pavón] went up to one of my friends to warn him, in words similar to these: do not compromise yourself with those who now win National Literary Prizes, soon all of this will be rolled back. (Arrufat qtd. in Ponte, *Villa 65*)

Arrufat, believing he has caught the revolutionary in a deadly contradiction, concludes: "Strange reasoning coming from a declared Marxist, to conceive of historical time as an eternal return" (qtd. in Ponte 65). The temporal dimension of this vision of the ideology of the revolutionary is striking in what it takes for granted: the time of the Revolution is teleological time without returns.[5] And yet the reason for the comments is the return of Pavón Tamayo and company. The return has no effect on the distribution of times in question. The reason for this can be gleaned from the commentary that Antonio José Ponte makes regarding Arrufat's observation. The emphasis is not placed on the temporal aspect of the remarks; rather it is a question of pointing to the totalitarian aspect of the political machinery of the state. "Understood from this standpoint," Ponte writes, "the cultural politics of the Revolution included equally the election and destitution of its repressive figures. . . . For no act, not even the most terrible, was beyond it" (Ponte, *Villa 65*). The absence of the supreme leader seems to need to be compensated with the symbolic return of one of its fiercest and most violent moments. And this goes to underscore that any changes in the level of repression are merely manipulative gestures of a political mechanism that covers the totality of life under the Revolution.

Were we to take this to its ultimate consequences, we would have to add that Arrufat's quip, regarding the contradiction entailed by a Marxism of the eternal return, could no longer be a way of pointing out an error of any kind. Rather, it would mean that the political machinery at issue also has the power to say that no time, no temporality, is beyond it as well. Yet this is not the way that totality and totalitarianism is usually read when it comes to its temporal implications. One can hardly blame Arrufat for adducing the clash between the rhetoric of the Eternal Return and that of the *tabula rasa* of the New as a central matrix from which to make sense of the cultural politics of the Revolution. In fact, this is one of the cornerstones of contemporary critiques of totalitarianism and its manipulation of the image of the past and the future.

Rafael Rojas, in one of the most influential critiques of the teleological matrix of the Revolution, presents the basic coordinates of the problem at hand. In the opening pages of his *Isla sin fin* (Island without telos, 1998), he invokes what he considers the characteristic gesture of all revolutions: a metaphysical pogrom in which one time has to be annihilated and a new one founded: "During the Paris Commune one could witness a group of revolutionaries . . . firing against the clocks of Churches and palaces . . . a destructive instinct against time, of total rupture with the past" (9). All revolutions, Rojas continues, partake in this desire to break time in two. In this they are messianic and present themselves as the advent of a new era of absolute redemption, but also as the incarnation of certain prophetic elements in the culture of the *ancien régime*: "Teleology is the discourse that organizes that closed representation of time, and identity is the syntagm that guarantees the becoming of that subject. A subject that is the Nation itself and whose teleology is safeguarded by the Revolution, i.e., by the moment that crystalizes the essence of nationality in history, by the traversal of a national identity from its origins to its destiny. . . . It is a question, in sum, of . . . an autotelic imaginary, always referring to itself, and which never opens itself to the exteriority of the world" (9). Rojas goes on to link this to the trajectory of modern subjectivity, which he calls "the ascendant march of National Spirit" (10). The Nation is the Subject of History and "the time of its becoming is the uphill [progress] of a triumphant self-consciousness" (10). He continually refers to this teleological structure in terms of closure (of history, of time, of the nation, upon themselves) while pointing out that such circularity presents a problem when it comes to imagining the future. The future is paradoxically left outside of the circle of teleology. The positivization of Absolute Spirit leaves the Subject of History without access to anything that is *to come*. Elsewhere he likens this closed temporality without future to a dead time, a temporal limbo (*El arte* 220).

Yet something curious happens to the circle of time in this description, which correctly identifies the logic of teleology.[6] It inadvertently opens up and is exposed to a different kind of temporality. The reel of time is unfurled. Teleology is grafted onto a History that is imagined as the linear story of progress and its stages: "for Marx," Rojas explains, "Hegelian teleology turns capitalism into the last stage of a classist prehistory, antechamber of Total Paradise." He adds: "In such cases the knowledge of the world is a mere image of itself projected on an external becoming, and its text, as Marc Bloch put it, 'an unrolled bobbin'" (*Isla* 73). One the one hand, the Revolution enters the dead time of teleology, of the self-referential event that is its alpha and omega, while, on the other, the modern tradition to which this process is ascribed seems to require a different relation to time in order to guarantee its historical necessity within the narrative of progress and development.

As evidence of this difficult temporal crossroads, Rojas adduces the archaeology of its manifestation in Cuban intellectual history. But the difference in temporal schemas goes unremarked. The intellectuals who shape the cultural field prior to the Revolution coming to power, figures like Jorge Mañach, Cintio Vitier, Virgilio Piñera, and José Lezama Lima, testify to the horrifying feeling of living in a time of political and cultural emptiness, of moving through the void of a neocolonial pseudorepublic. Cuba was for Vitier in 1945 "a land without *telos* or participation"; for Lezama, the island was incapable of accessing the fullness of its "political essence" (Vitier and Lezama qtd. in Rojas, *Isla* 76). However, for all of these figures, particularly for those associated with the journal *Orígenes*, edited by Lezama, the need for an insular teleology is directly opposed to this time of alienation—and it is for this reason that Rojas suggests that they pave the way for the Revolution. In 1953, Lezama put it in the following terms: "The triumph of temporality . . . seems guaranteed in that structure of absence or emptying out [that is] the clock"; Lezama adds that this clock measures and organizes "an awareness of hell in its imperial ticktock" (Lezama, *Obras* 594, 596). In a way that is not unique to Lezama, the romantic echoes here resound loudly and clearly: this is a call for the dissipation of the modern concept of linear time.[7] What we need to think is the specific way in which this rejection of modernity leads to the enthusiastic welcoming of the ultramodern paradigm of the Revolution—as if it were impossible to escape from the modern clock, which is thus not a single timepiece after all. For Rojas, this is not a paradox. As the cultural historian sees it, these kinds of declarations are instances of a country that imagines itself "teleologically," and he ventures that this would explain rather than complicate how we understand the enthusiasm with which the triumph of the Revolution was greeted in 1959 by intellectuals whose politics had until then seemed less than radical (*Isla* 76). Thus, the teleological collective desires of these intellectuals, as expressed in their various formalizations of Cuban history, end up serving as the building blocks for the narrative of the Nation as the Subject of History (190–94).

And yet, altogether, these considerations suggest a different image of modern temporality, one in which the linear and the circular meet. For what begins to appear is that the only way modernity, the putative linear unfolding of imperial capitalist time, could find the wherewithal to interrupt itself would be by invoking a temporality that would be both proper and improper. If one could speak of something like modernity's own image of itself, it would be the ideology of a single, empty, and homogeneous time. But it now seems that in fact modernity, and not any possible redemption or liberation from its political and economic deadlocks, is itself a mixed temporality that is constantly battling between a circular and a linear time—a linear time of alienation and a circular teleological time of redemption. The two need to be taken together, even in the very (im)possibility of such a synthesis. And this would mean that modernity is no longer the other of the revolutionary interruption of empty chronological time; rather, these are two sides of a single coin.

The problem at hand is not a mere quibble about the definition of teleology and our conception of the time of modernity. One of the favored contemporary methods of dealing with the problem of time and the Revolution is to insist on exposing the various temporalities that the teleological narrative of the Nation seeks to homogenize. José Quiroga does this while referencing Walter Benjamin: "The revolution had memorialized the past as a category that had been superseded, as an object that one could observe at a distance. But when the Special Period opened Cuba to the outside world, it was clear that Havana had been left in a state of suspended animation. For the foreign observer, as well as for many *habaneros*, walking around central Havana as late as 2002 invited the stroller, or *flâneur*, to apprehend different temporalities within the same structure" (32). The Revolution suspends time even as it accumulates temporalities. But what if the process that is being described here is not at all antithetical to the temporality of the Revolution as such? Moreover, what if this is the very logic of modern temporality finally coming to the surface, to be thought? It is telling that a figure like Slavoj Žižek, also invoking Benjamin, reads the same scene in a diametrically opposite sense in the opening pages of *Welcome to the Desert of the Real*. Looking at Cuba, "a country frozen in time," he sees "the growing inertia of social being/life" as the mark of fidelity to the Event of the Revolution: "It is not that the revolutionary Event was 'betrayed' by the Thermidorian establishment of a new order; the very insistence on the Event led to the immobilization at the level of positive social being. The decaying houses *are* proof of fidelity to the Event. . . . [W]hen Eternity intervenes in time, time comes to a standstill" (8). Whether one opts for reading the heterotopias where times accumulate or for the paean to order that testifies to the eventual suspension of temporality as the beginning of eternity, we are faced with an ethical problem that is often passed over in silence. Antonio José Ponte has called attention to it: "One hears frequently the affirmation that the regime that triumphed in 1959 has managed to banish Time from Cuba (. . . the most illustrious of her exiles). But such an affirmation would be inconvenient as it negates the biography of millions of people" ("La viga").

Perhaps I can put this differently. Beyond the negation of the biography of millions of people, the phenomenon of the perceived disappearance of time is uncanny precisely because it is the fiercest attempt by revolutionary politics to master and posit its own production of the temporal. Yet this production is not the production, not even at the simple level of an ideological or theoretical construction, of a simple or unique time. On the contrary, it is the positing of a multiplicity of times already from the side of the state. Thus, the biography of millions is not the only thing that is sacrificed if we neglect to take note of this. We also negate the complexity of the repressive apparatus that is made possible through this temporal refraction. This is remarkable on a different level, for it is also the indication, though on a purely negative level, of what a "time" that avoids the dialectic of modernity would entail if we are to begin thinking it.

It is the political dispensation and appropriation of liberated time that reduces the temporal appearance of an "other" (perhaps nonontological) guise of "time," which is not that of the Revolution or of modernity, and which can be termed thus because it is no longer the time produced by a subject trying to break away from time/s. This "time" would be the annulment of time, a phrase that Hegel uses to describe the becoming pure concept of the spirit in the *Phenomenology of the Spirit*, but this would no longer mean the introduction of Eternity or the suspension of the time of alienation. In what is perhaps the most profound antiphilosophical[8] move, this would be the time of the amorphous, or, time as formlessness—a time that is not time, if by time we understand the fundamental concept of the metaphysics of presence.

Time, the Ungraspable: Of Latin America as Modernity

> Since the 1980s, we Latin Americans have had acute difficulties placing our national societies in time—with various narratives competing among each other as available, but often rather unconvincing, framing devices. Any straightforward progressive or developmentalist narrative has lost credence. But emancipatory rhetoric, too, has tended to cede to a combination of sentimental gesticulation and realpolitik, even while it benefits from the backwind of the various disasters that were wrought by the Washington consensus of the 1990s to keep that rhetoric's image pure.
> —Claudio Lomnitz, "Time and Dependency in Latin America"

Claudio Lomnitz has drawn attention to the odd and perhaps unexpected parallels between contemporary and nineteenth-century Latin America, particularly in relation to the question of dependency. Beyond the emergence of neoliberal, neorepublican, and neorevolutionary discourses, he offers three elements that define our situation and that hark back to the postcolonial period. First, with the loosening of the grip of the United States as the policeman of the hemisphere, Latin America is once more a theater in which various powers (China, Europe, Japan, Russia, etc.) intervene more freely; second, the sense of isolation from the rest of the world, also shared with the Cold War period, in which it is felt that local opinion does not transcend the local level, that it goes unnoticed or unremarked; third, the sense that political representatives march out of step with the reality on the ground, "harboring an era of exalted discourse around citizenship and the rule of law" (356).[9] Taken together, Lomnitz concludes, these three elements point to a growing inability to locate Latin America in time: "we no longer know *when we are*"; and "this strange feeling is especially strong because of the odd nineteenth-century flavor of the political landscape in the twenty-first century" (348). However, the most important element in this description concerns the dissolution of the links between the United States and Latin American governments as the guarantor of "order," a dissolution that "makes it increasingly difficult to formulate a national time in any meaningful or convincing way. New dependencies implies fragmentation of interests and difficulties in shaping a convincing sense of direction for the national collective" (357).

It is necessary to consider this diagnosis, or this confession, in light of recent philosophical debates on the importance of thinking time, not only as a category for the accurate cartography of geopolitics but also for the very possibility of thinking. It would seem that it is only by knowing "when we are" that the specificity of our political location becomes intelligible. Furthermore, and this is the decisive point, this entails a relationship between a certain idea of time and the very possibility of politics that is far from self-evident—a relationship in which politics is only ever possible by way of a secure handle on time, a formalized relationship between time and action. In order to question that assumption, the philosophical underpinnings of Lomnitz's general argument need to be interrogated in more detail, even if he himself sets aside any general remarks on what these are. Giorgio Agamben's *The Time That Remains* would offer a privileged site for this oblique theoretical consideration of the matter as in it he makes his proposal by setting up a sort of triangle between the work of Alain Badiou, Jacques Derrida, and Agamben's own brand of messianism. It would also be of interest because the approach to the question of temporality here is explored by way of the Christian legacy, which is taken as a fundamental moment in Western thought, politics, and economics, leading to the formation of the contemporary global order. Further, the way that Agamben frames his argument in relation to Badiou and Derrida will serve as a way of preparing the way for the considerations made in the concluding section of this chapter.

On the one hand, Agamben's argument against Badiou centers on the use of Saint Paul as a poet-thinker of the universal that is produced as Sameness and Equality—which is to say, against the "present" that an event would create; to which Agamben counters that in Paul, despite the recurrent link between the saint and the idea of universality, what emerges in the end is not a universal man:

> The universal is not a transcendent principle through which differences may be perceived—such a perspective of transcendence is not available to Paul. Rather, this "transcendental" involves an operation that divides the divisions of the law themselves and renders them inoperative, without ever reaching any final ground. No universal man, no Christian can be found in the depths of the Jew or the Greek, neither as principle nor as an end; all that is left is a remnant and the impossibility of the Jew or the Greek to coincide with himself. The messianic vocation separates every *klēsis* from itself, engendering a tension within itself, without ever providing it with some other identity; hence, Jew *as non-Jew*, Greek *as non-Greek*. (52–53)

This is not inconsequential for the thinking on time that is at issue in this commentary on the Letter to the Romans, which Agamben reads as the fundamental messianic text for the Western tradition. The noncoincidence, the lack of ultimate ground, that the Pauline text reveals, produces not the universal of Sameness and Equality that Badiou emphasizes, but the problem of mastering representation. Now, in order for representation to be mastered, something must first happen to time. As David E. Johnson has pointed out: "Agamben attempts to overcome representation by suspending temporalization. In opposition to *chronos*, he posits the messianic present of *kairos*, which, he asserts, makes possible the stretching out, the suspension, of infinitely divisible *chronos*. The kairological suspension of temporalization, according to Agamben, allows for the mastery of chronological time. Without *kairos*, Agamben argues, *chronos* remains unfulfilled. . . . Without *kairos*, *chronos* exceeds our grasp; it is always beyond our reach, out of touch" (266; cf. Agamben 70–71).

On the other hand, Agamben's argument against Derrida centers on the idea that deconstruction is unable to master *chronos*, and, thus, infinitely divisible *chronos* must always remain unfulfilled for it: "Deconstruction is a thwarted messianism, a suspension of the messianic" (Agamben 103). The accusation would entail claiming that "deconstruction" is always on the sidelines when it comes to the "historic," since the messianic is fundamentally characterized by the wager that fulfillment is possible by "retrieving and revoking foundation, by coming to terms with it"; and he concludes: "If we drop the messianic theme and only focus on the moment of foundation and origin—or even the absence thereof (which amounts to the same thing)—we are left with empty, zero degree, signification and with history as its infinite deferment" (103–4). This way of presenting the argument forecloses the idea that there can be an engagement with history and politics that is not already the imposition of an appropriation of time. That is, it is the rejection of the lack of ultimate foundation in the name of politics. While it is correct to state that from the point of view of politics this void must be foreclosed at all costs, we will see in what follows that, so long as this move is made, the problems posed by modern politics remain out of our reach. Not only impossible to solve, which I am in no way proposing here, but also impossible to even think in a manner equal to the task.

The reason for this is structural. For in Agamben, radical as the kairological interruption may appear, it remains securely anchored in the very modern temporal crossroads we have begun to sketch out here. In fact, it is a Christian matrix that is at issue, as will become clear in the chapters that follow. What we are proposing, then, is this: if we refrain from thinking time as the formless void that is neither one nor many, neither *chronos* nor *kairos*, that is, if we avoid thinking the catachrestic time that is formless-time, however radical our political project, it will remain the imposition of an appropriation of time. Thus, when I write of the formless I am also writing of a relation to the political that is not itself political—perhaps I can refer to it as infrapolitical.

It is already possible to go back to Lomnitz's observations. For his description places itself within the horizon of this meditation by expressing a desire to fully master the representation of time—which is what he is looking for vis-à-vis concepts like "postcoloniality," "global south," and so on. Less obvious is the fact that it also opens the way to a consideration of the national as that which is truly modern—as Agamben would have it: part of "the epoch that is situated under the sign of the dialectical *Aufhebung*" (100)[10]—precisely *because* it is unable to master the representation of time, or, in other words, to become self-present to itself by mastering representation. As such, this would suggest a reason for the unruly relationship between modernity as a political condition for philosophy—structurally invested in a formalization of temporality that for this very reason would be inimical to the instrumentalization of the impossibility of mastering a time proper to the plasticity of capitalism.

Latin America, such as Lomnitz describes it, would, occupy the exact same place that God occupies in Hegel according to certain adversarial theological interpretations of the becoming subject of substance in Hegel's *Encyclopedia*. Lomnitz himself opens the way for this theological consideration when he quips that, in the region, the language of cultural emancipation, autonomy, sovereignty, and independence remains not only the cornerstone of hegemony in political discourse but also the symptom of a "Christian-inflected notion of emancipation in death that was transposed onto the chronotope of national liberation . . . a kind of equivalent of heaven and glory" (350).

When Latin America, as the subject of history, like God (the "substance-subject"), separates from itself through externalization or dependency, that either destroys the possibility of dominating representation (thus destroying the possibility of a "proper" temporal formation), or it forces thought to imagine time from a different perspective altogether. If Lomnitz offers a negative instance of the former, Catherine Malabou has formulated with clarity what is at stake in the latter with the concept of temporalization at the heart of her *The Future of Hegel*. By putting things in this light, it would be possible to turn on its head the commonly accepted image of modernity as the infinitely divisible line of "empty, homogeneous time"—against which, it is assumed, all other temporalities become atavistic remnants of the past. In fact, we would be displacing the problem of coevalness (in which the past and the present are captured by a single chronotope) since it is modernity that would be defined in this way, and no longer would modernity be coterminous with the authoritative coercion of the people, or of peoples, to fall into the rhythm of "contemporary" or "actual" chronological time. In fact, modernity would then be the unruly temporalization of an ideal of the homogenous that is never mastered. *Chronos* would no longer be able to hide behind the mask of sameness. The Lucretian classical materialist version of events would no longer be germane. The *clinamen* is not what comes to perturb a putative straight line of time because the standard situation of historicity is a chaotic, multitemporal, and multidirectional scribble. Thus, it is no longer possible to exalt the postnational or the postcolonial as multitemporal while assuming that the national can serve as an example of the homogeneous experience of time. But neither is it possible to imagine, as recent scholarship has demonstrated, that the imperial time of capital is empty or homogeneous.[11]

Malabou has shown how it is to the history of Christianity that we must turn if we want to think through this difficult terrain. Christianity will have been the religion of the pure event, and thus the religion of a very peculiar temporality. As much as we attempt to normalize this aspect of our experience, we live "the great revolution in time effected by Christianity," which "is the paradoxical inauguration of a non-recurring time. The time that makes history turn is the time which itself does not turn or return: a linear time radically distinct from teleological time. The essential reason for this is that the incarnation only happens *once*, and in a *unique individual* . . . . The unity of the divine and human natures can only be made manifest in *one* singular form" (116). To the extent that our calendar is the direct manifestation of this *turn* (before Christ, after Christ, regardless of the name we give to this pivot), we all live the unique and singular form of time Christianity has bequeathed us. It matters little that Saint Augustine, one of the key figures in this story, found the Psalmist of use in order to quell the anxieties of the Empire about a possible Christian rebellion: "God wanted time to be mixed"—this to cement the distinction between our time and the realm of eternity, which will be interwoven until the Last Judgment separates them (cf. Alliez 87). But this "mixture" is absolutely not the idea of multiple temporalities. On the contrary, it is the assertion of the single time of the Christian as he awaits the end of time. Christ *creates* this new time. And this creation is what places him apart from all other individuals (Malabou 120). It is the emptying out, or lowering, the becoming dependent of the deity, which puts time to the test. Malabou concludes: "This 'test of time' consists in the act of divine alienation, an absolute negativity which exposes itself within a finite negativity. Thus the *curriculum vitae* [life-process] of the divine appears as the articulation of two worlds, the sensible and the supersensible, the finite and the infinite. Christ is their living hypotyposis [the translation of the spiritual into the sensory]" (121). So far, then, we seem to be at the level of a more capacious schematizing power: the subject, and here it is a question of divine subjectivity, that is capable of creating or introducing a new temporality, that is wholly his own.

Malabou explains that for Hegel the time of Revelation is a specific time, which was philosophically expressed in Kant. In Hegel's interpretation of Kant the transcendental imagination is identified with intuitive understanding. This means that for Hegel the imagination is a synthesis of opposites (125). The alienation of God, such as Malabou reads it in Hegel, yields a decidedly different effect than the inability to master representation caused by the fact of dependency as understood by Lomnitz. Dependency, once set into a discernible pattern, is indeed capable of producing a clear chronotope, a stable mastering of representation and an image of time. It is in the phase of its becoming (those phases in which, like today, it is up for grabs which foreign powers will be able to gain allegiance) that time is undone, putting "us" Latin Americans in the difficulty of not knowing "when we are." In Hegel, God is "conceptualized as transcendental imagination," which "amounts to positing him as a *temporalizing instance*" which would then be able to hold all possible times together (126): "from the suffering of God to the vacancy in the sphere of the transcendental, the subject *takes its time.* The subject extends, stretches out, and unwinds the linear continuum whose source and starting point is the subject as Ego, as 'I'" (124). Hegel thus inscribes time, and not lack, within God. God, as transcendental imagination, is "pure vision *of* and *in* the temporal"; he is "identified with the process of 'to see (what is) coming'" (127).

Given these considerations, which turn God into the crossroads of time, Malabou is particularly interested in the interpretation that one can offer of the chapter on "Absolute Knowledge" in Hegel's *Phenomenology of Spirit*, the following passage in particular: "Spirit necessarily appears in time, and it appears in time just as long as it has not grasped its pure concept, i.e. has not annulled time. It is the outer, intuited pure self which is not grasped by the Self, the merely intuited concept; when this latter grasps itself it sublates its time-form, comprehends this intuiting, and is a comprehended and comprehending intuiting. Time, therefore, appears as

the destiny and necessity of spirit that is not yet complete within itself"
(Hegel, *Phenomenology* 487). Everything hinges on the way we interpret the
annulment of time proposed in this text. "For Heidegger," writes Malabou,
"the *Aufhebung* of time constitutes the Self's mastery of itself in its *parousia*,
a mastery which implies the final banishment of all temporality and the
advent of spirit's unchanging and indifferent present" (128). For her part,
Malabou posits that this is rather the death of a specific time, not of temporality as such: "The *Aufhebung* here does not apply to time in general
but only to a *certain time*: the time that has just been characterized as 'time
which lies ahead.' . . . Hegel is not considering time in general but linear
time, the time in which the subject 'sees itself as a passing moment'" (128).
The concept of linear time becomes the temporality of alienation. This is
the temporality that characterizes "a process intrinsic and unique to the
modern epoch of subjectivity," in which the subject is understood as a
structure of anticipation and temporalization (129–30). Since it is in God
himself that this movement is accomplished, and because *theos* is the end of
the development, Malabou stresses that to understand Hegel on this point it
is important to keep in mind the two temporalities implied. Another kind
of temporality is necessary for the sublation of the linear temporality of
alienation to be possible: "The criterion of completion assumed by modernity must come, in fact, from a time which is not modernity—from the
time of [circular] teleological fulfillment, within which the end is identical
with the beginning. For this is a time which can dismiss that other time,
the one that does not lie ahead. At the very moment when we believed
time had been dismissed, the two times meet and unite" (130).

For Malabou this crossroads of time is not only a matter of philosophical
debate. What is at issue is the condition of modernity, and our place in
it. As she puts it, the arrangement of Hegel's two times (teleology and
alienation) determines the future of those who no longer have time ahead
of themselves, for whom everything has been already accomplished. How
are we to understand this idea of "not having time ahead of ourselves"?
Malabou's answer:

> This situation creates the contradictory couple of saturation and vacancy.
> Saturation to the extent that the future can, in our time, no longer repre-
> sent the promise of far-off worlds to conquer. . . . The "new world order"
> means the impossibility of any exotic, isolated or geopolitically marginal
> event. Paradoxically, this saturation of theoretical and natural space is felt as
> a vacuum. The major problem of our time is in fact the arrival of free time.
> Technological simplification, the shortening of distances . . . bring about

a state where we must acknowledge that there is nothing more to do. The most sterile aspect of the future lies in the unemployment, both economic and metaphysical, which it promises. But this promise is also a promise of novelty, a promise that there are forms of life that must be invented. (192)

It is possible, nevertheless, to venture a different interpretation of the absence of time ahead, one that perhaps interrupts the holding together of times that Hegel formalized. This interruption would not have to be dialectical or antidialectical, but it would require imagining the annihilation of time in a different manner. What if our free time is not the time of unemployment (a time that after all is what holds the globe together today for capitalism), but that of thought vis-à-vis the unworking of the synthesis of time, a thought no longer held by the synthesis of the transcendental imagination? We are now in a position to reconsider Agamben's objections to Badiou and Derrida from a perspective that does not rely (or, at the very least, less credulously) on the very modern temporal matrix that is in question.

Badiou: Evental Time

What is evental time in Badiou? This question is of some importance when thinking about Latin America, as some of the strongest and most influential work being done today on the area takes its cues from the French philosopher.[12] According to Peter Hallward's survey of Badiou's work, it is against the grain of the chronological accumulation of time that "true time" traces a diagonal, a section that presents the absences and presences that articulate the various elements of a structure: "'every event constitutes its own time,' such that 'there is no time in general; there are *times*'" (Hallward 157). The time that an event opens is "the time of a properly eternal present, indifferent to both the inheritance of the past and the promise of the future. The subject of fidelity lives exclusively in an unfolding present, the present of evental consequences" (157). Hallward is right in pointing out the utter simplicity of Badiou's conception of time. The order of being, which is mathematical and thus timeless, is intervened by the declaration of the evental break. A time opens that is the time of the present, in which the consequences of an eternal truth unfold.

In the more recent *Logics of Worlds*, Badiou insists on this doctrine of the evental opening of an eternal present. An event is a separating evanescence, an atemporal instant that extracts from one time the possibility of another time, which presents us with a new time (385). It is the subject that is faithful to the event that builds the present, while the reactionary subject "extinguishes" it, and the obscurantist subject brings the present "to the night of its non-exposition" (55, 59). The examples Badiou offers are unquestionable insofar as he deals with jihadists and *nouveaux philosophes*. The issue becomes more complicated when we see it in the light of his reading of Pascal. An early reading of *Being and Event* by Lyotard broached this very same question in a way that will allow us to link it to the multiple times of Christianity.

Concerning Badiou's meditation on Pascal, in which the fidelity of the Christians is proposed as the model faithfulness to fidelity itself, and thus as the model for the fidelity to the event that opens the new present, Lyotard asks why the Jewish answer is not itself a militant one; the answer is that the opening of the event coincided with the decision to affirm the divinity of Christ (Lyotard, "Liminaire" 245). This is another way of posing the problem of the relation between the event and its name, which Lyotard suggests is a major difficulty precisely because of the lack of any serious engagement with the question of time in Badiou's doctrine. In the introduction to the Spanish edition of *Being and Event*, Badiou readily admits that this is indeed a serious difficulty, one which the developments of the 1988 book do not treat in sufficient depth (*El ser* 7). In order to tackle this problem, a temporality proper to the event would have to be considered in more detail, something he endeavors to address in *Logics of Worlds*. But even there, what results is a theory of time that remains ensnared by the allure of the presence of the present.

It might be more to the point, nevertheless, and in order to avoid a facile dismissal, to consider the conception of the present that Lyotard was working on at the time of his remarks on *Being and Event*. That is, I am not interested in taking sides; rather, what is at issue here is to illustrate to what extent the problem of time remains caught within the Judeo-Christian matrix and its translation into the politics of modernity. Published the same year as Badiou's magnum opus, Lyotard's *The Inhuman* offers the antithetical version of the present: "The presenting present cannot be grasped: it is *not yet* or *no longer* present. It is always too soon or too late to grasp presentation itself and present it. Such is the specific and paradoxical constitution of the event. That something happens, the occurrence, means that the mind is disappropriated. The expression 'it happens that . . .' is the formula of non-mastery of self over self. The event makes the self incapable of taking possession and control of what it is. It testifies that the self is essentially passible to a recurrent alterity" (*The Inhuman* 59). In one instance, the present is opened by the evental fidelity of a subject for whom there can be no other temporalities whatsoever, and this is the subject as disciplined master; in the other, what obtains is the deposed mind that is incapable of mastering a present that is ungraspable. The crux of the matter in both cases, however, is the particular determination of the present as such. Lyotard insists that fidelity to the evental inconsistency requires errancy, perhaps more than a theory of the supernumerary name ("Liminaire" 245); Badiou agrees that for him fidelity can also mean being disciplined with regard to the lack of discipline of the event ("Liminaire" 263). The central problem, then, is how to do justice to that which, for the time being, remains formless enough to evade, in Badiou's terms, encyclopedic capture. Whether it is an active, passive, or critical wager, I want to propose that the difficulty in grappling with the anarchic or formless is aggravated, not resolved, by putting the matter in terms of actuality or of the presence of the present—that is, in temporal terms. Our task remains to think time in all its radical complexity—that is, to think time as something other than a solution.

Both Lyotard and Badiou locate a place where time is lost, where we lose track of time as a single homogeneous order: the "event" and the "present" serve this function respectively. Badiou forecloses this loss of time by insisting on the present that the subject opens in following the consequence of the event; for Lyotard the dispossession of the self and of the mind is also a falling into a truly sovereign dispensation where passivity is the mode of the subject. Religion is undoubtedly the structure that underscores these different positions: however radicalized, one speaks in the name of Christianity and the other in the name of Judaism.

Bruno Bosteels has formulated what is perhaps the most trenchant critique of this residual Judeo-Christian matrix at the heart, not only of these two thinkers, but more generally, of the contemporary radical Left. "Badiou, Negri, Žižek," among many others, reveal a Left facing the "real difficulty of answering the demand for a political experience, including on a subjective level, that would be *essentially* different from the one it combats [Christianity and its ultimate absorption into the structure of the capitalist state, where the sphere of citizenship serves as the paradise in which civil society is redeemed]," and he concludes: "All of these thinkers, in fact, remain deeply entangled in the political theology of Christianity—unable to illustrate the militant subject except through the figure of the saint" (*Marx and Freud* 155). And yet the alternative he offers could also be traced back to the same matrix, for a reason that links his proposal to Badiou in one essential point: the lack of a serious meditation on time.

Bosteels argues that far from giving up on the subject, and the politics of subjectivity, it is a question of thinking against the internal limit of the subject's incorporation of the Christian or religious paradigm. It is a matter of turning to "the power of the subject against the domination of constituted subjectivity, as well as to open up the concept to that which cannot but remain unconceptualized. Such would be, after all, the possible role of philosophy or theory in the face of terror" (*Marx and Freud* 157). Yet what could the power of the subject that interrupts the domination of constituted subjectivity be if not the clash of a teleological closure with the linearity of alienation that has already been constituted and dominates? And what would this temporal crossroads be if not the time*s* of Christianity and the epoch that unfolds under the sign of the *Aufhebung*?

Another way of saying this would be to point to the need to oppose the materialist rereading of religion in Žižek and others, where the "Cheification of Christ himself" serves as the guiding motto to an even more radical return to the deposition of religion by revolutionary praxis: "In Cuba in particular," for he is writing of the cinema of Tomás Gutiérrez Alea, "any reliance on the analogy with Christianity also risks reducing the construction of socialism to a perpetuation of the political status quo for which this religion historically has provided an ideological alibi. It is for this reason that . . . [Gutiérrez Alea] patiently revisits the centuries-long legacy of Christianity as a near-insuperable obstacle . . . for the creation of the new man in Cuba" (*Marx and Freud* 113). Beyond any possible Žižekian reinscription of the Christian legacy into the thought/praxis of revolution, the surpassing of religion, it must be noted, was already accomplished by the Hegelian formalization of Absolute Spirit, where it was necessary to bring the mere representationality of religion into the concept. Moreover, it is the death of God through which, according to the dialectic, "substance has become subject" (cf. Derrida, *Glas* 231).

It would seem that in the case of Christianity, just as with the dialectic (which perhaps can be understood as the philosophical sublation of Christianity), the more one desires to break from it, the more one reproduces its most fundamental mechanism. What are we to do in such a situation? Where could the inner limit of constitutive and constituted subjectivity be found when we are dealing with a process that is absolute? For the proposition of an absolute religion, or an absolute philosophy (one that has opened up the concept to what cannot but remain unconceptualized), cannot and does not present a limit but, rather, the infinite proposition of the hetero-tautological dialectic. It is at this juncture that the work of Jacques Derrida needs to be revisited.

Derrida: "Time"

Derrida recounts: in absolute religion, such as Hegel understands it, separation or division is not overcome by reconciliation. The opposition remains as a representation that anticipates the ultimate truth, and hence the essential content of this representation remains external. The object in question is present, but it remains outside and ahead. The subject for whom this representation appears cannot be one with its object in the now, and the reconciliation has to wait (Derrida, *Glas* 219; I always cite, in the discussion that follows, from the column on Hegel). If this is what obtains prior to the Hegelian synthesis (the sublation of religion into speculative philosophy), it would serve to mark the limit of a pre-Hegelian modernity. So long as this exteriority remains, we are somewhere prior to absolute knowledge. By the same token, we would be in a zone where time, which would be defined as the representative exteriority itself, would be caught in the realm of objective necessity, nothing to be done to it, almost impossible to even notice it. Derrida sums this up in a single sentence: "Religion is representative because it needs time" (220). Let us remark, in passing, that any political praxis of subjectivity that has not yet produced its anticipated end result (e.g., communism) would come to occupy the place religion does here: it would have to be representative because it would need time. But occupying the same place that religion occupies before and after the formalization of Absolute Knowledge has its consequences. Namely, that the time of separation must be turned around; it must be "actualized and organized as the real movement that abolishes the present state of things . . . [and] find inscription in a concrete body" (Bosteels, *The Actuality* 239). Separation would then be that which is being destroyed by the actuality of that which is not yet here but as horizon. The age that places itself under the sign of the *Aufhebung*, modernity since Hegel, is forced to produce the historicization of eternity by pitting its horizon-al actuality against a present it needs to destroy, a present it sets out to transform, even as this present is only available as its own theoretical projection, its own theoretical fiction. We are talking about the crossroads of religion and revolution but also about the formalization of a stable present that can be handled so as to transform it, as if time were at hand, given in the form of an object here and now.

Moreover, the mere surpassing of this exteriority would only yield a further complication. If, as Hegel points out in the *Phenomenology of Spirit*, Absolute Knowledge is at once a deletion and a relief of time, what obtains is a "barely existing limit, exceeded as soon as it is posited," which "is already no more what it is yet and does not even give time to think its time. This limit is what barely presents itself between absolute religion and *Sa* [Absolute Knowledge]" (Derrida, *Glas* 220). Everything hinges on the strategic interpretation one makes of this deletion and relief of time, and any possible idea regarding a post-Hegelian modernity depends on it.

Absolute Knowledge, then, as the passage from representation to presence, produces the being by itself of the logos, its unveiled essence. Derrida calls this the final accomplishment of the phantasm: "The absolute phantasm: *Sa*" (225). And he asks: "What can there be outside an absolute phantasm? What can one yet add to it? Why and how does one desire to get out of it?" He follows these questions thus: "It is necessary to give oneself time"; but what kind of time, when the concept itself seems to be what makes it so difficult to imagine any thought of an outside in the first place? Derrida adds: not the time that remains, but "Time's remain(s)" (225, 226). The difficulty lies in "trying to think . . . a remain(s) of time . . . that would not come under a present, under a mode of being or presence, and that consequently would fall outside the circle of Sa, [but] would not fall from it as its negative, as a negative sound. . . . The remain(s), it must be added, would not fall from it at all. Everything that falls (to the tomb) in effect yet comes under [releve du] Sa" (226). Derrida opened *Glas* by observing that the words "here" and "now" are for us citations—and that we will have learned this from Hegel (1). Considered as citation, the question of "here-now" can nevertheless be staged, the better to go in the direction of "that element of the scene which exceeds representation" (Derrida, *Points* 11). What is at issue here, then, is a question concerning the possibility of time beyond any synthetic representation of it, yes, but the crucial point is not the aesthetic proposition of the theorist struggling with Hegel but that the only way of avoiding the mere substitution of one foundation or absolute ground by another depends on the possibility of assuming the here and now only as citation, as a theoretical fiction that envelops us almost to the point of blindness but that can nevertheless be staged so as to confront its fictionality, however obliquely. It makes no difference if this substitution of the foundation takes on the mask of the void or the form of the willful forgetting of the emptiness that haunts all institutions. What is at issue is therefore not merely to posit the vanguard notion of a postmetaphysical time, as if it were simply a question of proposing yet a different time-form. What is at stake is rather that the possibility of confronting the truth of what is given hinges on our ability to find a way to think the "fact" of this "thing" that is time beyond form, the nothing from which history is made.[13]

The remain(s) of time, or that time that is not without being nothing, point to a "time," or time, that is only "time" if we understand this word catachrestically, as the only word that we have available even though it is not up to the task. For this "time" is a formless time, the absence of time as a formalized structure of any sort, a time that lies beyond the columns (for instance the two columns of *Glas*). This is an uncertain time. And yet there is the need for infrapolitical deconstruction to make it appear, not as an aesthetic program but as a confrontation with the formlessness of history. "Forces resistant to the *Aufhebung*, to the process of truth, to speculative negativity, must be made to appear," while at the same time maintaining that "these forces of resistance do not constitute in their turn relievable or relieving negativities. In sum, a remain(s) that may not be without being nothingness: a remains that may (not) be" (*Glas* 43).

Beyond what can be decided by the subject of truth, it is his or her phantasm that is consequently belabored when here and now are taken to be something other than citations. What lies beyond that fantasy is not the tragic sublime of the political, and much less the philosophical idea of time or times as redemption, but the simple datum that the "time" that lies beyond the columns, beyond the philosophical projection of its form, whether it is declined politically or otherwise, is not the figurative imposition of anyone's "here" and "now." The rest of time: an unwieldy time that cannot be managed or imposed on anyone.

From the Mastery of Time to the Formless "Time" of Infrapolitics

A different perspective opens up if we return now to the opening scene of this chapter, that is, to the absent body of the sovereign and the uncanny reemergence of figures that symbolized the most forceful imposition of the time of the New on the subject of the Revolution. It would be tempting to think that the Revolution reintroduces Pavón Tamayo and company in order to compensate for the symbolic authority lost by the need to hide the ailing body of the sovereign, which as a living mortal being was beginning to clash with its ideal and eternal status as the principle of order for the whole of the community. As Castro put it: "Due to imperial plans, the status of my health becomes a state secret that cannot be divulged constantly" (qtd. in Ponte, *Villa* 49). But it is not the body of the sovereign that is at issue, for at the same time Castro was announcing the change in the leadership structure of the revolutionary government. It was Raúl Castro who would come to occupy his brother's shoes. We are dealing with the absence of a symbol, then. And not just any symbol, but the one that was able to master representation. The one that was verisimilar. In 2007, Fidel

Castro is still the stand-in for the domination and political instrumentalization in the present, of the *kairological* instant. It is for this reason that the return of the repressed past, and of the repressors of the past, a past that is still evoked as a secret even by those who lived it (cf. Arrufat in Barquet 138), had the disconcerting effect that it did. But this process ex-poses the true meaning of an entity, the subject of history, capable of creating its own time, and all its forms. It also illuminates the extent to which this modern and salvific political messianism does not contradict itself when it shifts from one temporal gear to another. On the contrary, this is its essence. If this is so, then the time of alienation that it promises to overcome is not an outside obstacle that is there to be definitively transcended but an internal apparatus of discipline that makes certain that there is acquiescence regarding the appropriation of the time of salvation. Antonio José Ponte suggests as much when he concludes that what the revolutionary regime gives to artists goes beyond any material good: what the state gives is "a time unfettered from any form of accountability"; the state gives "the time that remains after undoing all the equations that linked it to money. A time tailor-made for artists, ineffective, to be dilapidated. The time without borders within which the work [of art—*la obra*] is made. The time that they will never find in capitalism" (235). But this is merely the other side of the kind of time that Pavón Tamayo symbolized: the time of "punishment without borders" (236). Ponte adds: "It was clear that the State was capable of distributing with equal generosity the time of creation and the time of punishment" (236). When it is put in those terms, the narrative that Ponte constructs takes advantage of the modern aesthetic presuppositions concerning the revolt of the romantics against the hellish imperial ticktock of linear, empty, or homogeneous time under capitalism. As we will have a chance to observe in the next chapter, the sublation of this time of alienation is not the time of liberation but the time of (voluntary) slavery. The time without borders that Ponte invokes is actually the time that Che Guevara will offer to the workers as they are about to sacrifice themselves in order to produce the new nation. This is not a borderless time, then. It is the ideology of the borderless as it is subsumed under the political domination of the present. When the remains of time are yet again imagined as a new form of time, here and now, what obtains is an ideological temporality for which chains are tropes for liberation.

If we move forward in time and consider the image of Fidel Castro since the recent announcement regarding the normalization of relations between Cuba and the United States, we find that not understanding this modern and Judeo-Christian crossroads of time at the heart of the political machine of the Revolution makes it almost impossible to see what is at issue. Fidel Castro's image is no longer that of a hero but that of a retired family man, frail and in need of care. We see details about his private home life, the décor of his house, as well as close-ups of his decaying body, such as pictures of his hands. Ana Dopico has compared them to the hands of her father; to which she adds: "Those ancient hands . . . summon reluctant moments of identification. . . . It is an uncanny intimacy, an uneasy empathy. But it's there, the display of decay, the mortality of a 'historical' gerontocracy that has held three subsequent generations captive to a political primal scene" (Dopico). She suggests that what we are witnessing in these displays symbolizes the replacement of a particular mode of power for another, but she does not know in what sense: "What will the new modes of authority be, in whose service is this uncanny pathos being deployed? When Fidel's hands seem like your father's hands: what is the political meaning of such an image?" (Dopico). Perhaps the political meaning of an image that makes one identify the hands of the liberator/incarcerator with those of the father is openly displayed in the surface of the comparison itself. This is also the state's opportunity. It bides its time by creating it: this is the structure of the primal scene to begin with. The political primal scene is not simply the embodied promise of redemption but the uneasy empathy and identification it enforces on those who have to accept caring for the time of redemption as if it were redemption itself. One is captive to this primal scene whenever one thinks that further political intervention, a further and more rigorous way of mastering representation, will lead to the overcoming of one temporal predicament by another. Dopico concludes her reading of the family portraits of Fidel by asking: "How does one care for an uncanny exhaustion?" For her this is an open question, and its overtones in the context of the piece are immediately tied to the care for our elders. Nevertheless, I would like to suggest a possible reframing of this question.

The exhaustion here does not touch only on the decaying body of the sovereign, the liberator, the tyrant, and so forth. Neither is it tied to a particular mode of politics—even avowed communists can readily acknowledge Cuba's "outmoded conception of politics" without any further consequences (Badiou, *Ethics* 106). It concerns, rather, the very idea that it is only a further turn of the screw in the modern history of mastering time that is required in order to overcome the deadlocks of our frail and decaying modernity. Modernity, however, is frail and decaying not because anyone has done anything to it, but because it is increasingly hard to confuse its inner structure with a single (whether it is chronological, homogeneous, empty, coeval, etc.) temporality that can be redeemed by other modes of time itself. What comes to the fore, then, is that politics, modern politics, is nothing but this mastering of time and times, the ever-uncertain shifting of one temporality to another. And so long as we are guided, however uncannily or uneasily, toward identifying with the need to care for its exhaustion, it will hold us captive. The difficulty of the problem at hand is great. But the care of exhaustion only leads to further masterly representations of time in the name of politics. If time and politics are identified in this manner, then a borderless or formless time can no longer be the time of a politics as such. It must be the time of a politicity that will only show itself as the radical reframing of what counts as politics in the first place.

In the chapters that follow, I take this time, the time of the absence of time-as-a-formalizing-operation, as the guiding notion with which to read three intricately related histories. First, it becomes necessary to revisit the romantic literary tradition, down to its theoretical extrapolation in twentieth-century poetry and theory. The knot between politics and aesthetics here is also the crossroads of time as we have elaborated it in this chapter. Thus, the second chapter will lay the groundwork for the basic structure that emerges in the third, which is the politico-aesthetic form that the theory and praxis of Revolution becomes once it secularizes the theological categories that we have been examining thus far. Only then will we be in a position to confront the question of nihilism, which is the object of the fourth chapter.

2. Sovereignties, Poetic and Otherwise

> Honor of Mankind, sacred LANGUAGE,
> Ordered and prophetic speech,
> Chains of beauty that enwind
> The god bewildered in the flesh,
> Illumination, and largess!
> Now a Wisdom makes utterance,
> And rings out in that sovereign voice
> Which when it rings can only know
> It is no longer anyone's
> So much as the woods' and the waters' voice!
> —Paul Valéry, "Le Pythie" (translation modified)

Dictations: The Romantic Roots of *Foquismo*

In a recent study of the place of the *foco*, or the theory of the guerrilla, in the unfolding of the Cuban Revolution, Juan Duchesne Winter offers a temporally determined cause for the ultimate failure of Ernesto Che Guevara's strategy. His first claim is that it is in the narrative of *Pasajes de la guerra revolucionaria* and not in the theoretically inflected *La guerra de guerrillas* that the Argentine gives full body to the theory of the *foco*. "This is due," he explains, "to the ability of narrative discourse to display the *space of experience* as the work of human action" (*La guerrilla* 16). This space of experience is able to bring together past and future in the "present of interpretative action," which is to say that Duchesne Winter aligns himself with an interpretation invested in resolving the general aporias of time by reimagining or reworking Kant's productive imagination. The work of Paul Ricoeur is central in this regard, and Duchesne Winter openly declares his reliance on this model. He does so to an end that might seem surprising, as he turns to a model usually associated with the end of grand narratives but in order to account for what is arguably the last of the grand narratives: the guerrilla in Latin America. Without remarking on this, Duchesne Winter has thus given us a key to the function of aesthetics as one of the central aspects of the complicated process of formalization and institutionalization in the Cuban Revolution. Some preliminary remarks are in order for this to become more transparent.

The work of Ricoeur is often invoked as part of a broader tendency to proclaim "the end of time," or of History. Yet the turn to narrative could also be read as perhaps the last attempt at achieving a formal matrix with which to make time appear, for it promises an answer to the impossibility of producing a pure phenomenology of time. Paul Ricoeur has noted that this impossibility is a fact of the philosophical tradition at least since Saint Augustine (1:6, 83–84). For our purposes, what is important to underline is that Ricoeur's project does not intend to keep to that insight; his goal is rather to find other ways in which to produce a coherent thought on time. In fact, when considering the encroachment of a thought of the formless (*informe*) on modern narrative, Ricoeur notes that the need to do away with the formless is not due to anything like a requisite to better console ourselves, to protect against any exposure to the abyss of the groundless, but a mere necessity of discourse (2:28).

In the process, philosophy finds it needs to invite others to the conversation, hence the move toward narrative. Ricoeur writes of a three-way dialogue between historiography, phenomenology, and literary criticism; their intersection will mark the place where time is made to appear (1:177). Frederic Jameson, who has recently taken up this very same banner, summarizes: "What gives us an insight into the temporalities of (fictional) narrative is not the virtue of one of these accounts over the other, it is their very multiplicity as such"; to which he adds, following Ricoeur: "Time does not appear unless . . . these dimensions are held together in the 'configuration' (why not use Ricoeur's excellent term?) of a single [narrative] act" (*Valences* 497). Furthermore: it is literature that first makes time appear, or that first produces it, making visible "the great personification of Time from its multiple intersections. Time can only appear at the intersection between various times" (*Valences* 498).

It is impossible to ignore the power and reach of this kind of interdisciplinary apparatus for making time appear today. The ease with which we seem to avail ourselves of all possible temporalities in our various fields of research points to a defining fact of our contemporary situation, and not only in the humanities, and it is that beyond any antipathy toward the reopening of the ontological question by Martin Heidegger in the late 1920s, our default mode at present is to assume the active forgetting of the impossibility of a pure phenomenology of time. In essence, when we mark the place where time will be made to appear, what we are saying is that we have managed to give objective, measurable, observable form to being/time. We are dealing, then, with one of the most preponderant technologies for the forgetting of being available to us at present. The question becomes: What do we gain when we forget about the question of being/time? What we are supposed to gain, at least in theory, is the ability to sidestep the single homogeneous temporalization of modernity, capitalism, the nation, patriarchy, and so forth. With the multiplication of times we gain or regain some of the lost episodes of the history of those who do not get to write history books; in short, we gain access to the underbelly of History, which is thereby revealed as itself a narrative construction in the first place, or at least that is the plan. The problem, however, is much more complicated. And what I suggest in this book is that when we make time appear, this has more to do with our active participation in the process of caring for an exhausted modernity than it does with anything resembling a careful and radical engagement with the most difficult problems it has bequeathed us.

Let us return to the *foco*. Duchesne Winter is able to shed light on the internal structure of the doctrine of the *foco* itself by taking the narrativization of the guerrilla as his point of departure (as opposed to its more properly doctrinal exposition by someone like Régis Debray). In so doing, he is able to expose the theory even as the theory exposes all the contradictions that go into giving it its definitive form. The blind spot of Guevara's conception of the *foco*, then, is that it leaves out of the picture vast subjective and objective strata that went into the constitution of the Cuban experience. It is only by eliding those other considerations that Guevara, and the Revolution itself after him, is able to imagine that the *foco* as such is the cause of the victorious insurrection. Duchesne Winter states: "The so-called theory of the *foco* is the result of the form in which its most unalloyed exponent, Ernesto Che Guevara, elaborated the narrative plot of the Sierra Maestra insurgency so that it seemed to incarnate a sort of infinite Hegelian reason, with an apparently unlimited capability for self-determination and for the creation of the conditions for its own existence and development" (*La guerrilla* 17). As I showed in chapter 1, the temporality usually ascribed to this kind of Hegelian infinite reason is one that should, but does not actually, homogenize all other times, grafting them onto the course it prescribes for history. Yet, the narrativization of the guerrilla leaves something behind or outside. From a different perspective: the narratological exploration of the guerrilla illuminates all that its theoretical apparatus had to keep out in order to appear as a coherent program to itself. It gathers the remainders that fall from that infinite Hegelian reason. This infinite reason believes it is the totality, that there is nothing that falls outside of its reach. Its homogeneous time, however, is now illuminated and on closer inspection we can see that there was something excluded. This is the problem: if we make that exclusion appear as such, we have only succeeded in finishing the task of infinite reason; if we fail to make it appear, we have also failed at making time appear. And, within the confines of the logic in question, this means that we have necessarily failed politically. As we saw in the first chapter, it is because of these difficult choices that Derrida warns that everything that falls from Absolute Knowledge in effect comes under and takes over Absolute Knowledge. Perhaps it is for this very same reason that the remains of the infinite reason of the guerrilla can nevertheless be very easily and smoothly folded into the theory of the subject almost immediately.[1]

Duchesne Winter emphasizes that this conception of things was capable of producing a specific subjectivity, one that, following Alain Badiou's theory of the out-of-place, sunders the established order exposing the central contradiction at the heart of social space between exploiters and exploited (*La guerrilla* 24): "We attend to the phenomenological discovery and exposition of the political out-of-place from which emerges the subject in antagonism within the real conditions of existence" (*La guerrilla* 36). This subject, in turn, "acquires the imaginary dimension of the new time," even if this happens only in its projective dimension (*La guerrilla* 37). The new time of course is the time of a new law, the time after the destruction of the old order. And here things become more complicated, as the question of the foundation of that new order takes center stage. The *foco* posits a void between the destruction of an institutional circumstance that already exists and the construction of an alternative; it destroys one law by its direct action and does so on the grounds of the virtue of the new revolutionary program. This is a leap into the abyss, but one that immediately gives way to the task of covering the void over at any cost. Duchesne Winter then asks himself how new and how truly different is the new law that emerges. Does the interruption not imply a return to the myth of power that made possible despotic and arbitrary power in the first place? (*La guerrilla* 39). In forgetting about the impossibility of making time appear, what is actually lost is the idea that what matters here is not whether or not the new law is actually new or a reformulation of the old despotism. The fact that time has been made to appear in this context makes the real question disappear. What should have mattered is whether or not this revolutionary change in politics allowed itself to show the "fictional" or "narrative" and therefore unfounded nature of politics and the political. For the only thing new that could happen regarding the modern dispensation of oppression, resistance, and liberation would be the emergence of a politicity that is no longer solely concerned with erasing its ultimate lack of grounds. Obviously, this is not the case with the guerrilla, which immediately goes on the defensive, having to protect its own image and legitimacy.

The contribution Duchesne Winter makes in asking these questions is that he does not repeat the by-now classic liberal warnings about the revolutionary terror, for which all revolutions are an a priori evil, thus functioning as a plea for the conservation of things as they are. He wants to point to the dialectical return of that which is supposed to have been eradicated in the first place. I would argue, however, that by placing so much importance on the question of the return of the same, dialectical or otherwise, we miss the structure that fills in that void and, more to the point, that it is the reluctance to look at that abyss directly that makes possible the recommencement of hegemonic despotism. This is a tack that would not be, as far as I can see, antithetical to Duchesne Winter's reading of the narrativization of the guerrilla, as it is an aesthetic structure that is at issue.

I would like to propose, following the insights we gather from reading Duchesne Winter, that the structure that comes to cover over the void is not unique to the writing of Guevara but that he learns it from literature, and it concerns the passive welcoming of the other. Contrary to the by-now standard idea that theory turns to literature in order to destabilize or undo the hard-won ground of the militants in struggle, it is necessary to underscore to what extent it is literature itself that has been most instrumental in teaching the revolutionary how to cover over the void in question. I will not refer to all literature or to literature as such, not even to the totality of the work and thought of the authors whom I will mention throughout this chapter. What is at issue is the link between romanticism, modern revolutions, and the exhaustion of modern politics, particularly as this knot relates to the Cuban case. Though I will presently turn to three instances that are intimately tied to that historical reality, for the remainder of this chapter we will wander far afield into the realm of literature and theory with the hope that we will return to the Cuban context better equipped to understand the mixed temporalities of the Revolution after 1959.

Dictations: Martí, Vitier, Guevara

Allow me, then, to continue with three examples from the Cuban archive: one from the spiritual father of the Revolution (at least according to the programmatic ideology of the state), José Martí; the second concerns one of the most successful ideologues during the time between the end of the *pavonato* and through the post-Soviet era, Cintio Vitier; finally, we will return to Guevara's own *Pasajes*.

It is well known that Martí's poetry posits itself as a counter-rhetorical poetics. A poetics of the simple and the natural is at the heart of all his work. He points this out on more than one occasion by challenging a variety of literary or conceptual characters. One such figure is the "copista," a cultural functionary who operates via *imitation*, reproducing cultural models that already exist and have a generally accepted value ascribed to them. Against this kind of copyist, he proposes another: "When ideas are ripe for expression, they come of their own accord . . . when he who would be their vehicle does not expect it. . . . They emerge . . . as a sign of fire written in the shadows. He who sees them hunches over, as one who receives an order, to write. And after, the hand remains as if trembling from the pleasure of creation" (*Obras* 19:353). The "as if" of the last sentence is the crux of this passage. It is not an act of creation as such that takes place. That would be a human act, and, in that capacity, it would be a cultural act, mere rhetoric. The writing here takes place in a more mechanical or mediated form. What is said ultimately does not come from here, or from the subject doing the writing. Rather, it is the welcoming of a voice from elsewhere, which the copyist merely records. To describe this aspect of the poetic experience and the process of writing, Martí turns to a paradigmatic romantic metaphor, the aeolian harp: the poet is a "Harp . . . / Where the Universe vibrates" (*Obras* 16:91). The act of writing is the mechanism through which we receive testimony of that Other (realm or voice). But it is not the Other itself. The shadows that the fiery signs illuminate cannot appear as such. What remains is the trace of that other voice, which more than ever exposes the human voice as a "tosco alarde," a hoarse grunt, since the human voice only "thwarts" the manifestation of a Universe that "speaks better than man" (*Obras* 16:252). In the end, what the human voice can do, coarse as it may be, is give testimony of the experience as a whole, exposing the frailty of the subject and of subjectivity in general, which is itself revealed as the void that is momentarily occupied by the message from the true sovereign creative voice. The temporal aspect of this scriptural event remains obscure, however. When is the time when ideas are ripe of their own accord? What temporal crossroads is the scribe occupying when this sudden illumination takes hold of him? Only one thing is certain: it cannot be the time of the here and now, if by this we understand a time that is programmable or predictable, subject to the regular rhythms of the scribe. No, it erupts when he least expects it, and this occasion, this kairological instance, is essential to the experience being described.

My second example is significant for the way in which it "translates" the matrix of dictation into Christian, and properly Catholic, terms while, at the same time, doing so under the aegis of the first instance of dictation in the Western tradition: the Muses, and Mnemosyne in particular. It is also significant because it sheds some light on the kind of temporality in question. Cintio Vitier, in a text titled "Nemósine (Datos para una poética)," presents the *origenista* version of Martí's copyist. That is, a text that predates the Revolution as such, but that has become instrumental in explaining the primitive ground on which the Revolution's teleological matrix is said to take root (e.g., Rojas, *Isla*). Vitier is further implicated in the ideological use of Martí to the benefit of the Revolution, particularly in the 1990s. With him and his wife, Fina García Marruz, we have intellectuals who came of age under the influence of José Lezama Lima's Catholic vision of the history of culture, but who later on became defenders of the Revolution—their inflexion of that ideology cannot be underestimated, particularly for all that it reveals about the interrelation between aesthetics and the revolutionary political theology that concerns us here.

Invoking the Eucharist, the Form in question in what follows, Vitier states: "After we discover a form, there is no longer a before or an after, and we can only serve as its instrument, for the form is eternal and we are tied to death" ("Nemósine" 30). He speaks of a "tyrannical visitation" that makes of the poet "an adequate material . . . an artisan who at once obeys and is armed with astuteness," who, upon receiving the order, makes the work of literature an act that is "simultaneously free and necessary" (30, 32). For him, what is at issue in this experience is a moment of "synthesis," in which we are able to experience "unity in heterogeneity," and also a time where before and after do not apply (36). The time of successive nows is broken, and beginning and end are in harmony. For the Catholic poet, this gives us a "return to a lost unity and identity," which is the diametrical opposite of the nothingness of the moderns (36, 41). The example he offers is Jean-Paul Sartre's *Nausea*, in which we find, in the closing pages, the "miracle" of a creation that unfolds as the occupation of a body by something that "does not exist"; it is a record player that is in question here, a machine that reproduces music as the needle makes its way through the black gyre in which it is encoded (Sartre 239–42, esp. 242). "As Christians," Vitier posits, nothingness cannot be the foundation of the arts ("Nemósine" 33n1). It is important to note how Vitier relies on the very model that he is attempting to debar. The basic structure is maintained step by step, until we reach the final point. The emanation, that which gives the order and holds the "writer" as an instrument of its will, is not a void; rather, it is God himself, and, in this case, Christ in earthly form.

The ease with which this substitution is possible for Vitier would suggest that the structural places are the same in both cases; they just happen to be filled with different ideological content. No doubt the difference in that content is significant, for it marks the position of the atheist and the believer. However, instead of emphasizing the distinction between these two positions, the example can be adduced to illuminate a single structure behind the two. The contrast also sheds light on the ultimate function of this structure. It is a place where legitimation is garnered. For the Christian, as well as for the pagan or the modern subject that relinquishes autonomy, what is recorded, however mediated, presents a displacement that makes power and authority appear. The Muses return to the historical epoch of linear, successive time, in order to turn punctual facts into "poetic number," which is the measure of true history. They return in order to redeem alienated linear time. For the poet, "the only one who weaves the threads of history," the task is to be "indelibly faithful to what, having enthralled him, escapes from his mirror" (Vitier, "Nemósine " 37). The tyrannical prehension is not nothingness but is, rather, divinity itself, absolute fullness; the question remains, however, a matter of who gets to weave the threads of history. And the answer would be: he who harnesses the circular and teleological time of the Muses in order to disrupt the putative linear and programmable time of modernity's successive nows.

The trick, if we can put it in those terms, is to efface the truly modern character of the tension between the time of the Muses, circular and teleological, and the time of what could be called the ideology of modernity (linear, empty, homogeneous, the time of progress, or, more generally, the time of imperial capitalism), by pitting one against the other, and presenting one side of the (dialectical) opposition as the solution to the deadlocks posed by the other. If we are looking for the underlying structure that sends us in an endless circle, in which the solution reproduces the problems it was supposed to correct, this seems to be, in its most abstract form, a good site for interrogation.

If we now return to Guevara's narrative, where there are striking similarities with the two preceding examples, we will be able to gather the political import of the relay carried out by the Christian and aesthetic hypotyposis in question. In this key passage we find Guevara giving medical attention to peasants in the Sierra Maestra. He tells of an epiphanic moment regarding the link between the guerrilla and the people:

> The people of the Sierra sprout wild and without being cultivated [sin cuidado]. . . . There, in our work among them, the consciousness of a neces-

> sary change in the life of the people started to become flesh in us. The idea
> of agrarian reform became clear and the communion with the people was no
> longer theory but a definitive part of our being. The guerrilla and the peas-
> ants began to fuse into a single mass, without anyone being able to tell when
> in that long journey it had happened . . . that what was proclaimed became
> intimately true and we were part of the peasant mass. I only know . . . that
> [being among] the *guajiros* of the Sierra transformed a spontaneous and lyrical
> decision into a more serene force of a different value. The distressed and loyal
> people of the Sierra have never suspected the role they played in forging our
> revolutionary ideology. (*Pasajes* 71)

The awareness that the Revolution was necessary becomes flesh, and the
communion with the people is no longer theory. Unity has been achieved:
the guerrilla and the peasants are one. All of this happens without anyone
being the single creator of the new body, it is not even possible to pinpoint
when or where it happened. The instant of truth arrives, and the historical
necessity of the undertaking as well as the transparent incorporation of
the will of the people into the will of the Revolution is produced in one
singularly lyrical movement in which it is possible to claim that it is no
longer a question of political representation of the people by the Revolution, but of the Revolution being the presentation of the people as such.
The narrative is unable to present the time of the turn; this is a lost time
that cannot be subjected to objective measures. Rather, it is something that
is only given as "intimately true." Only the lyric form of the passage allows
him to give testimony of this event, and yet the lyricism of this movement
is exactly what Guevara posits has been sublated, changed into a force of
different value. The more romantic the trajectory of the revolutionary,
the more forcefully it must give way to something that is not at all lyrical.
On a different plane, however, we find that what Guevara is after is the
same thing that was at issue in Martí: the idealism of the Revolution has to
become a force of nature, sprouting in the wild, without being cultivated.
That is, without the lyrical mediation, without the parallel between the
wildflower (in all its originary ontological stability, *phusis*) and the people,
without the transubstantiation of the idea into flesh yielding intimate unity,
and without this force of nature forging revolutionary ideology—without
all of these paradigmatically modern aesthetic "moves," this passage would
be nothing but the declaration of one individual from Argentina who has
recently landed in a foreign land and proclaimed himself not the *representative* of the people but the people as such. (Ironically enough, we have a version of this very same scene without any of the lyrical dialectic that I have

been outlining thus far. It can be found a little over a half hour into part
I of Steven Soderbergh's *Che*. There, we find a line of peasants waiting to
see a doctor who tells everyone the same thing. No wild sprouting without
cultivation, no becoming-peasant, no passive forging of ideologies—only
the image of sweat-stained *guajiros*, all wearing earth-toned colors that
invoke not the lush greenery that the movie exploits so well but the ravages
of a civilization heavily invested in treating people like dirt: which is to
say, they represent not the world of *phusis* but the residue of a hypernihilist
process of cultivation.)

In this case, the tropology of dictation, of yielding to the will of the
other, which renders the subject a mere instrument at the behest of something inapprehensible (no one knows when or how these peasants occupy
the body of the guerrilla, only that this is absolutely true and unquestionable), is exposed in such a way that its ultimate function is also rendered
transparent. What resounds in Guevara's words is something like the sovereign voice we find in the concluding stanza of Paul Valéry's "Le Pythie,"
which appears above as this chapter's epigraph. This is a voice (Guevara's
own as an individual) that posits that its will is not the will of a single
individual. Rather, it is the utterance of a Wisdom that rings out knowing
that what resounds can only be the voice of the woods and the waves, of
nature. Again, it is a voice that commands the gap of a lost moment, when
time disappears. And the narrative is utterly unable to give shape to this
instant. It is as if the time that truly matters can never be made to appear as
such. Yet, in positing the occurrence of this event it does manage to make
other times appear as the intersection of heterogeneous temporalities that
indicate the guerrilla and the people becoming one. When time is made
to appear, it is as the dialectical synthesis of contraries that nevertheless are
maintained in the sublation. That is, when time is made to appear, what we
find is the dialectical elevation of one time by the force of another.

If this is the case, perhaps what needs to be interrogated more carefully
is not the narratological supplementation of philosophy (with literature,
history, and so forth), which breaks the master narrative of metaphysics
into multiple small narratives. For the metaphysics in question already
relies heavily on the form in which it makes multiple temporalities appear
together. That is, modernity is fundamentally and internally committed
to the constant confrontation of disparate forms of time. Instead, I suggest
taking a closer look at the time of lost time, the time of the void, and what
might happen when it is not filled in but, rather, allowed to resonate in all
its formlessness. Against the idea that this is something that was already
attempted, if not accomplished, by the romantics and their descendants (a

legacy most relevant to our theoretical tasks today),[2] we will have to show to what extent romanticism is still implicated in covering over the void.

Romanticism/Theory

Perhaps the most enduring idea on romanticism is that it is a search for unity in which the subject presents itself as the absolute sovereign. Christopher Newfield, writing of Emerson's view of the poet, offers a useful example of the kind of rhetoric that is most often adduced in this regard. He alludes to the ethereal flow of the universe that speaks or manifests itself through the poet: "The 'universal current' gives the poet life and . . . sustains rather than replaces the poet's power as sovereign law giver. . . . The true poet is the founding father . . . the sovereign . . . an objectifying ego whose practical freedom is manifested . . . by creating the world" (43). Modern poetry, particularly that which took its cues from German speculative philosophy after Kant, becomes increasingly invested in appropriating the figure of the sovereign as its own. There is no doubt that what happens to the concept of sovereignty in the hands of the poets, or even philosophers who, like Nietzsche or Bataille, sought to exceed the classical sense of the word, often bears little resemblance to the figure that decides on life and death. Nevertheless, the political revolutions of the time mark poetry with a desire that is certainly transformative (everything will be reformulated in the image of this sovereign), but it also places literature within an experience of time unknown prior to the two great revolutions of the eighteenth century, and which it will eventually have to confront. Hannah Arendt recalls that one possible name for this new time, as proffered by Robespierre himself, could be the time of the "despotism of liberty" (29). Here I want to follow some of the vicissitudes of that paradoxical temporality as it manifests itself in the form of a problem internal to modern poetry. That is, as it manifests itself as the aesthetic register of a "political" idea that had to be translated into the praxis of the poems (cf. Osborne and Alliez 9), and against which that same poetic practice became deformed, unformed, or opened to the formless, where it lingered a while and from which it eventually emerged, offering the experience of a different time that is the time of the absence of time, neither the atemporal realm of eternity nor the dead time in which it endured the dead time of the despotism of liberty.

One cannot compare Percy Bysshe Shelley's famous definition of the poets, "the hierophants of an unapprehended inspiration; . . . the unacknowledged legislators of the world" (297), to the fatuous narcissism of Robert de Montesquiou when he proclaims himself the "sovereign of transitory things"³—but the latter has the virtue of laying bare, in its self-serving directness, the underlying reliance on political concepts that characterizes much of post-Kantian poetry. And yet this sovereignty is more complex than the poet as figure of the Will allows us to think. If we take, for instance, fragment 209 of the *Athenaeum Fragments*, we find A. W. Schlegel describing the relationship between language and revolution in such a way that the concept of sovereignty itself emerges as a fiction: "Should a language bound by conventions like the French not be able to republicanize itself by having recourse to the power of the general will? The mastery of language over spirit is manifest: but its sacred inviolability follows as little from this domination as does the admission in natural law of the divine origin formerly imputed to all sovereign state power" (*Philosophical* 45). Language republicanizes itself by opening itself up to the power of the general will. This is not a power that exceeds language, for within this purview it is the communicative bond between the members of a community that defines the political even as it establishes the conditions for a republicanism modeled on poetic language. "Poetry is republican speech," writes Friedrich Schlegel in fragment 65 of the *Critical Fragments*: "a speech which is its own law and end unto itself, and in which all the parts are free citizens and have the right to vote" (*Philosophical* 8). It is in this sense that the Schlegels reimagined the tradition of political thought that, since Hobbes, took natural law as its point of departure. The most salient consequence of this shift is the subordination of jurisprudence to politics, and the deployment of poetry, and culture (*Bildung*) in more general terms, as the key phenomenon with which to think the possibility of a new world order. To take away the divine foundation of sovereign state power, imagined as an individual, required the general will to become the basis of republican political activity; humanity as a whole became one big family, thus sidestepping the transposition of the state of nature onto the sphere of international relations between states (cf. *Ideas* n. 152, in *Philosophical* 108). Chenxi Tang, who has offered an illuminating reading of Friedrich Schlegel in relation to international law theory, explains that for the Schlegels such a general will only exists in the realm of pure thought; and he adds that the Schlegels began

> what can be called the poetological conceptualization of the political. This poetics of the political addresses, first, the form of fiction, i.e., the way in which the empirical will of the majority stands in for the absolute general will, and second, the form of representation, that is, the way in which particular elected individuals or deputies stand in for the majority of the people.

> Insofar as the constitution concerns the form of fiction and the form of
> representation, the explication of republicanism boils down to nothing else
> than a poetics of the constitution. (38)

Far from positing an axiomatic egalitarianism, this poetics of the constitution requires special men, leaders, or mediators who will show the way
to those who "lack a center" within themselves (*Ideas* n. 45, in *Philosophical*
98). No one appoints the mediator, a mediator "appoints himself" as such:
"a mediator is one who perceives the divinity within himself and who
self-destructively sacrifices himself in order to reveal, communicate, and
represent to all mankind this divinity"—and only through this example
will others be awakened to perceive their own divinity (*Ideas* n. 44, in
Philosophical 98). The artist, or poet, who carries out this mediation cannot
pretend to govern. He can only educate, offering the state only one thing:
the formation of rulers and servants and the exaltation of politicians and
economists into artists (*Ideas* n. 54, in *Philosophical* 99). The poet is here a
mere instrument. He is to the nonpresentable or objectifiable general will
what the aeolian harp is to the wind/Spirit.

The aeolian harp came to represent the way in which the romantic
subject desired to be the voice of Nature (San Juan; Bloom 200; Abrams
26). Susan Bernstein puts it thus: "The Eolian harp is a kind of technical
supplement which would allow us to hear nature's own music, nature's own
voice, directly; it is supposed to bring about precisely one of the moments
of unity between man and nature for which Romanticism is famous" (75).
But, as Bernstein immediately adds, it is this supplemental aspect of the
instrument that should make us reconsider the role of this cornerstone of
a trope, as it turns the very symbol of unity into a mediation that points
out the unbridgeable gap between Other and subject: "The Eolian harp,
as a figure, presents not an immediate unity between self and other, man
and nature, but rather a temporary eclipse of separation that can only be
articulated poetically—that is, . . . figuratively, indirectly" (75). It should
be added that precisely because the suspension of separation takes place
figuratively and indirectly it does not actually take place as such. For a poet
to convey that the poem is a momentary eclipse of separation, he or she has
to suspend the expressive manifestation of that unity in order to inform
the reader about what is happening: if you suspend disbelief long enough,
the poem can give you the image with which to believe that the posited
unity is "real." This immediately turns into a metaliterary or metapoetic
event that makes the literary artifact into an object—and an object of the

literary precisely within that formation of the literary that is supposed to
be the acid in which all objects melt (Clemens 205).

Why is it so commonplace to consider even this metapoetic objectification as part of the dissolution of the object on the part of modern aesthetics?
Julia Kristeva offers a clear formulation of this assumption: "By its very
structure, insofar as it is a discourse of or on literature (let us say insofar as it
is a metalanguage) . . . , all commentary is condemned to treat the literary
experience as an 'object.'" This is so, she claims, except when we are able
to meet the challenge that writers "from Diderot to Baudelaire or Georges
Bataille" have posed to criticism: that "it is possible to speak *of* literature if
and only if we speak to literature" (*Pulsions* 41). Why does the metapoetic
apparatus involved in poetry's own representation of what it putatively
presents (in all of its paradoxical or contradictory "presencing") manage to
escape this objectification that obtains everywhere else? So it is not simply
a question of modern poetry's assumed autotelic character; modern poetry
is caught between its desire for pointing out the layer of reality that is the
text, as real as would be the world outside it, and its need to *represent* its
"presentative" "nature." (Is it any wonder that at some point the figure of
the sovereign will have to turn up in this scene?) Poetry is attempting to
capture the paradoxical movement of something that presents itself as it
withdraws; as it is left with nothing it turns to a metapoetic discourse that
becomes poetry itself. As the last mark or trace of something that gives
itself in its withdrawal, the poem becomes testimony or theory, a narrative
of the event of literature.

(This is why Mallarmé preemptively explodes Alain Badiou's theory
of the event—incapable of treating the poem as anything but theory of
the event, and thus not as a condition. Bruno Bosteels has already pointed
this out, but he assumes that the problem lies within the intricacies of
the theory of the event in Badiou and not in the historical materiality of
the literature in question qua literature—something that the recurrence
of the problem in treating Paul Valéry in the second volume of *Being
and Event* goes some way to suggest. This is why Bosteels can offer to
solve the problem by supplementing Badiou with Rancière. The point is
especially important as in Bosteels's argument it is here that his proposal
for a reconsideration of historical materialism begins [Bosteels, *Badiou and
Politics* 215–17, 221–23].)

A contemporary, and no longer simply romantic, version of this momentary "eclipse of separation," where the border between subject and object is
not operative anymore, presents us with an ethics of the wholly other. In

the preface to the 2006 edition of her *Dictations: On Haunted Writing*, Avital Ronell, writing here on Goethe, formulates it most clearly:

> Once we are . . . related and drawn to what withdraws, we incline ourselves in fateful submission to a power which comes from far away and for which writing is an offering. Conversation [the encounter with the Levinasian "face," *the wholly other in me*—a surplus that comes from elsewhere and that can no more be assimilated by me, than it can domesticate itself in me— Conversation:] tells us, among other things, that writing never occurs simply by our own initiative; rather, it sends us. Whether one understands oneself to be lifted by inspiration or dashed by melancholia, quietly moved, controlled by muses or possessed by demons, one has responded to remoter regions of being in that circumstance of nearly transcendental passivity that [Ronell calls] "Dictations." (xiv, xiii)

Transcendental passivity and the heteronomous response to remote regions of being—once again: the aeolian harp. However, a closer look at this trope reveals not so much a questioning of being but rather an immanent aesthetic-theology.

Take, for instance, Coleridge's treatment of the harp: "that simplest Lute, / . . . by the desultory breeze caress'd, / Like some coy maid yielding to her lover" (65, "The Eolian Harp" lines 12–15). For Coleridge, this instrument is the poet himself:

> Full many a thought uncall'd and undetain'd,
> And many idle fleeting phantasies,
> Traverse my indolent and passive brain,
> As wild and various as the random gales
> That swell and flutter on this subject Lute! (66, lines 39–43)

And yet there is reason for suspicion. Taken to its furthest consequences, where inspiration is the confusion of inner and outer, a yielding to Lover/ Being, Coleridge asks: Is this to reveal the wholly other as "the one Life within us and abroad"? Is this not a plea for an immanent vitalism that would place God and human on a single plane of being? This is why he asks:

> . . . what if all of animated nature
> Be but organic Harps diversely fram'd,
> That tremble into thought, as o'er them sweeps
> Plastic and vast, one intellectual breeze,
> At once the Soul of each, and God of all? (66, lines 26, 44–48)

Coleridge can only pose the question; he immediately retreats from it and its consequences, but the damage has been done. The wholly other (the breeze, the possession, the dictation of the wind, or of those remoter regions of being that Ronell points out) produces a folding of the distinction between the two radically different ontological planes Judeo-Christian thought assumes as first evidence. The poetic inscription of this event will produce a knot between politics, literature, and philosophy, which it is still our task to confront.

Carl Schmitt had identified this knot as a consequence of romanticism early on. Romanticism "ends as idyll with the absolute identity of the ideal and the real"—for this reason also it required a theory of human activity that complicated the autonomous mastery of the subject. Schmitt understood that the question about human free will and the status of human activity entailed a different answer than the one the romantics gave. They were convinced of the autonomy of their ontologically stable egos, but their freedom was only the freedom to "assent": "when the isolated subject treats the world as an *occasio* . . . the activity of the subject consists only in the fanciful animation of its affect. The romantic reacts only with his affect. His activity is the affective echo of an activity that is necessarily not his own" (*Political Romanticism* 94). At this point Schmitt sees no difference between romanticism and a rationalistic and authoritarian demand for the assent of political subjects "to the immutable nomological necessity of the event" of dictation—and of the dictator (94). He saw romanticism as the sentimental double of the latter.

Perhaps Schmitt was able to provide such a lucid reading of romanticism because of his own awareness of the void at the heart of the law, a void that he believes must be ordered and closed by the sovereign decision, but a void that is almost palpable nevertheless.[4] At bottom, however, it is not a question of Schmitt's solutions or of his reading being the definitive decoding of romanticism. For him, the problem was that romanticism was not politically effective, not that dictation or the dictator took center stage (Galli, *Genealogia* 199). However, this way of framing the question allows us to see that more than a doctrine as such, what we are dealing with is the opening up of literature to the void of being itself and thus to a post-doctrinal rhetoric. For that very same reason what we then encounter is an unexpected automatization of subjectivity that can go in many directions at once but that is therefore not immune to the most catastrophic declinations. And this provides an unmet challenge, one that I formulate in a way that would be completely alien to all the texts I have adduced thus far: to what extent has philosophy (or theory, or literature itself, and politics) refused to look into the abyss of the formless, opting instead, after however much coquetry with the void (the being of the void, being as void)? To peer into that void, which is already at the heart of the most modern of the modern artifacts we usually associate with linear temporalities of progress, entails confronting a time that *turns* the word "time" catachrestically.

The currently fashionable counternarratives that posit the coevalness or cobelonging of multiple temporalities will get us only so far and, in fact, might even run the risk of reproducing some of the effects that they seek to offset. Consider the historical configuration that Jacques Rancière has called "the aesthetic regime." He points out that one of its defining characteristics is the unity of opposites, particularly as this relates to the autonomy/heteronomy binary, but emphatically insists that the heart of the matter lies in the concept of history that is opened by this disposition. Modernity was not only the tradition of the New, with its putative ruptures and clear demarcations; it was also the invention of tradition. Rancière relies on a well-known narrative about modernity, according to which it is the implementation of an idea of linear history, of the history of progress, and of its transparent events separating before from after. He counters this with what is also by now a well-known counternarrative regarding the same moment, by insisting that the historical time of modernity is more accurately described as the "co-presence of heterogeneous temporalities" (*The Politics* 26; cf. "The Aesthetic"). No doubt there are good reasons for this corrective. Nevertheless, it misses a key dimension of the phenomenon at hand: namely, that the temporality of the dictation in question, of the kairological or occacionalist subject that is divided in the passage of the other, is not, strictly speaking, an experience of time as such but of the loss of time, however momentary it might be. It should be noted that this does not necessarily entail an experience of the eternal, or the annihilation of the temporal that takes place with the arrival of the concept or Idea. Rather, it is an experience of the formless, an experience of the void—and, thus, neither of the one nor of the multiple.

Maurice Blanchot, an author fundamentally inscribed within the completion of our still contemporary "closure of romanticism" (Lacoue-Labarthe and Nancy 124), synthesizes many of the central points at issue regarding this absence of time as it emerges in the space of literature. Whereas Shelley was able to write of the testimony of an unapprehended inspiration, because the writing-subject was unable to be the master and origin of the word that was nevertheless recorded, Blanchot begins by placing the emphasis on what seizes and cannot but seize. One is seized by the world, the things in it. The distance that separated one from the world collapses, and one is, then, held by everything that is outside, incapable of assuming a masterful stance. One is no longer an autonomous subject that organizes and uses objects. The distinction itself is blurred: "Sometimes, when a man is holding a pencil, his hand won't release it no matter how badly he wants to let it go: on the contrary, far from opening, it tightens. The other hand intervenes more successfully, but then the hand which one might call sick makes a slow, tentative movement and tries to catch the departing object. The strange thing is the slowness of this movement. . . . This hand experiences, at certain moments, a very great need to seize: it must grasp the pencil, it has to, it's an order, an imperious command" (25). This "persecutory," or, as the English translation has it, "tyrannical prehension," implies a different temporality: "The hand moves in a time which is scarcely human: . . . the shadow of time, itself the shadow of a hand sliding unreally toward an object that has become its own shadow" (25, translation modified). The act of grasping takes place in the shadow of time; there are no limits or demarcations but also no measure with which to ascribe authority or assume power: "What is written delivers the one who has to write to an affirmation over which he has no authority, which is itself without substance, which affirms nothing, . . . it is what still speaks when everything has been said. This affirmation doesn't precede speech, because it prevents speech from being the word that begins, just as it takes away from language the right and the power to interrupt itself. . . . To write is . . . to detach [language] from what makes it a power" (26, translation modified). Kafka's *Diaries* offer a glimpse of what this experience of time means for Blanchot. Faced with the temporally unfavorable circumstances that the world offers the writer, it would be tempting to search for a way to wrest from "the time of the world" (of work and obligations) more time to write. However, as Blanchot explains, this would be to lose all of one's time. It is not a matter of finding the most favorable circumstances, because that would entail the end of circumstances and thus the end of the limitations against which the work of the writer gains its tonality: "When one has all one's time, one no longer has time, and 'favorable' exterior circumstances have become the—unfavorable—fact that there are no longer any circumstances" (60). Circumstances are the limit of time, or time as limit, and writing must keep these limits within it as the datability that places it within the multiple temporalities of others. It is not only a question of exposing how literature gives phenomenality to this experience. For that would only be the time of circumstances. The elimination of circumstances is also not the point, as this would mean a limbo where life is put on hold, putting writing on hold with it. What emerges in this passage is an in-between through which we experience a time that is no longer a synthesis of any sort. "There are no favorable circumstances. Even if one gives 'all one's time' to the *oeuvre*'s demands, 'all' still is not enough.[5] For it is not a matter of devoting time to the task, of passing one's time writing, but of passing into another time where there is no longer any task"; Blanchot concludes: "It is a matter of approaching that point where time is lost, where one enters into the fascination and the solitude of time's absence" (60, translation modified). It is not possible to overemphasize the paradoxical nature of this remark. Blanchot is using the only words he has at his disposal in order to foreground the temporality of the absence of time. The word "time" is being asked to perform multiple and impossible duties in the passage. It must convey, at once, temporality and the absence of time. It is this distinction that I want to underscore when I write of formed and formless time: formless time is the temporality of the absence of time (a posthegemonic time of existence that does not seek to organize others into its rhythms). That Blanchot points to this experience but does not hold fast to his insight will become clear in what follows—though I am not interested in clearly separating my proposal from his even in the most perilous moments. It is simply a risk that has to be taken.

Ultimately, it is a question of how to think, not the standstill of all time, but the time of the absence of time as such. In this context, the possible and foreseeable objection that the proposal here would only be a further radicalization, a new and redeemed formal time, would miss the actual reach of what is being suggested. That sort of formalization would only be a new political instrumentalization of utopian ideals, and what is being questioned here does not concern a political translation in any form. Yet it is also important to stress that the experience that is being approached, however obliquely, is not an abstract or merely theoretical thesis. Rather, it is the most basic relation we already have had with time; for what is at issue is nothing other than our being in time. This is an experience that we all have, and the question is why we yield to the pressure to subsume it under the representational and political imposition that makes us transform our time of existence into the caring for the realization of an already exhausted teleological goal—a goal that is still, and will always be, to come. Thus, the time of the absence of time, or formless time, as I have been proposing in these pages, is not at all a question of a messianic redemption. To write, in the terms that Blanchot is adducing here, is to give in to the fascination that the absence of time produces in us. For Blanchot this means a time when nothing begins and initiative is not possible. It is a time without negation or decision, where here and nowhere coincide. It has no present or presence. In this time:

What appears is the fact that nothing appears, the being that is at the bottom of the absence of being, which is when there is nothing and which, as soon as there is something, is no longer. . . . The reversal that, in the absence of time, constantly leads us back to the presence of absence—but to that presence as absence, to absence as its own affirmation, an affirmation in which nothing is affirmed, in which nothing never ceases affirming itself . . .—is not dialectical. . . . In time's absence what is new renews nothing; what is present is not contemporary; what is present presents nothing, but represents itself and belongs henceforth and always to return. (30)

The shadow of time is where the image becomes "the formless presence" of what is absent (31). And yet, this is the moment when the sovereign reappears: that distance that holds us is "the lifeless deep, an unmanageable, inappreciable remoteness which has become something like the sovereign power behind all things" (261). What becomes of the other, of the sovereign power behind all things, when he is dead time? What possibilities are we giving up on when we are seized by the time of the dead sovereign? And is not our globe today supposed to be defined by that death?

It is not difficult to surmise that in Blanchot's approach to the absence of time, at bottom, there is a residuum of the Judeo-Christian crossroads of time that needs to be interrogated just as closely. For only when the temporality of succession is suspended does the sovereign power behind all things appear in its absence. The entire ex-position of this zone presents a difficulty for thought. Insofar as this is all concerned with the writer and writing in general, it appears as if it is only through the grace of this figure that being is allowed to "be" what it "is"—in its dissimulation, in order to "accomplish its work" (263n1). This way of posing the problem obscures the background of being as it precludes its presencing (being's presence as absence and absence as presence at the same time) from the plane of successive temporality. What should have been a starting point, that the dissimulation of being is always already there, exposing us to the void, the formless, and the absence of time, then, appears as a conclusion: we arrive at this zone, we approach it, we are taken by the experience, fall into the hold of the sovereign of all things. The consequences are not difficult to discern: (1) even with the emphasis on ambiguity, passivity, being taken hold of, and so forth, being appears as will annihilating the temporality of succession; (2) what should have been an opening to the abyss of the formless paradoxically yields a process that is structurally predetermined to exclude the void at all costs. For instance, when we admire the tone of a work, explains Blanchot, we are not referring to its style or to the intricacies of its language. What we approach then is a silence: "this vigorous force by which the writer, having been deprived of himself, having renounced himself, has in this effacement nevertheless maintained the authority of a certain power: the power decisively to be still, so that in this silence what speaks without beginning or end might take on form, coherence, and sense" (27). What speaks without beginning would then seem to collapse the ambiguity that lies at the heart of the ontological question. It is as if the danger posed by the sort of image that is the tool with which one grasps a thing ideally, which Blanchot refers to as "life-giving," were nothing compared with that which "threatens constantly to relegate us" to the absence of the thing as presence (262). The ontological charge of these considerations becomes increasingly hard to ignore. Rather than avoiding this challenge, I want to propose a possible way of understanding this retreat in the face of the abyss of the time of the absence of time. And it is to Heidegger that we have to turn at this point.

Heidegger, Noise

Allow me to illustrate by way of a reference to noise in Martin Heidegger's *Being and Time*. It has become increasingly difficult to ignore the experience of noise, even in music, where it illuminates a zone that is neither harmony nor disharmony. "Noise is immersive"; its effect is felt at the vibrational level rather than cognized in the manner usually reserved for the architectonics of composition (Toop 273). It is the multidirectional experience of the collapse of limits, where sound-objects are no longer discernible. Noise then can be seen as the abyss illuminating the presencing of the formless and the void, and of the absence of time that is not an escape toward eternity. Heidegger's 1927 treatment of this matter foregrounds the impossibility of ever having such an experience.

For Heidegger, hearing is an existential possibility that belongs to thinking itself. This is a way of connecting discourse with understanding and intelligibility. To hear aright is to understand. Hearing, in this context, is constitutive of discourse: "Hearing even constitutes the primary and authentic openness of Da-sein for its ownmost possibility of being. . . . Da-sein hears because it understands" (*Being* 153). Because this potentiality of hearing is existentially primary, something like harkening is possible, and harkening is even more primordial than hearing (it is "phenomenally more primordial than what the psychologist 'initially' defines as hearing"); Heidegger adds: "Hear-kening, too, has the mode of being of a hearing that understands. 'Initially' we never hear noises and complexes of sound, but the creaking wagon, the motorcycle. We hear the column on the march, the north wind, the woodpecker tapping, the crackling fire. It requires a very artificial and complicated attitude in order to 'hear' a 'pure noise'" (*Being* 153). The fact that we hear motorcycles, or the column on the march, provides "the phenomenal proof that Da-sein, as being-in-the-world, always already maintains itself *together with* innerworldly things at hand and initially not at all with 'sensations' whose chaos would first have to be formed to provide the springboard from which the subject jumps off finally to land in a 'world'" (153). To admit to the possibility of something like noise (and the experience of the absence of hegemonic time/s would be akin to it) would require that we construct the process whereby the form or the order of the world is achieved. Within this purview, everything would first have to be formed, and to be world-poor would be to be in a state prior to any such formalizing operation, faced with the pure chaos of sensations. For Heidegger, what is at stake concerns nothing less than the possibility of thinking through the confusion of today's world destiny (*Off the Beaten Track* 280).

In his reading of Anaximander's fragment, Heidegger posits: "What presences lets order belong," that which "presences a while . . . presences insofar as it lets the enjoining order belong" (*Off the Beaten Track* 269). The opposite would be things that hang on and pass their while attempting to aggrandize themselves, a "craving which leads them to seek to expel one another from what is presently present" (*Off the Beaten Track* 272). Reck-less Dis-order must be surmounted by "the presencing of what presence *is*." But this is to provide too simple an image of the fallen world that must be redeemed. Here is Heidegger's description (from a 1946 text) of that world of reckless disorder:

> Man is about to hurl himself upon the entire earth and its atmosphere, to arrogate to himself the hidden working of nature in the form of energy, and to subordinate the course of history to the plans and orderings of a world government. This same defiant man is incapable of saying simply what *is*; of saying *what* this *is*, that a things *is*. The totality of beings is the single object of a singular will to conquer. The simplicity of being is buried under a singular oblivion. What mortal can fathom the abyss of this confusion? In the face of this abyss one can try to shut one's eyes. One can erect one illusion after another. The abyss does not retreat. (*Off the Beaten Track* 280–81)

Perhaps this abyss of confusion is a version of the non-relation that Da-sein was not supposed to sustain initially. Would it be possible to speak of Da-sein maintaining itself together now with "sensations" even when these were posited as a chaos that would first have to be formed in order to provide the springboard from which the subject would jump off finally to land in a "world"? Yes and no, for the way the issue is posed is in itself the symptom of confusion. The vibrational immersion of noise is neither chaos nor order, since only in the plane of sound composition would that distinction have any bearing. Hearing, then, would be something closer to what Jean-Luc Nancy has proposed in his meditation on listening, where "hearing" is displaced from "hearing say," and thus hearing as making sense, to hearing sound—he wonders: "perhaps it is necessary that sense not be content to make sense (or to be *logos*), but that it want also to resound" (6). But then the noise of the world could no longer be grafted onto the distinction between order and disorder; it would be a more complex relation or, perhaps, a simpler one: "A blow from outside, clamor from within, this sonorous, sonorized body undertakes a simultaneous listening to a 'self' and to a 'world' that are both in resonance" (42–43).

The same could also be extended to a reading of absent time in Blanchot. In Blanchot as well what we arrive at ultimately is the formalization of writing. That is, writing is only ever what has already gained sense, coherence, and form (27). It is for this reason that the figure of the sovereign reappears in what is otherwise a context that can easily mislead the reader into thinking that what is happening is anarchic. For example, commenting on this absence of time, Gerald L. Burns asks about its nature in order to identify "anarchic" time and dead time as a futureless time of waiting (161). As appealing as this sounds, calling the absent time of Blanchot anarchic time seems nevertheless inappropriate—and even shocking if we consider the importance of "the sovereign over all things" that emerges once the time of successive moments has been suspended.

It is the work of Paul Celan that brings this entire tradition to a close. Or perhaps "closure" is not the appropriate term: Celan brings back to the starting position the question of the sovereign within poetry: the question of a king more majestic than any actually existing sovereign. Thus, he makes explicit what the text of absent time in Blanchot presents to us as the tacit unworking of the sovereign for whom authority and power are no longer possible.

Sovereignties Otherwise

Derrida writes of the poem's setting itself free from art, through art, in Celan—of a time that "disqualifies or discredits the presence, the self-presence of every living present"—and this "in order to make a strategically essential and necessary reference" not only against "Husserlian phenomenology and to the transcendental phenomenology of time," but to the thought of self-presence that singles out the human "I" as a privileged site "from Descartes to Kant and to Heidegger" (*Sovereignties* 110, 131). He begins by pointing out that in "The Meridian," Celan uses the word "majesty" in two different senses: to indicate the present-now and as part of the lexicon of monarchy. This monarchy alludes to the sovereign that the French Revolution deposed. Among Celan's references to the work of Georg Büchner (as this speech is being spoken on the occasion of the poet being awarded the Georg Büchner prize in October 1960), there is a particularly important sequence in *Leonce and Lena* that introduces us to an art in which "time and light are no longer recognized" (Celan 174). Also, in it "we find ourselves 'in flight to Paradise'" as "'all clocks and calendars' are soon to be 'destroyed' or 'proscribed'" by the Revolution (174). After various declarations of enthusiasm for the Revolution, Lucile proclaims, to the surprise of everyone present, "Long live the king!" To elaborate on this declaration, Celan finds it necessary to inscribe anarchism into his narrative: "To be sure, [Lucile's statement] sounds like an expression of allegiance to the *ancien régime* . . . . But these words—please allow one who also grew up with the writings of Peter Kropotkin and Gustav Landauer expressly to emphasize this point—these words are not a celebration of the monarchy and a past which should be preserved. They are a tribute to the majesty of the absurd, which bears witness to mankind's here and now" (175). Derrida points out that in using the word "majesty" in this manner Celan places "one majesty above another"; and this is "a bidding up [on sovereignty] that attempts to change the sense of *majesty* or of *sovereignty*, to displace its sense, while keeping the old word or claiming to restore its most dignified meaning. There is the sovereign majesty of the sovereign, of the King, and there is . . . , more sovereign and otherwise sovereign, the majesty of poetry . . . as it bears witness to human presence" (*Sovereignties* 117).

Celan's anarchist past, or what he reports as such, needs to be remarked here—for it is not a political point that he is making. Anarchism is not invoked as the actually existing form of a specific politics. What is at issue in Lucile's statement is the possibility of a poem, or of a literature, that cuts the wires that moved the poets, wires that turned the poet into, as Celan puts it, a marionette or a mechanical contraption. This is another figure for the effect of the dictation of the sovereign of all things, which Blanchot also coded into the tyrannical or persecutory "prehension" that moves the hands of the writer, even as it introduces the shadow of time.

Art, writes Celan, "is indeed a problem . . . which is hardy, long-lived, and transformable"; and he adds: "But when art is being talked about there is always someone present who doesn't listen very carefully" (174). The one who doesn't listen very carefully, according to Celan, "has perceived language and form"—without, at the same time, perceiving "breath": "direction and fate" (174). Celan identifies in Büchner's character Lucile someone who "perceives language as form and direction and breath" (178). She is also capable of an act of freedom that stands in stark contrast to the action of the other characters in the piece. They move as if on "the basis of a dictum" so "foreign" that Celan describes it as the confirmation of the triumph of the puppet and the wire (175). Lucile, on the contrary, does not forget to speak in the first person, the "I," as opposed to the "one"—which Celan ascribes to those interested in art, and who in losing their "I" have become puppets or marionettes. This is not the "I" of egology but a libertarian "I," and yet this is a libertarianism that can hardly be simply identified with the political ideology of anarchism. Rather, it is the "I" of the an-archic, which merely registers it own being in the world, the "I" that keeps its dates, registering not the preprogrammed march of History but contingency as it touches and un-forms it. Lucile, who is blind to art and whose language is personal, is the true face of poetry for Celan. It is she who will pledge allegiance to the sovereignty of now, a different time that would be open, not to sheltering the dictum or influx of the outside, not to the recording of "mechanical devices," but to "a concentration which remains aware of all of our dates," and which "faces that which appears" even as it is able to "question this appearing and addresses it" (182). What results is not a copyist, or the hierophant of an unapprehended inspiration; neither is it a matter of being held. "It becomes dialogue"; Celan adds: "Only in the realm of this dialogue does that which is addressed take form and gather around the I who is addressing and naming it. But the one who has been addressed . . . also brings its otherness along into the present, into this present. In the here and now of the poem . . . , this one, unique, limited present, . . . does it allow the most idiosyncratic quality of the Other, its time, to participate in the dialogue" (182). The poet is not attempting to critique or to "expand" art by surpassing a threshold. He insists that he is using a "well-known" term when he speaks of the wholly Other (180). He does not want to appear as the vanguard in a linear progress that renders this other obsolete. But he needs to open both the I and the Other to a dialogue that is foreign to the one-sided dictation of the sovereign of all things. This he offers not as a way of innovating or renovating art but as a way of accompanying it into his own unique place of no escape, a place that is the concentration that remains aware of all his dates.

Derrida is concerned with showing how Paul Celan "signals toward an alterity that, in the inside of the 'I' as the punctual living present, as the very point of the self-present living present, an alterity of the wholly other, comes not to include or modalize another living present (as in the Husserlian analysis of temporalization, where, in the protention and the retention of another living present in the now living present, the ego comprises in itself, in its present, another present), but—and this is a wholly other matter—lets appear something of the present *of the other*, 'letting the most proper of the time of the other' [speak also]" (*Sovereignties* 131). This is the difference between my present and the time of the other, a temporality that cannot be "reduced, included, assimilated, introjected, appropriated" (*Sovereignties* 133).

Yet again we come face to face with a text that is doing the utmost in order to foreground the time of the absence of hegemonic time. Perhaps the difficulty of the task can be illustrated by pointing out the way in which Derrida finds it impossible to think posthegemonic time without addressing the other, which might immediately give the impression that what is at issue is an ethics of respect for differences. But this is not the case. It is not a matter of including, appropriating, or reducing the other.

But the difficulty is also Celan's. That the poet concludes his speech with remarks in which this time is imagined as circular, turning with the poles of the earth, I believe indicates that what is happening here was not taken as far as it could have been taken, particularly if we consider the enormous effort that he put into reimagining the dominant poetics of his time. For the distinction between linear and circular time should, by now, have started to seem suspect—one of the most important tools in modernity's arsenal when it comes to delineating the contours of the contemporary. The tension between these two temporalities is in itself also the legacy of the modern sovereign. Everything hinges on what the "I" is capable of letting be of the Other. Yes, it is its time, thus co-belonging to a present of disparate and irreducible temporalities. But this time ensues only when it is the "word" of the Other that is listened to. It is only insofar as we can *speak* with things in this manner that we are faced with the question of their whence and whither (Celan 182). Is this too much to concede to *logos*? Is not Celan's own conception of poetry as a turn-of-breath (*Atemwende*) already moving in a zone below or above the forming logos, already resonating before and after the word? Yes, breath is *pneuma*—it is not possible to simply deny this connection—but breath is also tone and resonance. And is this resonance not the only way that the awareness of our dates unsettles and unworks the perception of language and form, language as form, of he who does not listen very carefully?

It is not possible to equate the romantic lineage, and its theoretical consequences, with a welcoming of the formless, for the same reason that it is not possible to assume that the revolutionary rupture with the past can, as politics, acknowledge that its own condition of possibility lies in the void that un-founds all politics to begin with. It is this same foreclosure that leads Guevara to offer his most lyrical developments as the description of the process through which the Revolution morphed from a romantic to a properly materialist historical project. Even in its most extreme extensions—that of Celan, for example—we can still sense the difficulty of thinking the formless temporality of the absence of time. The problem of foundations, or the lack thereof, even when treated directly, is referred to a higher, though absent, foundation that moves the strings that dictate, from an ontological level, what happens on the plane of history. Nevertheless, the question of what rights revolutionaries have to change the world is played out in this maneuver. As I show in chapter 3, the political instrumentalization of this schema relies much more openly on the temporal relays we explored in chapter 1 than in tarrying with the abyss that does not retreat. The next chapter, dedicated to the mixed times of the Cuban Revolution, as an instance of what, following Malabou, I referred to as the "crossroads of time," will show to what extent these "times" form the background against which the contemporary form of nihilism comes into sharpest focus. We will then move to a sustained meditation on contemporary nihilism in chapter 4.

3. The (Mixed) Times of Revolution

Why Lezama? Why Now?

José Lezama Lima came of age under the sign of neocoloniality.[1] Which meant that his first political experience was politics as farce. The Republic was a pseudorepublic. Everything political took on the hue of the counterfeit. Rather than imagining that this was an accident that could be corrected, that there was a true politics, and that it was a matter of locating and activating it, Lezama's early orientation shows a young intellectual who assumes the opposite. Politics is always counterfeit. Neocoloniality, a scene in which colonial rule goes under the name of democracy, with all the formal institutions necessary to give credence to the idea, does not offer us a distorted image of politics, which would only need to be corrected in order for true political agency to manifest itself. Rather, it gives us a glimpse of the true nature of politics even in the metropolitan "centers" supposed to be in charge of moving the strings attached to the "periphery." Thus, it is not merely a question of reforming or rectifying the state, as if it were a matter of righting a wrong, and as if a pure politics were possible with enough care and effort.

In an often quoted, but rarely interrogated, text from 1949, Lezama notes that the state shows an utter lack of imagination and that this is clear to all. He calls this ruin, the exhausted image of modern politics, a "disintegration" that needs to be set aside but not confronted frontally—critiqued but not engaged on its own terms (*Imagen* 205). The text is often adduced in order to place Lezama in the Latin American tradition of intellectuals like José Martí, José Enrique Rodó, José Vasconcelos, and others—which is to say a group of intellectuals concerned with the identitarian matrix of Latin America usually marshaled in the name of an alternative ethical modernity (Rojas, *Isla* 30–32). Whether one reads this as a positive or a negative assessment,[2] the crux of the matter is that Lezama is all too quickly grafted onto a political grid that the text itself wants to leave behind. In fact, it is precisely because Lezama's position is read only from the standpoint of the possibility of an ideal, noncorrupted politics that this text can be used as representative of a conservative rejection of modernity, and, beyond it, why Lezama can be charged with paving the way for the teleological view of history and culture ascribed to the Revolution itself. The charge in that regard is that the putative political cynicism that is involved in thinking the Republic as a fake, puts in place a nihilist germ that will find its true destructive manifestation with the triumph of Castro in 1959. Yet, if we turn to Lezama's text in search of the answer he poses in the face of the disintegration evinced in the political sphere, we would be hard-pressed to sound convincingly political. "Erotic knowledge," "knowledge of the other" and of "the opaque multiplicity," the "inebriation of the Romantics," "the search for the secret" (*Imagen* 206)—hardly a materialist program for militants looking to reactivate the revolutionary and "true" identity of Latin America.

In place of making an argument for or against, an option that remains wholly within the political dispensation of the problem, I want to propose that it is high time that we set aside the compulsion to either castigate or redeem Lezama for the obvious Christian legacy with which he thinks, and start analyzing its implications in a wider context. To this end, it will be useful to think of Lezama's early position, beyond any political correctness, as an infrapolitical one: that is, as a retreat from the political that nevertheless does not abdicate the politicity of that withdrawal but rather points to the absent center of all politics in order to open the way for what might, perhaps, be a different way of existence beyond the demand to care for the exhaustion and ruins of political organization. Were this to be the case for an early Lezama, our task and difficulty would appear to lie in how to then make sense of his public enthusiasm for the Revolution during its first years. And further, whether or not his posterior disenchantment with the repressive cultural politics of the Revolution would represent a return to the early position or a different relation to politics. Yet, just as the disintegration of the state and of politics in general did not simply entail an even more radical politics, with the case of the Revolution we need to examine the precise manner in which he modulates the Revolution as such. In fact, as paradoxical as this might appear, his way toward the formless is through Christianity and the Revolution. The poet places the Revolution in the context of a tradition that was defined solely by all that it lacked, all that was absent: "The unknown is our only tradition," which makes for a strong fascination with that which is unrepresentable: "The attraction of toppling the columns of limitation or the laws of the contour" (*Lezama disperso* 188). It is for this reason that Lezama can state that "a revolution does not express a form,"[3] that it cannot configure or produce the last stage of the process it transforms but is, rather, a moment of "ecstasy" (understood by Lezama as a cumulative march, moving faster with each new instant): "The instant of this fact [i.e., the Revolution] oozes secular accumulations, five thousand years that open their eyes and communicate their *andantino* to history, a secret march of man toward his joyfulness" (*Lezama disperso* 99).[4] The secularization at issue here is the cause behind the acceleration of history leading to the Apocalypse and thus bringing man closer to Paradise. It is a Christian narrative that lies behind the poet's understanding of the Revolution, which becomes one more step toward the end of the world.[5] But it is also this narrative that informs his ideas on formlessness. By pointing this out I wish to emphasize that the writing of the formless does not constitute an easy way out of all the complications that modernity and the politics of the Revolution pose to Lezama and to us. It is not a question of imagining that the formless will be a better and true emancipatory narrative; this would entail, in fact, returning to the tried and failed paradigms that substitute the putative linear time of the modern with the multiple or circular times of redemption. The point is to map the way in which Lezama begins to inscribe his dates on his writing, up to that place where cartography is no longer possible. The writing of the formless, which I begin to approach here, though the slow unfolding of it will only occupy center stage in the second part of this book, must first be squarely and unflinchingly placed in the context of Christian time—perhaps the first religion of the formless as such, even if this fact is only unconscious.

Christianity, Apocalypse, Revolution

Before dismantling Christian doctrine, Lezama appropriates it for the poet and poetry. This displacement puts the pastoral figure in a place where he is not wholly at home. With Castro's victory in 1959, it is the Revolution itself that will become written into history passively, a writing that takes place without an author that shapes the new state order. For the Revolution was seen as "a poetry without poet" that achieved the highest goal imaginable: to penetrate into "the mystery of the unanimous" (*Imagen* 20).[6] (What, if anything, happens afterward I will leave aside for the moment.) It is often claimed that the incarnation of God on earth is the basic structure through which Lezama frames the triumphant entrance of Castro and his men into

Havana. It is almost never remarked that if this is so, then, with the Revolution, we enter the realm that lies between the two deaths—a realm that is already the site of the resurrection but prior to the second death of those whose names are not in the book of Eternal Life. And this place has its own particular temporality, which would then have to be checked against that of the Revolution. I intend to show that Lezama is correct in identifying the two events in question (though one is wholly imaginary). And that, far from this being a problem, it offers an important window through which we can begin to outline a proper temporal dimension of the Revolution and of modernity in more general terms.

The doctrine of the resurrection is a theory that Lezama outlines up to a point, but one that he puts to the test on rare occasions. That is, even though for him it is the poet alone who is in charge of the image that offers knowledge of the resurrection, seldom does Lezama himself offer his reader an image of what takes place after the second coming. Here is one example that dates back to 1955, from the last section of the poem "Aguja de diversos," later published as part of the 1960 collection *Dador*:

How do they wait for the second death? The dying
of his other death, already situated between death
and the other death after the valley of splendor.
Did that resurrection entail seeing anew
those gaps and the frozen
standstill of the steed? Or thinking about the essences
that had made signs in its eyelids?
Always the same helplessness, and the trembling
when writing the history of the one resurrected.

[¿Cómo esperan la segunda muerte? La de morir
su otra muerte, ya situado entre la muerte
y la otra muerte después del valle de esplendor.
¿Aquella resurrección entrañaba ver de nuevo
aquellas aperturas y el detenimiento
congelado del corcel? ¿O pensar en las esencias
que habían hecho signos en sus párpados?
Siempre aquella indefensión y el temblor
al escribir la historia del resurrecto.] (*Poesía* 304)

The poet trembles at the thought. What could the history of the resurrected be like, what can a history/story after the end of time be? Consider the following cluster of images: "El resurrecto, situado ya entre la muerte y la muerte / en el valle de la piedra irradiante, avispero de centrales metales, / pues el germen no puede reabsorberse en la flor/ de otro germen, sino por el ensanchamiento de su vientre / de enigmáticas refracciones pisciformes, que llega a laminarse/ como la piel que recubre los granos adoríferos, las monedas / los muertos, los arcos asirios, conmemorativos/ del arco del antílope" (*Poesía* 304–5). Reconsider it in translation: "The resurrected, situated now between death and death in the valley of the irradiating stone, wasp's nest of central metals, since the germ cannot be reabsorbed in the flower of another germ, but for the widening of the gut of enigmatic fish-formed refractions, which is laminated as the skin that covers the odoriferous grains, the coins of the dead, the Assyrian arches, commemorative of the arches of the antelopes." There is no verb that can be attributed to the resurrected, they are "situated" within a whirlwind of images where what is commemorated also belongs to the same "present." The history of the resurrected is a history without the linearity of verbs; it is, rather, the story *of the Verb*, which turns all other actions into its own attributes.

What is at issue here is not a dead time. Lezama elaborates in a text from 1966: "From the Epiphany until the Resurrection there is the participation in the identity of the temporal, the *tempus habemus* and the *tempus destruendi* become one in the identity of the gyrating sphere" (*Obras* 949).[7] Would it be fair to say that this is Lezama's time that we are reading about in this sentence (Cf. Brett Levinson's *Secondary Moderns* 70)? Would this not make of this time (or times, as the case may be) the time of a subject, that is, a subjective image of time that refers us back to a phenomenology of time, when in fact we are dealing with the paradoxical temporality of the Deity as Christianity imagines it? What would the consequences be for anything that, leaning toward the postmetaphysical, or its deconstruction, burrows its way into these times in order to draw its implications? Would it entail a Christianization? What can there be of the phenomenon of the equalization of "the time we have" and "the time of destruction" in the perfection of the sphere that emerges only after the resurrection (since it is only then that the sphere appears: "The day of the Resurrection we will present ourselves in the perfect form, that is, as spheres" [Lezama quoting Origen in *Obras* 948])? From Lezama's own perspective, in order to answer these questions, or in order for the answers to mean anything to the reader, he or she must already be in the position of the Christian, at least momentarily: "History has been written upon . . . the accomplished fact. . . . But now we know that history has to begin to be valued starting from what will be destroyed. That is to say, vast temporal extensions, which did not crystalize in any form, will become equal to the great extensions that did reach the realization of their form, but which were destroyed. Thus only the *imago* can penetrate into the world that did not realize itself, of what can be destroyed, and of what was razed" (*Obras* 949–50).[8] The *imago*, then, would touch on the time that did not become time. The image, as opposed to the imago, has a different role, more directly linked to the resurrection, as it is what makes knowledge of resurrection possible: "Were we to be denied the image, we would have no knowledge of the resurrection" (*Obras* 1215).[9] For the Christian, this is an essential aspect of his doctrine. As Hegel pointed out in his *Lectures on the Philosophy of World History*, something of God must be revealed, otherwise the Christian would be no different than the heathen and would worship like the Athenians at the altar of an unknown God (212). It is poetry where "one lives in the image the substance of the resurrection," but "as preview on the mirror," wrote Lezama in September 1958 (Lezama Lima, *Obras* 820).[10] A basic stance toward history emerges for the poet: what exists will be destroyed, and this for imperative reasons. A text from 1956: "It is not only the resurrection of a God . . . but of a whole people [*pueblo*] in unanimity, preparing its resurrection in the image as the geometry of the thought of God" (*Obras* 778).[11] The categories begin to blend one into the other, as the poet is in charge of the only possible knowledge of resurrection that is available for this people. Without this knowledge and the hope of resurrection, there is no possible plenitude (*Obras* 838, 868). Sage, teacher, pastor of the people on the way to salvation, this is a multivalent and multifaceted leader in charge of those who shall be saved from the second death. Revelations: "whoever conquers"; those who in the first resurrection will join in the reign of one thousand years; those whose names are found in the book of life (2:11, 20:6, 20:14, and 21:8). The resonances are clear, and it is not difficult to understand why the relay to the sovereign is so seamless once the Revolution comes to power. In Lezama's peculiar language, Catholicism is "the most powerful inextinguishable that man has created, inciting us to the most violent irreducibles" (*Obras* 476).[12] A more accessible formulation: "Until the arrival of Christ, Pascal used to say, there had only been a *false peace*; after Christ, we may add, there has been the true war—that of the partisan, that of the witnesses dead in battle, the one hundred forty-four thousand, offered as first fruit to God and the Lamb" (*Poesía* 158).[13] Yet, for all of the responsibility incurred by the poet, after "Aguja de diversos" Lezama will give us very little regarding the resurrected and the resurrection. Though he often made reference to the resurrection and made a poetics out of it (vis-à-vis Heidegger, he famously declared that he was not interested in being-for-death but that his work took being for the resurrection as its guiding motto [*Obras* 819–20]), we have very little to go on regarding this (non) "time" after the second coming. The time that we have and the time of destruction are united in the perfection of the gyrating sphere. A fragmentary version of this dynamic also appears in the same poem. "Now," it begins, but already this is an impossibility, this "now" indicates the "present" of plenitude—earlier in the same poem Lezama had already warned his reader, "My representation requires objects that escape it [que la burlen]" (*Poesía* 291): "Now time does not crack . . . / but blows, erasing . . . succession of the hands / toward the whirlpool, truncated whirlpool" (*Poesía* 296).[14] The new swirling synthesis (of the "time we had" and the "time of destruction" in the time of the rotating sphere) is truncated in this case because we are dealing with one that will go down into the lake of fire, otherwise the linear time of succession along with the time of destruction melds with the gyring time of plenitude. It is here that all "times" meet and become indistinguishable from one another.

Lezama did write other things about the second coming. Not poems but panegyrics to the Revolution. For instance, the endlessly quoted passage about the Revolution being "the replacement of God willing [Dios mediante] for a God right before us [Dios delante] . . . God right before man" (*Lezama disperso* 187);[15] to which he adds: "The image comes ajar in an absolute time. When the people are inhabited by a living image, the state reaches its figure, for the plenitude of a state is the coincidence of image and figure. The man who dies in the image, gains the overabundance of resurrection. . . . The Cuban Revolution is nothing but the resurrection of the veridical Cuban state. . . . Not a revolution within a prior state, that never existed, but the creation of a new state order, just and overabundant" (*Lezama disperso* 187, 190–91).[16]

The just and overabundant state, which is to say the state-as-resurrection, points to the unthinkable that has happened, which is true because it is absurd, and that is also why Lezama believes in it with such fervor—a Christian pattern transposed into the key of the modern *ius revolutionis*, and a going beyond the columns. In a lecture delivered at the Federación Estudiantil Universitaria, in 1959, Lezama, wishing to link his experience in the revolts of 30 September 1930 to the recently triumphant Revolution, offers the following image of the temporal upheaval it constitutes. The poet writes of a stair of stone that connects the 1930 rebellion with the Sierra Maestra; the experience leads him into the time of the Revolution in which he finds himself now engaged in the transposition and displacement of everything that was the case before: "I transposed [transponía] sites, encounters, spells, losses, to philosophical categories. . . . The stair does not only secrete immediate history, hot as a turn of the sun, but also a philosophical concept. . . . In opposition to the passage of time, the voice that raised itself [the nonpersonal creative force behind the revolution as a poetry without poet] in its articulation came to offer the scrutiny of circles" (*Imagen* 102).[17] In opposition to the mere passage of time, what appears is the circle of the concept coming to itself. A text entitled "Comienza la era poética," also about the Revolution, sums up the temporal mixture that obtains in this particular exceptional event: "In such occasions time and intentionality are so well soldered together that they form, within time as successive quantity, a separate whirlpool, as if frozen by the vision" (*Imagen* 114).[18]

For the time being, I want to call attention to this mixed temporality that is attributed to the Revolution-resurrection. It is not a simple or linear time, which would be the time of alienation—though Lezama is too quick to imagine that the temporality of modernity is in fact a single homogeneous one. Neither is it the end of time, as a dead, static eternity. It is a veritable cross between the time of causality and alienation, the time of its destruction, and the "remolino" of the sphere as the emergence of the perfect form in resurrection. It is the cross between the line, the erasure of the line, and the spiral. But this mixture of times, which is far from an empty homogeneous image of any sort, is nothing other than the "creation of a new state order." I want to argue that this is not a contradiction but, rather, an extremely lucid appraisal of what is at issue in the emergence of order, particularly in the case of the state, which would be in the position now of producing the geometry of thought that before pertained only to God.

Perhaps it would be possible now to entertain a paradox internal to the reading of "Aguja de diversos." If the resurrection concerns the triumph of the Revolution, then it must also imply a certain degree of immanence, or of a secularization of certain transcendental ideas fundamental to the Christian narrative. It is possible to read something of this sort in the poem in question, as part of the sections that were added for the post-Revolution publication of *Dador* in 1960 (the poem nevertheless concludes with the same meditation on the resurrected before the second death):

> The foundations do not have to be in the depths;
> the skin, the surface of the sea and the face of the blade,
> remain insoluble, and the coarseness of the knife
> does not manage to inaugurate enmity nor senseless
> dispersion, for the face seems to root itself

in the second root of what is proper, in the voracious
identity that sinks and continues as the cavalry
extended on the interminably homogeneous sheet [lámina].

[Las bases no tienen que estar por los profundos;
la piel, la superficie del mar y la cara de la hoja,
mantienen su indisoluble y la tosquedad de la cuchilla
no logra inaugurar la enemistad ni el enloquecido
dispersarse, pues el rostro parece enraizarse
en la segunda raíz de lo propio, en la identidad
voraz que se hunde y continúa como la cabellera
extendida en la lámina interminablemente homogénea.] (*Poesía* 297–98)

This segment of "Aguja de diversos" begins by singling out the surface of the sea: a sheet, skin, or a blade that has directionality because it has a face but is insoluble. The sheet (lámina) is interminably homogeneous. Everything will be on that surface. However coarse the surface of the sea might be, the voice will find the necessary breath. It would be tempting, while exploring texts like these (which appear more often than is imagined in the poetry), to read Lezama as does Iván de la Nuez. For de la Nuez, Lezama saw in the island a site "with the necessary immanence" (131). For him, Lezama stands as a welcome corrective to a Latinamericanist tradition that understands the emergence of the nation as the dialectical overcoming of a time when the "civilized" stood next to the "barbarians." This tradition is dominated by the idea that Latin America moves from the chaos of an unformed reality to its most perfect formalization in the state (de la Nuez 131–32). Such a developmentalist narrative is unworked by the persistence of formless fragments that occupy the present even after the nation comes into being. And the author of *La expresión americana* is of help, as he teaches us how to avoid a logical and linear image of history: "If Lezama gives us the means to escape such a conceptual situation, this is because in his *poetic system* the text, writing, or poetry are the guidelines (chaotic and imprecise) of a culture. To achieve this, he gives a noble and 'philosophical' value to the singular, to the amorphous [*informe*], that whose permanence is disposable and mutable" (de la Nuez 132). I am sympathetic to this reading, and in my own way wish to contribute to this line of thought.[19] Nevertheless, some difficulties have to be noted.

The first concerns the way in which the evocation of immanence sets itself up too quickly as a response, in the negative, to the dominant view of Lezama as a poet of the transcendental. According to that tradition,

Lezama would be a belated Hegel of the tropics, an out-of-step romantic flailing about in an unconscionable search for the Absolute.[20] In view of so neat an opposition between immanence and transcendence, it is hard not to want to resist it as a false problem/option. Moreover, the opposition would risk obscuring those aspects of Lezama that relate directly to the Christian legacy. In trying to save Lezama, once again, we risk losing sight of the real import of his writing.

A second difficulty: a closer look at "Aguja" immediately presents obstacles to the immanentist interpretation. Section 13 continues:

> The surface of the sea does not reflect the incontinence of its entrails;
> the sheet in covering over the cloacal mouth
> is not ruffled by the occult schism of the words.
> The severe fundaments of the sea foam
> is not born of the unceasing questioning of the entrails.
> The face and the roots have the same canal
> to particularize the slight gust of wind. And the face
> buried in the air or the root that flies
> inside the earth, both have the same emergence
> for the voice and the breath to find themselves.

> [La superficie del mar no refleja la incontinencia de sus entrañas;
> la lámina al tapar la boca pocera
> no se frunce por el oculto cisma de las palabras.
> La severa fundamentación de las espumas
> no nace del incesante interrogar de las entrañas.
> El rostro y las raíces tienen el mismo canal
> para particularizar el airecillo. Y el rostro
> enterrado en el aire o la raíz que vuela
> dentro de la tierra, tienen el mismo surgimiento
> para que la voz y el aliento se encuentren.] (*Poesía* 298)

What is being interrogated there is the foundation of the formless and "impermanent foam," which cannot be ascribed to the depths or to a hidden source; probing into what lies behind the surface is not what makes possible the birth of the severe foundations of the sea foam. If we were dealing with pure immanence, the expectation would be to place formlessness on the side not of the effect but of the cause, which is to undermine the priority of the cause, only present, then, in its effects: for "the cause immanent in its own effects is representable only in the form of its effects but *qua* cause it is formless and unrepresentable" (Casarino xxxiv). This cause, as such, would be an absence, formless because void. Where does the "obscurity" come from then? There is a third term, held in common by the opposition of face (surface) and roots (depth): it is a canal, a passageway, through which the "airecillo" (a gust of air that is the spirit, *pneuma*)[21] becomes something in particular. In the last section of the poem, Lezama writes of "the figure that unites spirit with the germ" (*Poesía* 305). The hypotyposis confuses all the senses, the sky is the earth, up is down, roots fly, while taking on the rhetorical form of the chiasmus (flying takes places underground, burial takes place in the air). The crossroads that emerge do so for the voice and breath to encounter each other. It is not hard to surmise that Lezama is dealing here, in his own very peculiar language, with the trinity: or, as he puts it elsewhere in the same poem, "el triángulo de diferencias" which is "la superficie sin tiempo" (*Poesía* 293). What needs to be asked, then, is, What does this "lack of time" entail?

If the trinity, the incarnation, and the projection of these Christian structures onto the arrival of the Revolution, if all these elements play an important role in setting up his enthusiastic response after January 1959, when Castro appears to the poet as the second coming, then it would be tempting to force the section that I have quoted above to speak of a political incarnation, a becoming immanent that relates to the sea change in Cuba's history.[22] With the Revolution, politics enters a phase in which it is no longer subject to the dictates of a transcendental order, but in which that order is forged here and now and there is no other ontological zone that underwrites it. Yet this would make of immanence exactly the ground from which someone like de la Nuez wants to find a line of flight, and emphatically not the solution to the identitarian logic that he critiques. Lezama, who had read Donoso Cortés, would be too close to the reading of the *ius revolutionis* that the Spanish jurist offered, in which, with the eradication of God from politics, what emerges is a human being that illegitimately appropriates all the attributes of the deity—thus opening the age, not of revolutions, but of despotism.

Even critics who seek to extricate Lezama from the nationalist teleology of the Revolution agree that for the poet the Revolution was a messianic event. Most recently Juan Pablo Lupi, after correctly pointing out the poet's aversion for narrow historicist images of the world, asks: "Doesn't this [acceptance of the arrival of the messianic event] open the way for . . . what Lezama's historiographic speculations seem to oppose all along?" (234). Lupi proposes that Lezama subtracts himself from this messianism. The Revolution does appear to Lezama as an event, he explains, but it does so under the sign of "el *potens* . . . en la infinitud," which discloses "not a teleology, but the wondrous and unexpected fulfillment of a historical desire out of a virtual infinitude of possibilities"; in the end, he concludes: "The revolutionary event becomes subsumed under the 'poetic reason' of infinite possibility, and this historiography . . . is radically *non*-teleological" because it places the event in history and opens it to its future ruin (240). Lezama's vision of history and the imaginary eras "constitute the prophetic foreshadowing that the present *will be (mis)read and ruined* in unforeseeable ways in the future" (242).

This reading, however, leaves a fundamental problem unresolved. If Lupi is right, Lezama is able to conceive of the Revolution as an event precisely because he applies his own Catholic formalization of the event-Christ to Castro's arrival: it is true because it is absurd, it is true because it is the unworking of Reason, and so forth. If this is the basis on which all events are opened to their future ruination, then it is also true of the Christian story insofar as history is concerned. That is, if this is the reason why Lezama escapes the retroactive narrative of a single event that is here for all time and orders past, present, and future, then the same must be said of Christianity. And it can be said of Christianity for a very simple reason: for that doctrine all historical events will be subject to ruination, culminating of course in the time of destruction, as Lezama puts it. So the poet's vision of history is saved precisely because he subjects it to a higher end: the return of the true Messiah and the end of time. And it is precisely this foretelling of the future ruin of the triumphant revolutionary that we find in the additions made to the poem "Aguja de diversos" for the 1960 edition of *Dador*.

We begin to discern the general pattern of the poem, for the additions after the Revolution do not concern a new ending in which the "resurrecto" is imagined as a new state order. Lezama changes the beginning, where he follows the vicissitudes of a sovereign soon to meet his ruin, a sovereign who had made his terror into his "soplo"—*pneuma* (*Poesía* 289). His time is time "chopped by men" (tajado por el hombre) (*Poesía* 292). This time, the time of "successive years," is ruled by a higher authority, one that "abounds in its inexistence": "the pleasure of terror recovers a difference whose center of similarity is lost," and the spirit that animated the terror of the sovereign is met by a "surface without time," a third person that is "increada en la distancia" (*Poesía* 293). Then, time "blows, and erases . . . , the succession of hands moves toward the whirlpool, truncating the whirlpool" (*Poesía* 296).

We are faced with a paradoxical image of Lezama. On the one hand, he is supposed to have accepted the event Castro = Christ. As Ponte puts it:

"The *origenistas* . . . find in the 1959 revolution the end of time, the Parusia, . . . the second coming . . . , Hegel's Prussian state, the last of the imaginary eras and the last effort of the historical imagination" (*El libro* 110). This Hegelianization of Lezama, and this is something that always goes unremarked, would also amount to declaring the end of his Catholicism. But it is only via his Catholicism that we seem, thus far, able to imagine *both* that the poet was more critical of the victorious Revolution and *also* that he simply put Castro where he had put Christ before the Revolution. On the other hand, if we reject the transcendentalist vision altogether, as is the case in de la Nuez, we then run the risk of an absolute secularization of the divine that yields a plane of immanence but also a despot, a reading that forces us to think immanence in the terms of a conservative Catholic tradition—for which, immanence is simply the plane of human hubris.

These readings, taken together, are not able to account for the mixed temporality that Lezama ascribes to both the Revolution and the resurrection. As a whole what is obscured also concerns the way in which the displacement of religion for revolutionary politics would entail a radical discontinuity, on Lezama's part, with his stance as a Catholic displeased with "republican" politics pre-1959. In fact, this shift would imply that Lezama had given up on his Christianity altogether. For not even by way of liberation theology can Christianity see the second coming in the face of a merely human revolutionary hero. To address these questions in all their complexity, we must first get a firmer grasp on the temporalities of Revolution itself.

The Times of Revolution

Let us consider the way in which Che distinguishes between the Cuban experience and the Russian one. On the one hand, Guevara will insist on a break with Leninism. In his "Notas para el estudio de la ideología de la Revolución Cubana," for instance, he opens by declaring: "This is a singular revolution in which many have found a disjunction regarding one of the basic premises of the most orthodox revolutionary movement, expressed by Lenin thus: 'without a revolutionary theory there is no revolutionary movement'" (*Obra* 507). The specific difference concerns the role of theory in the Cuban experience. And the implications this had for the idea of the party, which became one with the armed forces on the ground. Theoretical considerations are not dismissed out of hand, but the way to the knowledge that would be derived from them is not the same. There is access to a truth, the same that theory was to yield for Lenin we might add, but it is gained in a more immediate form: "Revolutionary theory as the expression of a social truth is above any statement; that is to say, revolution can be carried out if one interprets correctly the historical reality and uses in the appropriate manner the forces that intervene in that reality, even when one is unaware of the theory" (*Obra* 507). A year later, in April 1961, he returns to the question of the singularity of the Revolution, and this time he is even more direct in attempting to downplay the exceptionality of the Revolution: "We accept that there were exceptions that gave its peculiar character to the Cuban Revolution . . . , but it is no less established that all revolutions follow laws whose violation is not possible for society" (*Obra* 515). Guevara is no longer attempting to explain the validity of his approach; he is attempting to show that the Cuban Revolution simply was in perfect accord with true laws of revolution in general. Even the singularities in question are part of the general laws of all revolutions. This has the paradoxical effect of bringing the argument full circle but as if it were dialectically sublated. We start by saying that the (theoretical) laws of revolution have to be broken depending on the reality on the ground; this decision is incorporated into a narrative that explains what could seem to be a subjectivist bent as a better and more consistent way of being in touch with the truth; and, finally, the ironclad and universal truths return, but, now, as the overcoming of merely theoretical knowledge. The vanishing mediator in this dialectical overcoming is the lyrical moment when the guerrilla becomes one with the people. The transubstantiation makes them the obedient vehicles of the general will, even as it transforms the aesthetic mechanism that made that metamorphosis possible in the first place into a material manifestation of the truth, rather than a poetic or idealist projection. Theoreticism, idealism, lyrical flight—all of these maladies of the bourgeois intellectual are set aside for good. The shift produces the results that the romantic poets had hoped for, but with one major difference: this is real, material history that we are talking about and not merely words on the page.[23] Guevara places the Revolution on a path that is beyond any subjective reach, "a fundamental logical path derived from the immanent laws of the social process" (*Obra* 526).

On the other hand, once the immanent laws of the social process are revealed, the effects for the theory of the subject are clear. There are at least two important *consequences* of the Cuban struggle in this regard. The first is the lesson that the future of revolution in Latin America will depend on the successful alliance between guerrillas and the peasant masses. The second: "The masses do not only know of the possibilities of victory; they already know their destiny. They know every day with more certainty that, whatever tribulations history throws at them during short periods, the future is of the people, because the future is one of social justice" (*Obra* 525). In terms of the temporal self-awareness of the Revolution, the results are striking. This process does not only give them access to the other, with which they have become one. (I have pointed out in these pages that what is taking place here responds to a modern model of self-legitimation via the Other. It is not the guerrillas who dictate, but the masses who teach, and while this learning happens, the guerrillas simultaneously incorporate the masses and make them one with their own being—thus sidestepping the question of political mediation or of representation.) It also gives them the certainty that the earthly time of history is no longer their own. This accounts for the self-assured Castro who, in a February 1957 interview with Herbert L. Matthews for the *New York Times*, stated that the guerrilla's fight against imperialism is "a battle against time and time is on our side" (qtd. in Prentzas 50). This was still the situation in 2007, when Castro spoke of the post-Soviet era of triumphant globalization: "I was fully convinced that it was . . . [globalization] that had to be resisted. . . . Wait patiently, for globalization to collapse" (qtd. in Lambie 2–3).

As tempting as it would be in this context to attempt to explain the recent announcement regarding the normalization of relations between the United States and the Revolution taking this temporality as a point of departure, I would argue that it would perhaps be misleading to claim that the second statement is the sign of a decaying leader who has lost touch with reality, and history has proven him wrong. Certainly, the new era that is dawning with the promise of "normalization" will mean a more aggressive integration of the island into the global economy. But the issue here is lost. It is not that globalization won against the Revolution. It is that the banner of a regime of politics that is beyond the reign of the finite, a politics that claims that it is itself the end of history because it manages the whole of life according to some putative universal and ironclad logic that is simply "the way things are" is equally applicable to globalization and to the logic that we see unfolding in our reading of Guevara. And this internal link becomes further illuminated if we delve deeper into what is at stake for the subject that has been liberated by the Revolution.

The common assumption is that, faced with the difficulty of achieving production goals, Cuban socialism sought a solution that was not tied to the incorporation of capitalist logics. Rather, with Guevara what emerges is the management of consciousness in the form of moral incentives. But this entails, paradoxically, a theory of the subject shaped by capitalism. The remnants of the past in the human material that should have become the new man were an obstacle that had to be overcome—and this meant the complete reformation of the subject in light of unselfish and participatory values (Chomsky 11–12). George Lambie is aware of the dialectic this will set in motion, which he explains in an approving tone:

> While the initial surge of political will and popular commitment were important in initiating the Revolution, there had to be a learning process in which the masses, by changing the world around them, also changed themselves. This symbiotic development was vital to the consolidation of the Revolution, and over time received support from state structures in education, health care and a whole range of initiatives that promoted the "general will." In the beginning, however, huge problems had to be overcome to precipitate a transformation. Cuba's underdevelopment had produced a highly unequal society, and those who constituted the mass support of the Revolution were mainly from the poor, undereducated, disadvantaged sector. (125–26)

The new Cuba had to deal with the fact that the masses that gave it its direction and its legitimacy, while being the source of innovation, as the guerrilla itself was to claim for ideological reasons, were not equipped to actually run the country and thus had to be transformed so as to accommodate to the mandates of development.[24] This is tantamount to saying that the very motor of the Revolution was not "up to speed" with "the times," and it is the times that have the final word. In the end, the masses have to submit to the narrative of development and its polyvalent temporalities—which means either that the masses were too far ahead of the conditions on the ground or, on the contrary, that they were as Marxism-Leninism had posited, behind the contemporaneity of the contemporaneous. It becomes increasingly hard to determine which temporality is marking the time of the new Cuba, whether it is that of the peasants (who had forged the ideology of the Revolution in the Sierra Maestra according to Guevara's diaries), that of the workers (who were not up to the task of production and thus had to be constantly reminded of their importance and of their need to rise to the challenges of the modern economy); or if, on the contrary, it was the time of the global economy which Cuba could not possibly escape. The issue only gets more labyrinthine once we take into account the way in which "work" and the "worker" were treated in the ideological evangelism of the leaders and in the propaganda material they commissioned to idealize and romanticize this figure.

Guevara's critique of the socialist camp, so we are told, was that they had disregarded "the moral and spiritual factors of socialist societies"; and, as the Cuban philosopher and historian Juan Antonio Blanco continues: "If you disregard the spiritual factors and only attempt to deal with economic factors, you are not going to get rid of alienation. For both Che and Fidel, socialism was not simply a matter of developing a new way of distribution. It was a question of freeing people from alienation at the same time" (qtd. in Chomsky 42).[25] But this assumes that alienation is still a fact of the new revolutionary reality, that the victory itself did not equal the qualitative transformation required by the ideology of change. This is decidedly not how Guevara understood alienation.

In August 1964, Guevara delivered a speech on the role of work in the creation of a new revolutionary consciousness. In it, all of the tensions at play come to a head in their most fundamental form. He began with a poem, which he did not attribute to anyone in particular, in part because it was to be an example of a defeatist attitude coming from a different world, "another world that we have already left outside vis-à-vis work." What he wanted to point out by quoting from that poem was the "bourgeois" desire for a sort of labor that is a "return to nature" or for the transformation of day-to-day life "into play" (*Obra* 400). This is a line of thought that he identified with a world that was no longer the world that existed in Cuba after the triumph of the Revolution. Though he does not say it, it is an archi-romantic desire that he is presenting in his opening lines—a desire that goes back to Schiller's *Letters on the Aesthetic Education of Man* (1794), where it was through play that infinite or absolute time would emerge for the artist: "Let the artist endeavor to give birth to the ideal by the union of the possible and of the necessary. Let him stamp illusion and truth with the effigy of this ideal; let him apply it to the play of his imagination and his most serious actions, in short, to all sensuous and spiritual forms; then let him quietly launch his work into infinite time" (Schiller). Guevara is not talking about artists; he is addressing the worker in this instance. "But," as he continues, this only goes to prove that a dialectical change had occurred: "The extremes meet, and that is why I wanted to quote those words to you, because we could ask that desperate poet to come to Cuba, to see how man after surpassing all the stages of capitalist alien-ation, and after being considered a beast of burden tied to the yoke of the exploiters, has found once again his way and has returned to the path of play. Today in Cuba work acquires a new meaning, it is done with a new joy [alegría]" (*Obra* 400). Something seems odd. The poet could come to Cuba to find this kind of play-labor, but he will still be able to find men and women who have returned to a previous state. And this return is even more problematic once we find out that these human beings are not quite there yet, as "the man who works with the new attitude," whom the poet should come to Cuba to see in the flesh, "is perfecting himself" (*Obra* 401). Revolutionary Cuba is a new world where alienation has been surpassed and the worker's labor is joy, yet in the act of work what is at issue is the becoming perfect of that joyous worker, who must contribute to the development of a properly socialist consciousness in order to "prepare a new stage of society . . . in which there will be no classes, and thus there won't be any difference between a manual worker and an intellectual, between laborer and peasant" (*Obra* 401). Thus, we are and we are not in the time that comes after alienation. Alienation and liberation coexist for the time being. The time being, however, is defined in essence by the fact that a first death of alienation has taken place, which means that this is also the time when the worker awaits the second death of alienation. This is a properly spiritual plane. Guevara refers to the workers who are already doing their part as those who have the "spirit of sacrifice, the spirit of communism and the new attitude toward life" (*Obra* 412). Guevara speaks of the new Cuba as a site where the alienation of the worker has been superseded; labor is play. Nevertheless, this image of liberation stands in sharp contrast to the image of a leader who appears in front of the worker to count their hours, to divide them into "normal" days of work, and to offer them the calculations regarding the more than twenty-one thousand days that the state had received in volunteer work in the months preceding the speech (*Obra* 404). One imagines the poet he invited to the island to witness the new labor, of play and joy, calling him out on this wielding of the infernal ticktock that measures the time of work.

The time of capitalism survives within the time of the Revolution as a reserve, a denegated remainder that can be instrumentalized by the state to great advantage. It is the internal survival of this time that masks the constitutive link between the Revolution and global capitalism, and presents it as if it were an external and contingent accident that prevents it from reaching its full potential. In other words, the Revolution cannot under any circumstances eradicate this time, because it is the only historical time it has—with the proviso that it is not a single time to begin with but the multiple times of modernity as such. In its approach to this difficulty, the Revolution opted for a path that was tragic and heroic in the technical sense of those terms: it attempted to do the impossible. We can say, today, that the difference between the old and the new radical governments in the area touches on this point in a fundamental sense: from Chávez to Morales there is now no desire to claim that what they do politically concerns the eradication of alienation or anything of the sort; their first move is to accept that globalization is the only game available (Chávez Frías 4). The transition from one mode of radical politics to the other is possible only because there is already in the temporality of the Revolution, its tradition and archive, its saints and villains, not a gap that separates its "time" from that of the imperial, capitalist, colonialist enemy, but a fundamental continuity. Moreover, it is the Christian crossroads of time that more capaciously serves as the only possible background against which the radical difference between socialist and capitalist Cuba can be perceived as such. As the central matrix from which both derivations of the modern political order spring, it should not be surprising that its "spirit" is the only wind in the sails of redemptive actuality—an actuality that was always only capable of biding its time until the second death and the time of plenitude.

It is to this Christian and Catholic strain within Cuban socialism that the leadership of the island has always turned in times of adjustment, beginning not with the Special Period, but before with the Rectification campaign of 1986, which found its emblematic figures in José Martí and Che Guevara (Chomsky 61). This is also why the "Catholic national utopianism" of someone like Cintio Vitier finds its heyday during the difficulties of the 1990s (cf. Prieto). Yet, only by ignoring all the contradictions hidden under that ideological narrative does religion become able to do its political work. That is, it can only function, and be politically effective, if the ideologue proffering it is willing to overlook that it is the very foundation of both politics and religion that are compromised. Our engagement with Lezama has shown that it is possible to enter into this political scene from a different, less intrumentalized, angle. In fact, what I have outlined in this chapter regarding Lezama's manner of working through the revolutionary sea change remains wholly out of reach of the political institutions that demanded that he take care of them. The Catholic background is at the center of his displacement of the political, but not in the sense that this is usually imagined when it comes to the relationship between religion and communism. Lezama did not resist communism in the way that a religious order resists the demand for secularization (that is, by positing a higher absolute authority that trumps the legitimacy of the state). He did it by taking the idea that since the first death of Christ, nothing that can happen in the realm of history can legitimately wield any real authority. We are all as in a void: and all our institutions are the more or less enduring fictions that seek to cover over that abyss. If this image nevertheless relies on a teleological and theological bedrock, it has been mobilized in a way that is certainly not that of the history of the ecclesiastical and statal orders that have most benefited from them. In the case of both politics and religion, we need to come to terms with a politicity with which politics wants nothing to do, and a religiosity with which religion wants to dispense. Thus, it is not a matter of indicating that Lezama was of this or that political persuasion, and then using him as a means to approve or disapprove, just as it is not a question of dismissing or defending his faith. Rather, it is a question of illuminating to what extent his texts are a record of the inability of big projections like state, religion, history, politics, and so forth to suffuse and cover over the entirety of existence with their dissecting grids. Would one be able to tell if Lezama was an "idealist" or a "materialist" in shifting onto the underside of these monolithic institutions (and monolithic even and perhaps especially when they operate in the name of inclusion and diversity)? The question itself crumbles to pieces if we take his thinking seriously. For what it would show us is that "materialism" might, after all, be the name we will have reserved for all the scholastic exercises that have been adduced in order to legitimize the "idealism," and utterly nonmaterial self-representations, of revolutionary politics since the nineteenth century. Politics, on the contrary, cannot bear the weight of that elucidation. And we cannot sidestep it without paying a price. For if we do not see the Revolution's own temporal crossroads, we are not only tempted but already at work to identify solutions that are nothing but the deadlocks we were attempting to dissolve.

What I am suggesting is not a more radical unveiling of the ever-darker side of the revolutionary process. Perhaps more modest, my proposal concerns the various ways in which not paying attention to this temporal meeting point (where alienation meets the spirit, where the linearity of development meets the circularity of teleology) leads to our own misperception of the limits of some of our most fundamental political and aesthetic concepts. Where these logics are played against each other in order to solve the conundrums each poses to the other, the question of nihilism hides itself in its most cunning guise: as the critique of nihilism as such. It is to the role that nihilism has played in this story that we must now turn.

4. Nihilism: Politics as Highest Value

The theological underpinnings of the Cuban Revolution are often confronted as if it were a nationally circumscribed problematic, even as its analysis reproduces dynamics that are perceptible and operative on a much broader scale.[1] Yet something is erased when the national furnishes the only framework to think through this difficult terrain, and it concerns the specific role of politics. This might seem paradoxical, for how could politics be disregarded when it comes to revolution? Politics becomes invisible when the only viable strategic maneuver to dismiss a political position hinges on the accusation that an authority in power is not legitimate—for it is the foundation as such, or the lack thereof, that should be in question. That is, when we ask about the legitimacy of the foundation of any politics, we are thereby assuming that such a foundation is readily available. However, as we saw in chapter 3, there is another way. If Lezama is an indication, it concerns putting the very idea of foundations in doubt. In other words, to lose sight of politics means to assume the inevitability of the ruinous presuppositions of political (dis)order. Politics, then, becomes the air we breathe and begins to appear as a necessity for life—imperceptible because it is the environment in which we move. In this chapter, I want to focus on the role that theology plays in organizing the forgetting of the non-necessary status of the political, and further, the forgetting of the lack of ground on which it is erected—that is, the role of political theology in positing politics as the highest value.

In this chapter, I trace some of the contemporary manifestations of nihilism as it pertains to the communist horizon, radical or Left-Heideggerian theory, and the case of Cuba in particular. A central aim is to show to what extent the willingness Lezama demonstrated to look into the void at the heart of politics is the kind of courage that goes by the name of nihilism. Beyond that, I want to begin to examine to what extent the accusation of nihilism is itself the nihilist covering over of that abyss. Nihilism in this sense takes on a different meaning, for it is no longer an accusation leveled against the unbeliever or the reactionary subject. Rather, it becomes a name that identifies the various ways in which the being of the void, the paradoxical there-ness of the lack of foundation, is denegated. The chapter concludes by illustrating the role that the temporalities of politics play in this eradication.

Postfoundationalism as Forgetting of Being

How do we stand with respect to nihilism? Oliver Marchart's book *Post-Foundational Political Thought* (2007) is a good place to start when considering this question, even if in a preliminary fashion. His book is, among other things, an attempt to separate Leftist-Heideggerian theorists (including Jean-Luc Nancy, Alain Badiou, Claude Lefort, and Ernesto Laclau) from the charge of nihilism that is usually leveled at approaches that posit the absence of a final or foundational ground, whether it is in terms of politics or philosophy. I quote Marchart, who quotes Laclau's words to this effect: "There are no necessarily pessimistic or nihilistic conclusions to be drawn from the dissolution of the foundationalist horizon. . . . As Laclau underlines, the 'abandonment of the myth of foundations does not lead to nihilism' since the 'dissolution of the myth of foundations . . . further radicalizes the emancipatory possibilities offered by the Enlightenment and Marxism'" (156). What is odd about this particular defense against the accusation of nihilism is that the theory of postfoundationalism is predicated first and foremost on what Heidegger called the ontological difference. And in Heidegger's own thought, we find that taking the ontological difference seriously would make it impossible to treat the problem of nihilism as a mere pitfall that can be avoided or as an obstacle that can be simply surpassed—for nihilism must instead be thought in its essence, and thought must first learn how to gather itself in the nothing that it is (see Heidegger, *Pathmarks* 291–322). Marchart, on the contrary, states that nihilism, which for him is another name for antifoundationalism, is the assumption of the absence of foundations, even if one thinks of foundations as contingent and partial. And according to him, this "would result in complete meaninglessness" (14). Marchart's project is geared toward avoiding such an abyss.

My aim here is not to delve into the intricacies of the theory of postfoundationalism as Marchart elaborates it, but his insistence on sidestepping the problem of nihilism does serve to illustrate one of the recurrent symptoms of the incursion of the question of being into politics. In Marchart's case, the basic problem remains how to accept the deconstruction of metaphysics while remaining politically relevant. All answers to this problem that leave the very idea of politics and its temporalities untouched (even while declaring that the political is contingent, finite, and ultimately without ground) risk reproducing the very metaphysical matrix that they explicitly critique. I do not pretend to offer an image of what a different conception of politics would be; I simply want to elaborate on certain problems that are essential in approaching that question.

One way of illustrating the underlying problematic behind the question of foundations for politics is by turning to the work of Carl Schmitt. It is well known that Schmitt defines the sovereign as "he who decides on the exception" (Schmitt, *Political* 5). In turn, the exception, he states, is principally characterized by "unlimited authority," and this "means the suspension of the entire existing order"; he adds: "In such a situation it is clear that the state remains, whereas law recedes. Because the exception is different from anarchy and chaos, order in the juristic sense still prevails even if it is not of the ordinary kind" (12). The state is above the law, and this superiority has nothing to do with its anarchic or chaotic character. For the exception to be intelligible in the first place, there must be a normal situation. Thus, another definition of the sovereign is in order: he who "decides whether this normal situation actually exists" (13). Since "there exists no norm that is applicable to chaos," the entire apparatus of sovereignty according to the political theological model is to begin by legislating the anarchic and the chaotic, the formless, and the ab-normal, out of existence (13). This stratum becomes a nothingness that stands in opposition to the all that is nevertheless divided into two: the situation and the exception. The anarchic is vanished, but only because it is taken over and domesticated by the act of decision, which is the only absolute principle—but a principle that, precisely because it is a decision, cannot be an *arché*. This displacement is at the heart of the contradictory dynamic that Schmitt's sovereign enacts: he constructs by destroying, determines by in-determining, forms by deconstructing (Galli, *Genealogia* 338). "Authority," Schmitt writes, "to produce law . . . need not be based on law" (Schmitt, *Political* 13).

Carlo Galli has pointed out the extent to which we are dealing here with an abyss that is proper to the crisis of modern political thought, and that leaves the order that the sovereign is able to produce haunted by its diametrical opposite: "Through this creation of form and of order the sovereign draws energy from disorder itself, from the exception; neither is this abyssal act given once and for all, rather disorder and exception remain, within the order, as an always present potential" (*Genealogia* 339). It is tempting to imagine that this problem emerges only with the demise of the Christian social mediation. However, this would obscure the fact that the Christian mediation, and before that the Imperial Roman mediation (with its law and its *humanitas*), and before that . . . we could keep tracking this crisis all the way back to the most fragmentary of pre-Socratic remains we have at our disposal—all of these steps back are iterations of the same attempt at domesticating the nothingness from which order emerges. Galli puts it thus: "The modern rationalist project (Lockian, Enlightened, Positivist) of making politics turn upon the individual, of turning the political mandate into an impersonal and legal function, and of rendering politics transparent and in continuity with the rationality of the subject, according to Schmitt's text, is shipwrecked: in order for a rational and impersonal order to have normative validity there must be a personal, prelegal and prerational mandate, founded on that normative Void that is the decision" (*La mirada* 65). Galli immediately adds that Schmitt is not a nihilist on this score, but he must come to terms with modern nihilism: "with the absence of foundation" (*La mirada* 65). In Schmitt, there is the recognition that "the only possibility of something concrete in the modern age lies in the awareness of nihilism and the opposition to its formal concealment, that is, the merely formal . . . determination of the political order" (Galli, *La mirada* 65). Modern political existence, for Schmitt, is defined by this founding absence, this Void-of-Order. This lack is the decision, and assuming it as the unfounded foundation of the law is the only way to be "scientific" regarding the modern situation. In this, Schmitt assumes, on the one hand, that order is necessary but impossible to realize perfectly; and, on the other, that this is a historically specific situation. The only way to face this moment is by remembering and activating the remembrance that the public order emerges from the contingent. This understanding of the lack of foundations, and not a Heideggerian approach based on the problem of the ontological difference, seems to be more attuned to the elaboration that Marchart makes of postfoundationalism. For the Heideggerian approach to the ontological difference, as Emmanuel Biset has shown in his own reading of Marchart's book, cannot be reduced to the dualism of an ontic politics and an ontological realm of the political without welcoming back the classical metaphysical matrix and its foundationalist thought (on this point, see Biset).

Even a cursory description of Marchart's approach to foundations reveals closer affinities with Schmitt than with Heidegger. He explains that, since it is not an easy task to get rid of foundations altogether, postfoundational thought pays closer attention to "what is excluded by the erection of foundations"; these contingent foundations are "an ontological weakening" of foundations that does not go all the way to doing away with them—and adds:

> What distinguishes [antifoundationalism from postfoundational thought is that the latter] does not assume the absence of *any* ground; what it assumes is the absence of *an ultimate* ground, since it is only on the basis of such absence that grounds, in the plural, are possible. . . . Hence, post-foundationalism does not stop after having assumed the absence of a final ground . . . for what is still accepted by post-foundationalism is the necessity of *some* grounds. What becomes problematic as a result is not the existence of foundations (in the plural) but their ontological status—which is seen now as necessarily contingent. (14)

There is a shift involved that turns the attention away from the object and toward its conditions of possibility. Laclau calls this kind of operation transcendental, but I want to ask whether it is, properly speaking, a metaphysical operation as well. The fate of any possible "Left-Heideggerianism" is at issue in this question. For it is by taking the ontological difference (between being and beings) that this operation is said to be possible in the first place. As Marchart puts it: "At stake in post-foundationalist thought is the status attributed to foundations, whereby the primordial (or ontological) absence of an ultimate ground is itself the condition of possibility of grounds as present—that is, in their objectivity or empirical 'existence' as ontic beings" (15). Against thinkers who dismiss the relevance of the ontological difference for politics (like Rancière, Rorty, or Oakeshott), this understanding of ontological difference qua difference is essential for postfoundationalism. A plurality of contingent and temporary foundations ground the social field empirically, but it remains impossible to find a final ground for that plurality. To hold these two ideas together at once is to admit that the impossibility of the final ground "cannot be of the same order as empirical foundations themselves" (15). The absence of *arché* ends up being the very legitimating mechanism for the multiplication of finite foundations, which will take on the form of a decision—as was the case also in Schmitt. The empirical order must then be able to posit its own finite principle. It is not universal, and it is openly accepted as contingent, but it remains a principle. And what makes it possible is the transcendental absence of an ultimate principle.

We can think this description not as postfoundationalism, but as a thoroughly secularized version of the transcendence and rescendence that obtains when the location of value(s) is no longer above but here on Earth. As such, it can be used as a description of what "modernity" or "enlightenment" actually were supposed to be, even as it is with modernity and the Enlightenment that this operation becomes the basic ideological matrix for a disembodied and unlocalized universalism that we know today to have been in crisis since its very inception. Would this not then mean that postfoundationalism is simply a rehabilitated form of modern thought as a whole? If this is so, then postfoundationalism "attends" to the ontological difference the better to forget about being, in Heidegger's sense of the term. But more generally, what is at issue in this forgetting has a very specific political consequence: this flattening out of the ontological difference prepares the way for the accusation of nihilism to be leveled at whoever does not forget what is essentially at issue in thinking the difference between being and beings as difference and not as a stratification of "ontic" and "ontological" "levels."

Nihilism Today

The accusation of nihilism is not made today primarily as the condemnation of a lack of faith in a concept of politics that is easily traced back to its metaphysical legacy, even if it is couched in postfoundational gestures such as we have explored in the case of Marchart. Take the case of Alain Badiou as a starting point. As Benjamin Noys points out: "In *Being and Event*, Badiou diagnoses . . . active nihilism as 'speculative leftism,' the belief in the absolute event that all too easily folds over into accepting the unalterable reign of power" (160). This folding over turns belief in an absolute event into the disbelief that will obtain in the case of all "real" events, as there is no such thing as an absolute event in the first place. For Badiou, speculative leftism is the belief that it is possible to commence from nothing, and he cites Nietzsche and the belief that it is possible "to break in two the history of the world" (Badiou, *Being and Event* 210). But again, this is imagined by this doctrine as the preparation for disbelief in all events that do take place, events that take on a more dialectical and less pure form. Thus the accusation of nihilism is bounced back to those forms of thinking that have attempted to work through the problem of nihilism, but now with the added caveat that nihilism is what these theories themselves produce and not anything that describes the state of humanity in whatever sense we wish to give to that expression. The result is striking as the fight against nihilism continues, but it is now a fight against those who think the problem. The banality of nihilism must be dismissed or critiqued.

Justin Clemens, in his Badiou-inflected *The Romanticism of Contemporary Theory*, has shown to what extent, within Badiou's doctrine, this means to identify nihilism with anti-Platonist trends from Nietzsche and the romantics down to the various deconstructions of metaphysics that are loosely collected under the heading of "theory":

> Romanticism is obsessed with the problem of nihilism, which it often codes as "Platonism." The abiding force of the problem is such that its effects can be discerned across an immense range of contemporary theory—and even in writers who may seem hostile or indifferent to nihilism's appeal. Furthermore, the problem of nihilism is irreducibly bound up with the problem of aesthetics. For Romantics, art is the non-place in which the historical distress of the world is best discerned and analyzed, although by no means resolved. (194–95)

The problem of nihilism, Clemens concludes, can be circumscribed to a series of philosophical or theoretical theses: concerning "irreducible multiplicity and subjective finitude, the necessity to delineate the end of metaphysics, the rejection of technoscience, and so on" (195). In "The Caesura of Nihilism," Badiou sheds light as to what is the bottom line in this sort of proposition in terms of a materialist concept of politics. So long as philosophy is critique, fixated on exposing the finitude that haunts every Idea, we are active nihilists; for "philosophy has no other legitimate aim except to help find the new names that will bring into existence the unknown world that is only waiting for us because we are waiting for it" (Badiou, *The Adventure* 65). The new world has to be named by philosophy; this is its political task. Anything else would be to call for the nihilistic disenchantment of all hitherto existing values and a call to inaction.

Commenting on this identification of nihilism with the inactive and impolitical, Bruno Bosteels has asserted that any effort to link this to a progressive or leftist agenda would have to contend with Geoff Waite's indictment of Left-Nietzscheanism (Bosteels, *The Actuality* 123–24). Though it is not a matter of proving one's progressive or leftist credentials, it is worthwhile to take Bosteels up on this suggestion—not because in the end a true theory of the Left will emerge but because it will shed light on the way that politics, as such, has taken up the place of the highest value and has thus been theologically inflected in order to defend it from the corrosive effects of so-called nihilist thought. Bosteels does not point to any specific place when citing Waite, but one could do worse than this passage: "Historical arguments linking Nietzsche positively to 'the Left' can be compromised by demanding that the historians who make them define what they mean by 'the Left'—a term that too often means a cowardly liberalism that has been more part of the *problem* . . . than any *solution* to it. A powerful, even fascistoid-liberal tendency has long been more in league with Nietzsche's corps/e than in effective combat against it" (Waite 145). In essence, the issue is with any theory that by its radical critique will fall into a tacit or unwitting defense of the status quo. Nietzsche is a revolutionary thinker for Waite, but a revolutionary in what sense? He finds his answer in what he considers "*the* most significant moment in all Nietzsche criticism," that is, Stanley Rosen's "Nietzsche's Revolution." In Nietzsche,

> Rosen writes: "An appeal to the highest, most gifted human individuals to create a radically new society of artist-warriors was expressed with rhetorical power and a unique mixture of *frankness and ambiguity* in such a way as to allow the mediocre, the foolish, and the mad to regard themselves as the divine prototypes of the highest men of the future." And, as Rosen concludes this part of this argument, "Nietzsche intends to accelerate the process of self-destruction intrinsic to modern 'progress,' not to encourage a return to some kind of idyllic past. The more persons who can be convinced that they are modern progressives (or postmoderns), the quicker the explosion." In short, "Nietzsche is a revolutionary of the right in his radical aristocratism and antiegalitarianism," *but* he needs the willing cooperation of a workforce in this bizarre, even murderous and suicidal project. Furthermore, Nietzsche seems to have *succeeded*, for Rosen, at least in part and negatively: namely, "in enlisting countless thousands in the ironical task of self-destruction." (Waite 166)

Waite leaves unremarked the apocalyptic Christianization of Nietzsche that this reading implies. It is telling that to arrive at this long quotation, which settles his argument for the moment, the author has to spend so much energy touting the need for a proper philological reading of Nietzsche's text. He faults people like Richard Rorty for not having read deeply enough in the work of Northrop Frye. Likewise, Heidegger, Lukács, and Freud, among an overwhelming number of others (since for Waite, Nietzsche is the philosopher of the contemporary world, the most influential on a global scale, the dominant ideologue in the context of the *pax americana*), all of them, according to Waite, simply ignore the philological question of method when appropriating the texts of the German philosopher. Philology, then, is opposed to hermeneutics. Hermeneutics, we are told (via Sorel as quoted in Rosen and reported by Waite), entails an expression "of middle-class fear of the violent and repressive nature of truth . . . a cowardice which consists in always surrendering before the threat of violence"; and for the author this indicates that hermeneutics is "condemned to death" and that "its disappearance is only a matter of time" (163). Philology, on the contrary, has a more Gramscian connotation for Waite: not only as a practice of communist scholarship but also as a practice of communist action beyond the academy. Gramsci's "living philology" is, for Waite, the "highest possible standard against which to judge any text" (79, cf. 145–66). The current appropriation of this argument goes under the guise of an attack on the melancholy leanings of a putative self-defeatist Left, preventing the revolution by its fixation on failure and its unwillingness to produce the new world that is waiting for us.

Perhaps the most important recent incarnation of this philological imperative is the claim that "theory" or "postmetaphysical" thought is today a major hurdle against the promise of a better world, even serving as the philosophical equivalent of savage capitalism and its democratic processes (see Bosteels, *Badiou and Politics* 262). Yet, if "'finitude' has today become a dogma that risks keeping the empirical form being internally transformed" (Bosteels, "Translator's Introduction" xxvii), perhaps it is not a "dogma" that we are talking about in the first place. On the one hand, this position assumes that "the revolution," or the "new world," is prevented from coming into being by the perhaps unwitting speculative efforts of certain theorists—that is, it seems to throw the political field onto the desk of the philosopher/theorist up to a point. On the other, it wants to offer a dialectical recasting of the very opposition between theory and praxis, in which theory is no longer the work of leaders separated from the masses, or philosophers in a position external to actual emancipatory political sequences. Thus, the work of the masses themselves, the work, that is, that goes on in those actually existing political sequences, has to be displaced from a purely practical consideration and reimagined as dialectically engaged in the production of both theory and of a torsion or change within the historical situation as such. This shift is not a merely theoretical move, for it has been achieved "as an effort of the intellect of the masses" themselves: "Political movements, in other words, are also and at the same time theoretical acts; conversely, all theoretical or philosophical configurations are likewise to be read as political interventions—say, as diagnostics or as prognosis, whether overt or esoteric. But the crucial point not to be missed is that these insights are but two sides of the same coin. Otherwise we risk smuggling in through the back door the straw man's argument that we thought we kicked out of the front door, namely, the dichotomy of theory and practice" (Bosteels, "The Efficacy" 661). And further: "To protest is to know; to know is to transform; and to learn is to be controversial. If the theorists are the masses themselves, instead of the vanguard leadership detached from them, then this is what theorists are for in times of riots and distress" (662). It is impossible to give here a full account of the subtle and complex theoretical footwork that has to take place for this dialectic to make sense. Nevertheless, several remarks are in order to understand what is at stake both in Bosteels and in what I am proposing in these pages. We could start with the idea that for Bosteels, following Badiou, the main interlocutor here is Left-Heideggerianism, a loose label that is sometimes applied to Badiou himself. For our purposes here what is important to underscore is that Left-Heideggerianism is meant to designate those thinkers for whom the work of Heidegger is a fundamental point of departure, but who ultimately assume that in Heidegger there is no answer to the question, "What is to be done?," and thus no useful link between theory and praxis. What results is a theorization of the social that sees in it the appearance of an unstable or un-founded totality, always precarious and always contingent. The attempt to close this gap, so the argument goes, would result in terror. For Bosteels, this radicalization of the Heidegger-inflected principle of anarchy remains unable to give a satisfactory answer to the problem of theory and praxis. It leaves the theorists in a very traditional position; according to Bosteels: "The philosophy of radical democracy rarely exceeds the frame of traditional political philosophy, inasmuch as it is still a question of deliberating the uses and disadvantages of different modes of organizing society. In other words, it judges politics from outside . . . starting from a necessary comparison of various types of symbolic ordering" (*Badiou and Politics* 270). This externality is no less unacceptable than the relative externality of theory when compared to the isolated and autonomous praxis of the militant, according to which theory only happens in the streets. The dialectical relation between theory and praxis, if it is to avoid the adventurism of ultra- and speculative leftism, involves two tasks that go to the heart of Bosteels's proposal. The first is to provide an ontology of actuality, or of the present, which Bosteels associates with Foucault but ultimately defines as the theoretical task of mapping the events "whose configuration marks our present"; the second is to cover over the void that so-called anarchic poststructuralist thought makes so much of, in order to define the subject of truth capable of transforming that empty space itself (269). Or, in other words, the task is to define the present and to find the subject of truth that will be able to transform it according to a universal prescription—as opposed to a contingent hegemonic articulation without ultimate grounds.

The reference to Foucault is more than a little odd here, particularly as it is set aside right away in the name of a more Badiouian formulation regarding events. In Foucault, the ontologies of the present had more to do with exposing the contingency at the heart of any present circumstance, precisely because it is one of the traditional metaphysical moves to assign the status of necessity to what is present—a status that goes straight to the heart of the principle of reason. In Bosteels as well, the contingent is meant to emphasize the fact that what is present is not necessary and can therefore be transformed in a radical way consistent with emancipatory politics. But the principle of reason creeps back in with the suggestion that it is possible for theory to offer a univocal representation of what the present is. And this brings us back to the issue of an answer to the question, "What is to be done?" The possibility of an answer to this question is tied necessarily to the possibility of knowing what the present is. As soon as a clear picture of what the present is appears, there also appears a set of consequences as to what needs to be done. However, the problem is how this picture emerges in the first place, and whether it is possible for it to emerge without returning to the most traditional philosophical grounds. But even beyond the more philosophical questions, it would be an issue that affects the most trivial organizational principles in constructing our critical arguments. For instance, is what defines our present the fact of a "deep unity" between postmetaphysical thought and the structure of the market? (262). However subtle the qualifications one adduces in making this reduction, the fact that it can be seen as an instance of reductionism, at the very least, exposes the impossibility of defining and representing the present except as a subjective wager regarding what is and is not actual, or is actual only from a certain perspective. This is the subject that displaces the void, the subject of truth, the subject of revolution. To be in disagreement with that subject about what the present is, means to be a reactionary subject, a subject unwilling or unable to believe in the truth professed by the militant subject. It would be tempting to invoke here the current commonplaces about how disagreement as such is what lies at the heart of politics, and to say, for instance, that the present is neither one side nor the other but the tension that the disagreement sustains, and thus that the present is the multiplicity of presents that are therefore configured. But this would be simply to multiply and complicate the requirements necessary to fully delineate what the present actually is. What I submit is that the real issue lies in the impossibility of giving form to the present and that this impossibility can only be overcome by sheer voluntarism and reductionism. This means that, up to a point, I am in agreement with Bosteels's critique of Left-Heideggerianism, insofar as what he says can also be read as a diagnosis that the necessary absence of foundations of the social often, as was explained in the pages above with regard to Marchart's proposal, substitutes for or acts as yet another foundation with which to cover over the an-archic at the heart of the political. But if the Left-Heideggerians do this unwittingly, Bosteels does it fully conscious that it is ultimately a question of displacing and forgetting the void. That is, the issue of the forgetting of being in the twenty-first century is no longer a question of what has gone unthought, but of a willing forgetfulness that is justified in the name of making the work of politics possible. And its first task is to dismiss all that the theorist knows about the difficult and treacherous traditional philosophical baggage regarding the presence of the present for thought. But the here and now, particularly after Hegel, does not let itself be pried open in this form.

However dialectically mediated, the theory/praxis dyad remains completely folded into an epistemological search for ultimate foundations, the final ground, from which knowledge is obtained. That is, the dialectic of theory and praxis remains wholly within epistemology itself. But it also posits that nihilism is the measure of the distance staked out from the nonmelancholic proper Left that defines what the "here and now" are, which is to say, the distance that separates critique from true politics as the highest value. Furthermore, by pointing out the obstacle that the melancholic poses to this highest value, the true progressive does nothing other than unwittingly underscore the finitude of what he or she assumes to be the correct political path. For, one cannot kill God as if it were a choice; not even Nietzsche made such an extravagant claim. The void at the heart of the political has little to do with a proverbial theoretical pudding[2] that is offered and can therefore be accepted or rejected as if it were a matter of choice. This void is not an aesthetic or imagined supplement; it is the first evidence of modern political experience, particularly after the great political revolutions of the era. That is, it is not a conservative gap installed in order to dismiss or discredit the emancipatory energy of the militant; rather, it is what the militant, unaware of all its consequences, first exposed in saying that the king was not a necessary feature of the political landscape. And that his beheading, far from being a catastrophe, was the only way of making life more bearable. But the void does not pick sides; the day after the revolution that void is also there already gnawing at whatever new institutions are put in place. The paradox of historical materialism is that it is unable to come to terms with the materiality of this emptiness. And this is the central paradox of nihilism today.

But it would be a mistake to think that this is only a question of/for contemporary theory. In fact, it would be possible to show the extent to which an approach labeled Left-Nietzschean, or Left-Heideggerian, or even Left-anti-Platonist, which is to say the thought of the displacement of politics as a category of metaphysics, appears today as the enemy and nihilist adversary across a wide ideological spectrum. This is not because it is always the same concept of the political that is at issue but because politics is placed in the same structural position: as the highest value against which nihilism is measured. For the moment, I will call the dislocation of that site the task of infrapolitical deconstruction. But my aim here is to show the extent to which its disavowal operates under the guise of a defense against nihilist thought across a variety of fronts. For this reason I want to look at two examples taken from the Cuban archive that are usually considered as antithetical. The work of Rafael Rojas and Cintio Vitier is representative of the thought that defined a specific moment in time concerning the possibility of either defending the nation against imperialism or thinking through the possibility of a politics of multiplicity that does not think history teleologically.

Politics or Nihilism

Rafael Rojas is perhaps today's most emblematic neorepublicanist critic of the Cuban Revolution. He, too, understands nihilism as any force that helps undermine the respect of active involvement in politics, now understood as civic virtues and values. There is no distinction between politics and the political in Rojas, no "true" politics outside of the sphere of politics that is already here. One either is a republican—endowed with a civic vocation and involved in "public affairs"—or a nihilist. Understood in these terms, nihilism has two modes: gestational nihilism (the retreat from the political sphere, which implies reducing the value of the present state of affairs to nothing, to a mere farce or simulacrum), and active nihilism (which would be the revolutionary takeover of the public sphere in order to redeem it). Following Zygmunt Bauman, Rojas subscribes to the thesis according to which gestational nihilism is said to prepare the ground for the active nihilism of a revolutionary politicization of the public sphere (*Tumbas* 145). This is a link that he will exploit in reading the generation of writers and intellectuals of the last prerevolutionary decade in Cuba: "perhaps," he writes, "the most nihilist in Cuban intellectual history" (*Tumbas* 151).

Rojas argues that the retreat from politics that characterized many of the important literary figures prior to the Revolution placed them in a void, constantly thematized in their work, and that made them unusually prone to misperceiving the new regime as a political and cultural panacea. It is almost painful to read the texts that document the overnight change in figures like Virgilio Piñera, Fernando Ortiz, José Lezama Lima, José Rodríguez Feo, among others. As if by magic, they all underwent an ideological sea change that had important consequences for their understanding of literature and its place in society. They willingly put themselves at the service of a revolutionary leadership that was condescending at best and vicious at worst. However, this shift toward Revolution, according to Rojas, was not one toward civic values, that is, proper politics. Rather, all of them, some more and some less, assumed a revolutionary posture that turned gestational into active nihilism (*Tumbas* 163). The long incubation finally gives its fruit in the enthusiasm that emerges upon the revolutionary event at the end of the 1950s. The discrepancies between the imagined relation between literature and politics, that feels so abrupt, are explained by the underlying nihilist stance that underwrites the position of these intellectuals before and after the Revolution came to power. This stance does not preclude that the prerevolutionary nihilists can and in fact are subsequently exposed to the despotism of the new revolutionary nihilists in power. Rojas rounds out his reading by turning to Albert Camus's model of the rebel and rebellion. Camus, the anti-Sartre, provides an image of the writer-as-rebel that for Rojas seems to have been telecasted to the young Cuban revolutionaries as a warning of the pitfalls that remained ahead.

The historian is interested in grafting Camus's rebel onto the overarching thesis that nihilists metamorphose into revolutionaries, but he adduces this example without placing it in the Cuban context in which he is so well versed. The reason for this is not difficult to surmise. If he had mentioned that in 1952 a long chapter from *The Rebel*, "Nietzsche and Nihilism," had been translated by Rodríguez Feo and published in *Orígenes*, his narrative would have been more complicated. For one, all of the figures involved in the metamorphosis from nihilism to revolution would have had access to the text to which he himself turns in order to find an alternative. On another front, it would have, perhaps, required a reconsideration of the very thesis on nihilism that makes his reading possible. Camus's text is intent on showing not a proper theory of the political (revolutionary or republican as the case may be) but on emphasizing that whatever is understood by politics, it only emerges in the absence of a theory of the proper discipline and activity of political actors, all of whom are thus faced with the limitations of their own partial positions (Camus 306).

Enrique del Risco has contested Rojas's claims regarding the causal link between nihilism and revolution by accepting Lezama's enthusiasm as authentic and by insisting instead on the deeply rooted nationalist myth of the Revolution. The Revolution, in its empirical facticity, was able to revive what Lezama had assumed to be dead (217–18). While I agree that the concept of nihilism, understood in these terms, is insufficient in explaining the shift that occurs with the advent of the Revolution, del Risco's recourse to the deep strata of nationalist mythology makes it impossible to confront the question of nihilism at all. This reading also risks occluding the overarching significance of Rojas's questions in an extranational setting, thus reducing his own, otherwise illuminating, argument to a narrow inquiry into the truth of Lezama's texts and intentions. But it is these acts of occlusion that nihilism unfolds.

On a different score, Rojas's recourse to Camus obscures the specific role that *Orígenes* plays within the broader ideological framework of the Revolution. Of course, it is ultimately as state-centered voices that figures like Fina García Marruz and Cintio Vitier emerge in the 1990s. But their role as agents of the state and representatives of a defense of the Revolution, to whatever degree this agency obtains, goes together with a complex ideological background that is not politically homogeneous, and not only because of religion. It might even be possible to claim that it is not primarily as Marxists or Socialists, and only relatively more so as revolutionary ideologues that García Marruz and Cintio Vitier emerge in the 1990s.

Both Vitier and Marruz came of age under the deep influence of Lezama. Both collaborated intensely in what has come to be known as the *origenista* project. And after the death of Lezama, they were the figures that did the most to memorialize *Orígenes* as a family and as a proto-Revolutionary mobilization of literature. This, they claimed, had to take on a baroque obliqueness. And this obliqueness left them open to facile accusations of escapism. Their central aim was to produce the emergence of a truly great art on the island, which meant, for them, an art that left behind the individualism of the moderns, the false radicalism of the vanguards, and the opportunism of the poetry that exploited the local and ethnic reality of the island and the continent as the display of the exotic for European consumption. This vision of things is not universally accepted. And in the pages of this book it is challenged insofar as the image of Lezama that I am interested in offering to the reader has little to do with Vitier and Marruz's ideologico-aesthetic program. But it is an image that has required intense and sustained effort to contest. In essence, they became the representatives of *Orígenes* and Lezama himself, using this legacy in their defense of the Revolution. It is to that defense that we must now turn. What is at issue concerns two central problems, on the one hand, to show that they are more complicated than simple ideologues of the state, and, on the other, that even in their divergence they join figures like Rojas and Bosteels in positing politics as the highest value.

They emerge as critics within the system, critics whose first order of business is to defend the Revolution against imperialism in all its forms, but critics nevertheless. Thus, it is true that they frame their interventions as attacks on the free circulation of ideas and as a stopgap from criticism more generally. But this would be an incomplete picture. For within the very limited margin they allow themselves for thinking through their situation critically, they tend to do so from a leftist position that is not always welcomed when it is a question of fortifying the strong leadership of the party. In this sense, they come closer to a tradition of which Camus's anarchism is an important part. This is not to say that they do any better for this reason. Their position relies on premises that cannot be questioned and on the uncritical acceptance of the Revolution's own rhetoric.

It is with their brand of nationalism that nihilism takes a precise form in critical discussions on Cuba since the fall of the Soviet Union, particularly when it comes to the relation between literature and politics, and, more precisely, to the work of José Lezama Lima and those associated with the journal *Orígenes*. This was a time when, in John Beverley's epigrammatic appraisal, their "Catholic-utopian nationalism" took "the place of an increasingly bankrupt orthodox Marxism" ("Introduction" 6). It came to function as a supplemental *Paideia* in order to better answer for the crisis the Revolution had to manage in the 1990s. Thus the resurrection of *Orígenes* served as an ideological pharmakon, meant to calm the ailments of the Revolution on a more "spiritual" (and also anarchist or libertarian) plane. The upshot is that nihilism reappears with a vengeance exactly when God, to allude to Nietzsche's maxim, could no longer have been said to be dead, as it is with the spirit that we will have to contend once again.

Vitier's efficacy in the ideological scene of the 1990s, though undeniable, needs to be reassessed as it occupied a place of enunciation that was paradoxical at best. One only has to look at Vitier's condemnation of the massification of the Cuban educational system, which he insisted was to blame for the inability of Cubans to identify themselves with the message and teachings of Martí—a confrontation with the institutionalization of the Revolution all the more significant as this lack of deep understanding of Martí, so Vitier argued, was the reason why the Cuban exodus had not been prevented: "Today our country only has great problems. . . . To the general scarcity on every front, we have to add the scar left by those who leave. . . . We know very well who is the culprit behind that massive exodus" (*Resistencia* 149). Thus far Vitier is simply stating the official line of reasoning: the true cause of the problem is U.S. imperialism. But then he adds: "There is an undeniable fact that is beyond any possible explanation or argument: those who leave, risking their lives, are Cubans who did not hear the word of Martí. Is that their fault or ours?" (149). And he concludes:

> Our duty is to prevent that from happening moving forward, because Martí lived and died for them. Our revolutionary education has not been sufficiently successful "for the good of all." Perhaps the massive scale that was its obligation conspired against the quality that was its ideal. In any case, almost thirty years after the triumph of the Revolution, we face increasing disbelief and disenchantment in greater sectors of our youth, those who are illiterate as well as the intellectual minorities. We know this youthful nihilism, which finds expression in the philosophical current called "postmodernism," is a universal phenomenon but that in this country it is not a dominant trend. Yet in this field the intellectual minorities have an unexpected responsibility, and the Revolution, as massive as it might be, has to see in every demoralized youth, in every political unbeliever, in all marginal and antisocial elements, an undeniable and painful failure. . . . Let us make our maximum effort to make it possible for Martí's word to reach them. (*Resistencia* 150)

The nihilism of the young in Cuba is not, as Vitier and Lezama would have argued in the prerevolutionary context, due to the efficacy of the nothingness of modernity. It is now lack of belief in and disenchantment with the Revolution itself that is at issue. Only Martí's word would correct this wrong. And here again it is a question of a living philology, capable of extracting the truth out of a text in order to offer it as a guide to true political action.[3]

Without a doubt the political bedrock in the passage quoted, which dates to 1992, is assumed to be not only stable but also absolute. As Vitier puts it elsewhere, for him the reality of the Revolution was indisputable; it was to be compared to a flagpole, firmly staked in the ground, which allowed for an endless struggle for freedom, symbolized by the chaotic movements of the flag waving in the air: "the tense freedom of the flag" ("Resistance and Freedom" 252). In framing this image, Vitier makes clear allusions for anyone familiar with Lenin's *What Is to be Done?* (cf. Lenin 5:354–56). "In the face of the enemy, ideas have to become entrenched, united for resistance, without fissures"—the fact that the call for unity is directly followed by a remark on the "freedom of the press" makes the parallel with the 1902 text by the leader of the Russian Revolution difficult to ignore. Yet here the purpose is far from being a linear grafting of one ideologue onto another. For the pole of "necessity" (which alone granted the measure of true subjectivity, of the subjectivity that knows scientifically what is to be done), this pole, cannot be, for Vitier, as dominant as it was for "proper" Marxism-Leninism: "A trench is not a parliament," concludes Vitier ("Resistance and Freedom" 252). In fact, for him, as for Fina García Marruz elsewhere, what is to be done is to produce a synthesis between the ironclad ideology of Revolution, insofar as it has Marxism-Leninism as its official precursor, and what in their poetic reading of politics is seen as "the libertarian spirit of Martí" ("Resistance and Freedom" 249).[4] Libertarianism is not a category that socialism can accept without some friction. This strange "anarchist" *Paideia* is summed up in the formula Vitier offers as the way forward: "We should be as free as the words of a poem. But the words of the poem *are owed* to the poem, they are committed to it and are at its service, as our freedom and criticism should be at the service of our resistance" ("Resistance and Freedom" 252).

The libertarian or anarchist supplement to the revolutionary process of institutionalization does not happen for the first time with Cintio Vitier and Fina García Marruz. They come to occupy a place that was already available in the early 1960s. The paradigmatic figure in this regard would be Manuel Gaona Sousa, who was part of the anarchist contingent but who, beginning in November 1961, had a change of heart and declared himself a loyal subject of the revolutionary process (Fernández 84–92). His function was to lend credibility to the Revolution's public relations efforts with the international libertarian movement, which was an important effort in maintaing a certain image of the revolutionary process as different from the previous revolutions of the century.[5] But while the Revolution needed to pay attention to these ideological matters for practical reasons, it was steadfast in the belief that anarchism constituted a dangerous element, particularly because of its ties to a labor movement that had to fall in line with the new productive exigencies of the regime. Guevara was unequivocal on this point: the "masses building socialism" were "not pure" and carried "along with them a whole series of bad habits inherited from the previous epoch"—including their collective organization against their bosses (*Obra* 401). Then, as in the 1990s, it was a question of forming or producing the proper subject. But in the 1990s the alibi of production and of bringing organized labor into the fold of the Revolution was no longer the crux of the matter.

Whereas Guevara was concerned with eliminating the remnants of the past so that the New Man could finally emerge, though this figure was already somewhere beyond the alienation of capitalism (a mark of the temporal undecidability at stake here), in Vitier's case, on the contrary, it is a question of reactivating an even more remote past, of calling attention to the void at the heart of a Revolution faced with the nihilism of the young, in order to fill it with the spirit of Martí. I want to conclude this chapter by offering a brief example of the image of time that emerges in each one of these cases. That is, the image of time that emerges once a definition of nihilism makes politics, in whatever form of declination, the highest value.

The Time(s) of Politics

In a piece titled "Discurso de la intensidad" (1993), while attempting to offer some edifying Martían wisdom, necessary in order to overcome "the most difficult hour in Cuba's history," Vitier asks: Is Cuba "an infinite island, a challenge for reason, or made out of the infinite, of infinite desire, like poetry?" (*Resistencia* 171, 168). The infinity in question has a lot to do with the concept of time that Vitier ascribes to the Revolution, which, he posits, Lezama prophesized in the first verse of "Muerte de Narciso" (1937): "Danae weaves golden time through the Nile." The thread of time moving in the circles woven through the ever-changing flow of the river—this is a tempting image for Vitier, who offers his own exegesis: "Tightening and contracting, concurrent with flashing swirls, sovereignty of light, opening with a certain unconcealable majesty" (*Resistencia* 168). Vitier is clear on the fact that this image is to be opposed to the linear concept of time: "If history were for us only successive time, that *fatum* [that history is subject to erosion and ruin] would be incontestable. But we believe in another history, a protoplasmic one, . . . a creative history, that of the infinite possibility which emerged precisely out of our 'impossible' historic succession" (*Resistencia* 168). The sovereignty of the doodling lines of times tightening and contracting, swirling, emerges precisely out of the immanent situation that the Revolution has to counter. Note that here Vitier is not emphasizing, in the way that Lezama did in a passage quoted above, that the Revolution emerges out of nothing. This is a more dialectical vision of history and of the event in question, even if the resulting image of time is more complex than that of a crossroads of time. What is the name for the path of a weaving thread making its way through the flow of the river? It certainly is not a simple image of time that would emerge. Yet Vitier opposes the multivalent temporal dynamic of revolution to the simple linearity of modernity's putative "successive" time. It is this gesture (to counter the simple temporality of the enemy with the richer and more dynamic one of good politics) that begins to appear with the effacement of nihilism.

The same gesture is present in one of Vitier's sharpest critics. In the concluding remarks of *Motivos de Anteo: Patria y nación en la historia de Cuba* (2008), Rafael Rojas offers his own meditation on temporality, in large measure in order to counter the vision of history that Vitier represents. An error in the title of one of Vitier's essays on Lezama turns the word teleology (*teleología*) into theology (*teología*). Rojas reads the misprint as a reflection of a failed nationalist mentality: "The construction of a destiny was, in fact, the religious formula . . . that parts of [Cuba's] nationalist Catholicism had found to organize the archive of national culture in order to hand it over to the socialist State"; the procedure consists in "simplifying the plural history of a community" (*Motivos* 378). Rojas's last move in this book is to subtract Lezama from that image of history. The poet's concept of futurity, according to which every present constructs its own future by way of its horizon of expectations (which Rojas likens to the theories of Reinhardt Koselleck), has been verified and proved by the unfolding of Cuban history already.

> Today it is evident that Cuban time did not end with the Revolution. . . .
> The past, as Lezama wanted, is finally exposed to multiple interventions, which cannot be submitted to a single criterion of national "truth." The future, or better, the futures, are yet to be constructed, and not in a providential or teleological manner, but with the same . . . diversity from which the present is made. The subjects of Cuban culture that are still to come will have to, of necessity [a fuerza], reproduce in that diversity, which does not admit ideological, religious or moral ontologizations. Those subjects will be conceived by the "universality of friction . . ." and will speak the serene and permeable language of democracy. (*Motivos* 378)

Perhaps Rojas moves too fast in setting up the problem as the confrontation between a single and homogeneous temporality and a better, more diverse one. This gesture sidesteps or erases the multiplicity of temporalities that structure revolutionary time—just as revolutionary time does the same to the "time" of capitalism. The historian is thus exposed to some of the same problems that he ascribes to the position he is critiquing, particularly if we consider that making politics the highest value also reintroduces, even if inadvertently, a deity into the public sphere. That is, as was noted in the opening pages of this chapter, already in the first phase of the Revolution it was not a question of dead time. Furthermore, it is possible to argue that the rejection of the various ontologizations that Rojas identifies in this passage is undermined precisely by positing proper politics as the effacement of nihilism.

The same fundamental gesture also appears in the neocommunism of contemporary theory. Bruno Bosteels, quoting Badiou, states: "Contemporary nihilism . . . consists . . . in defining the Good only negatively by way of the need to avoid Evil. 'Evil is that from which the Good is derived, not the other way round,' as Badiou writes in his diagnosis of the ethical turn. 'Nietzsche demonstrated very neatly that humanity prefers to will nothingness rather than to will nothing at all. I will reserve the name nihilism for this will to nothingness, which is like a counterpart of blind necessity'" (*Marx and Freud* 68). A proper leftist politics will only emerge upon the eradication of all that, fixated on willing nothingness, prevents the real transformation of the present alienation. This is a program that Bosteels outlines in the closing section of *The Actuality of Communism* (2011), where he emphasizes the need for the proper progressive Left to recognize "an eternal or ahistorical kernel" that "would open up the possibility of changing the very terrain upon which history plays itself out" (*The Actuality* 278). The dualism of ontological and ontic levels, which need to be linked somehow, is already at work here, though not under the banner of postfoundationalism. Yet it is from the same premises that the tasks for theory in the current situation should be decided, according to Bosteels. For him, the first would be writing "a history of communist eternity," "that of the different aleatory sequences of the communist hypothesis in a strict immanent determination"; the second, communism "must also be actualized and organized as the real movement that abolishes the present state of things" (*The Actuality* 278). On the first count, Bosteels argues against a linear logic of necessary stages and in effect paraphrases the basic premise of the theory of the event in Badiou: that an event emerges in a situation and not out of nothingness (to think so is the mistake of speculative leftism, and thus of nihilism, according to this theory); on the second, while assuming that the Left as a whole would want to adopt the name communism as its own, he admits that all the fights and disagreements of the Left would concern what one understands by that particular embodiment and organization of communist politics (the party, or the state—the negation of both—or the multitude, and so forth), and it is in this latter acrimonious zone that subjectivity emerges. Elsewhere Bosteels has commented on the difficulties of producing the New Man, with reference to the case of Cuba in particular, and of how it cannot be by way of eliminating the old in view of the new, whether it is a bourgeois subject that needs to become revolutionary or a religious one that needs to be secularized. In fact, these two kinds of subjectivity appear as two dimensions of the same problem, as a true emancipatory politics would entail traveling "down the road to the religious alienation that lies at the root of political and economic alienation" (*Marx and Freud* 122). The time of such a subject would have to be a new subjective present (Badiou, *Logics of Worlds* 51); but then the world this subject occupies and transforms would have to be somewhere in between, in transition, both in order to maintain the requirement of immanence and to avoid the Christian carryover of a subject that simply destroys an old self.

The image that best captures the crossroads of time that this assumes is that of the horizon, which is derived from the rhetoric of Bolivian vice president Álvaro García Linera. The actual body that incarnates the idea-in-history will have to declare that the horizon is not actual (this is patently clear from García Linera's statement), whereas the theorists who appropriate this horizon need to re-mark it as the actuality of the present: "This and nothing else is what the invocation of the communist horizon is meant to produce or render actual once again: a complete shift in perspective, or a radical ideological turnabout, as a result of which capitalism no longer appears as the only game in town and we no longer have to be ashamed to set our expecting and desiring eyes here and now on a different organization of social relationships" (Bosteels, *The Actuality* 228). So far, this is the horizon of the present of a subject faithful to the communist Idea. Since that subject is here-and-now, the Idea of communism is also here-and-now: it is an actual body that is present. But this means, at the same time, that the noncommunist situation, the world that has to be transformed, in which this subject emerges, and the now of the subjective wager coexist. Furthermore, that situation is then touched by a temporality that is beginning to blur the line between history and eternity more and more. Bosteels, citing Jodie Dean, writes:

> "Horizon: . . . tags not a lost future but a dimension of experience we
> can never lose, even if, lost in a fog or focused on our feet, we fail to see
> it. The horizon is Real not just in the sense of impossible—we can never
> reach it—but also in the sense of the actual format, condition, and shape
> of our setting . . ."; Jodi Dean explains in her own riff on the notion of the
> communist horizon that she also borrows from García Linera. "We can lose
> our bearings, but the horizon is a necessary condition or shaping of our
> actuality. Whether the effect of a singularity or the meeting of earth and sky,
> the horizon is the fundamental division establishing where we are." (*The
> Actuality* 228)

If the dimension of experience we can never lose is not an impossible illusion, that imaginary line where earth and sky meet, but the condition shaping our actuality, why resort then to the image of the horizon? One pays homage to García Linera by doing so, but in his own formulation the image had rather different connotations: "The general horizon of the era is communist. . . . But at this moment it is clear that this is not an immediate horizon, which centers on the conquest of equality . . . But we were serious and objective, in the social sense of the term, by signaling the limits of the movement" (qtd. in Bosteels, *The Actuality* 226–27). Horizon here entails a movement toward something that is to come, which will have to be constructed. If this is a stage-ist reading of the passage, which Bosteels dismisses as inappropriate, then what emerges when it is read by the new communism begins to sound and look more like the not-so-new and only questionably communist temporal image not of classical or orthodox vulgar Marxism-Leninism, but its Guevarian variant. For what the passage states is that "the movement" has to be properly formed—given its "limitations"—by a very serious "we" that knows better, because it is the nonmediated expression of the truth on the ground. However, being serious and objective means pointing out the limits of the movement on the ground. Things have changed, and the new progressive governments in the south are providing the Cuban state a new mechanism for biding its time, but the romantic dialectic that informs the radical materialist rhetoric remains the same.

Perhaps it is time to reconsider the problem of foundations from the perspective of the *ex nihilo* without any further qualifications, that is, from the perspective of a thoroughly a-principial thought. That the nonfoundation of change is always the void would then mean that no political praxis/thought would be able to avail itself of necessary reason, even if this reason returns in the form of a stable, though contingent, image of the present. The precariousness of this praxis/thought would constitute the edge or the border between what forms and unforms it at every turn. This proposal does not require that we delimit the proper space of literature, politics, science, and so on, with every autonomous region as separate conditions for thought. But we would need to frame the problem some ways beyond the columns that cordon off the romantic legacy that has most often been associated with the formless, the sublime, and the tragic, as so many instances of the void that structures the whole, even in its vanishing. Because this form of praxis/thought is not a vanguard, I want to approach it in all its contradictory detail by offering a patient reading of its unfolding in the work of Lezama Lima in the second part of this book. I do not want to give the impression that in doing this I will have offered a definitive image of the poet's oeuvre, and this not because of the usual false modesty of literary criticism. I say this with properly methodological ends in mind: I do not intend to do anything other than draw out a facet of Lezama's writing that is barely audible, barely readable, and that does not constitute the "program" of any one of his "books." That is, I intend to roam through Lezama as the formless roams through his writing.

Part II

Writing of the Formless

Lezama's Critique of T. S. Eliot's Difficulty

Lezama's theories cannot be reduced to a system of aesthetics in the philosophical sense of the term. Neither can they be reduced to a set of concepts that one would be able to define and use elsewhere. This is because in his theory of the arts there are no transhistorical constants that give sense to the history of forms. Even in a more specific or circumscribed setting, his method of reading rests on the idea that no two styles can be the same and, as an extension, that there are no two ways of putting together the materials that give rise to his "concepts." As he explained in his 1957 lectures, *La expresión americana*:

> We approach the question of forms with the understanding that the metaphorical subject . . . destroys the unacknowledged pessimism of the theory of historical constants. Our point of departure is the impossibility of two similar styles . . . the impossibility of the identity between two apparently concluding forms[; our point of view derives] from the creative force of a new concept of historical causality, which destroys the pseudo concept of temporality according to which everything is directed toward the fragmentary time of the present. (62–63)[1]

In this passage, Lezama outlines the basic premise behind a writing that is geared toward making its appropriation impossible; that is, in it we find a way of explaining why Lezama's writing is difficult to paraphrase as well as almost impossible to mine for working concepts that can be transplanted from his text. The singular encounter between the lived time of the poet and the historical materials that he re-collects and brings together produces, or at least should produce, a writing and a thinking that does not stand as representative of an idea, a movement, or a transhistorical constant.

It is not a matter of positing the uniqueness of an individual style, for this is only part of what is at issue here. The writing results, in the end, from the singular style of the writer as it is in-formed by a specific relation with a historical time that is not ordered and directed toward the configuration of a present, in whatever form that present might take. It is not hard to see why this stance toward history and toward the act of writing would result in texts that are often considered opaque and almost unreadable. And Lezama opens his lecture with a direct reference to this difficulty: "Only what is difficult is stimulating" (49).

However, because it is a matter of making a key distinction, Lezama immediately asks: "But, in fact, what is difficulty?" (49). In the text, his main interlocutor is T. S. Eliot, and the target of his remarks is the notion of difficulty held by the author of *The Wasteland*. Eliot attempted to separate (good) poets, who managed to think while keeping everything under a unifying logic, from the (bad) poets who accepted the "chaotic, irregular, fragmentary" experience of "ordinary man" without resolving the chaos into a "new whole" (Eliot 64). This tension between fragmentation and wholeness, which for Eliot appears in all the poetry of the modern period, is the reason why "poets in our civilization . . . must be *difficult*" (65, emphasis in original). From the standpoint of Eliot's theory, Lezama's difficulty is dictated by the historical moment in which he writes; also from that purview, his success as a poet depends on his ability to surpass that fragmentation—which entailed, as Eliot envisioned it, becoming more and more "comprehensive" (65).[2] On both counts what we find is an imperative that goes for all poets. First, there is the fragmentary configuration of the present that is the same for every poet (a fragmentation that, nevertheless, does not preclude the possibility of producing a unified image of the now). Second, there is the poetological imperative to make it cohere, to suppress the fragmentation of the present by making a new whole. For Lezama, on the contrary, the "present" is not one for all, because the present is configured singularly in every case based on a particular relation with the past. That relation is determined by the way in which history returns to a specific writing. Moreover, the only imperative that he admits is the imperative to welcome that very messy relationship with time into his writing—decidedly not a way of producing a new whole. (In fact, even at the level of the sentence, we find that Lezama's writing constantly frustrates the search for a coherent whole.)

Lezama asks about a more exact definition of difficulty precisely in order to avoid the scenario proposed by Eliot. To that end, Lezama marks the opposition between, on the one hand, what is "given" by history, and, on the other, what the contingent and unexpected intervention of the meta-phoric subject does with the material that is given by history (*La expresión americana* 49). The "encounter" does not yield a synthesis, or the discovery of universal constants. Rather, it produces a mixed causality in which the boundary between original and copy, cause and effect, before and after, begins to blur (62). The linear relationship is the hallmark of the inadequate interpretation of cultural historiography. If, according to Eliot, the unity that made the fragments cohere had been lost, Lezama had no desire to join in Eliot's search for it—as he cautioned: "Let us not fall for that business of a lost paradise, for our origin is something that resists our grasp" (*Poesía* 164).[3]

Lezamian "difficulty" has much more to do with the unavailability of the origin than with a transcendental continuity of culture that compre-hends the whole within a single logic. "Resistance" becomes, for Lezama, another word for difficulty, and he uses it as such in the opening sentence of *La expresión americana*: "Sólo lo difícil es estimulante; sólo la resistencia que nos reta es capaz de enarcar, suscitar y mantener nuestra potencia de cono-cimiento" (49). A sentence that we could translate in the following terms: "Only what is difficult, only the resistance of the origin to become present for us, only that absence, is capable of banding, arousing, and sustaining our potential for knowledge." Thus, what made poets "difficult" for Eliot—the unified image of the here and now as the fragmentation of the modern world as it passed into the poem—does not present a particularly "stimu-lating" problem for Lezama. Not only is the present not-one, but also the image of the whole, of the ground or foundation, is, for Lezama, always already an absence that resists being captured in any form.[4]

Given the central place that the notion of resistance has in the Latin American political tradition,[5] Lezama's choice of word on this score is significant and needs to be remarked. Even with Levinson's illuminating intervention on this point (*Secondary* 61ff.), it is necessary to recall, and it cannot be emphasized enough, that by aligning the impossibility of the origin, the whole, the foundations, and so forth, with what is usually assumed as the banner for the only possible form of politics in Latin America, the poet is also pointing the way toward a different understand-ing of the political. This other understanding would be unrecognizable as such by anyone invested in the idea of resistance that dominates the political landscape in the Caribbean and Latin America, but also, beyond that geographical delimitation, by all the dominant modes of thought of the Western tradition since the Greeks. That Lezama arrives at this position by taking the Christian doctrine at its word, and thus exploding it from within, is indicative of the kind of thought that we will be tracking in the following pages. The difficulty in question, then, is not only Lezama's but is also our own, for it is a matter of pointing out the way in which a religiosity that is incompatible with religion as a sociopolitical institution, and a politics that is beyond the reach of the political grid, give specific character to a writing that is constantly probing how to make its marks without forgetting the void: the absence of origin and foundation. Writing of the formless in this precise sense: a writing that wants to give testimony of the being of that absence, a writing that does not foreclose the abyss in the name of a consistency that will redeem our world, a writing for which time (the past, the present, the future) cannot be offered as a clear synthetic image of any sort. And it is in this sense that writing of the formless means writing of the end of time and times as pastoral formalizations that guide our sense of what counts and does not count as politics.

Meta-phora and Out-of-Place: Aposiopesis

Lezama's metaphoric subject does not stand as a figure of the fusion of subject and object. For the poet, this would entail the subject becoming one with its own ground. In finding its foundation, resistance would disappear, as it is the absence of a secure ground that resists ever being presented as such. Ground is exactly that from which the metaphoric subject seeks to differentiate itself. In what follows, I rely on the opposition between, on the one hand, the movement and the surface implied by that movement, which can be associated with the workings of metaphoricity, and, on the other, the nonground, or out-of-place, implied in the differentiation of metaphoric subject and ground that takes place in Lezama. Here the metaphysical tradition of a topology of discourses (putatively ordered by systematic philosophy) comes to the fore as a problem.

Western metaphysics since Aristotle has relied on a spatial metaphor meant to think the grid of places that constitutes the real and its adequation to thought. Whatever lies outside of that grid, whatever is not correctly placed, is immediately disqualified from discourse and from *being*. This is the case with the *reductio ad absurdum* that Aristotle carries out in his *Physics* in order to disqualify thinking about the void. A void would interrupt the possibility of measure, and, by extension, it would make thinking impossible. The political application of this topology of discourses/beings ultimately produces a system of distribution and legitimization, and it is possible to track its path into the system of what Barthes called the "old rhetoric." If we consider the rhetorical equivalent of a void, this becomes clearer, at the same time that it will take us to the very limits of the system.

Thus, aposiopesis[6] (the interruption of discourse, reticence, ellipsis) is a figure of thought when used as a properly rhetorical device. What is essential about the use of this figure is that it is intricately linked to what is or is not *aptum* according to public opinion, insofar as the interrupted thought would otherwise go beyond what is considered appropriate either intellectually or affectively (Lausberg § 411). Only secondarily is this figure used in order to convey the impossibility of expressing a situation (§ 411, 3); its center of gravity is the social situation that the orator addresses. Aposiopesis marks the interruption of language within a system of rules meant to teach the most appropriate use of language. This makes it into the structural element within the system that most clearly indicates to what, other than language itself, the *ars rhetorica* as a whole is subordinated: namely, the dominant social formation that is addressed. The paradoxical status of this figure within the conceptual paradigm of philology is that it marks the interruption of discourse only in order to safeguard the continuity of the situation (*stasis, status*) that makes discourse possible in the first place. But, at the same time, it can be seen as the crack in the historical ground that constitutes, through an opening toward an-Other side, the excluded side of history, the possibility of listening to "all the words without language that appear to anyone who lends an ear, as a dull sound from beneath history, the obstinate murmur of language talking *to itself*" (Foucault, *History* xxxi–xxxii). Discourse, in this context, means an articulation of the organs of language with an established, given situation (personal, social, objective) (Lausberg §§ 2–6), in which a system of laws (*ars rhetorica*) regulates ways of saying (§ 28). But it is also the articulation of silence and language as the relation of language to itself—language at the point where it leads not to continuity but to a constitutive exclusion that appears as a tear in the fabric of discourse.

What is at issue, concerning this other side, is the articulation of a moment that appears to be "heterogeneous with the time of history, but ungraspable outside it" (Foucault, *History* xxxiii). Foucault, in a Nietzschean reference, understands this as the confrontation between "the dialectics of history with the immobile structures of the tragic" (*History* xxx). The structurality of this confrontation, which will win out to the same extent that history will be the written document left behind by the victors, entails the silence of all that would reveal a discontinuous moment. Aposiopesis serves as an alibi that ensures the continuity of the system as a whole. At the same time, it points to what dominant social relations determines to be beyond the realm of the proper, of the *aptum*. In the most general sense, the parts are judged to be good insofar as they manage to persuade. Persuasion, however, leads right back to the system of places that characterizes the common situation: for persuasion is what one tries to achieve vis-à-vis the "dominant" parts of the situation in order to maintain or change it (Lausberg § 6). Whether as popular opinion, or as a relation of power, whatever falls within the category of "saying well" is a part that submits to the structuring principle of the whole. Interruption of the whole from without is ruled out.

Of course, within the logical coordinates of the entire system of the *ars rhetorica*, putting things in this manner would be inconceivable, since within the continuity of the rhetorical situation (and by extension the reign of philology as a "science" of literature), a figure has no rights other than as a tool to persuade the hegemonic state of the situation one way or another. What goes unquestioned is the right to that hegemony. Altering or deconstructing the power relation between dominant and weak parts of a situation, so that what is overturned is the idea of "the dominant" as such, would require a "rhetoric" so entirely transfixed that it would probably not be recognized as an *ars rhetorica* at all. For what would have to be rethought would be rhetoric's assumptions regarding the role of language within the social sphere. Within the logical domain of rhetoric, language, and whatever uses one might make of it, is objectified and appropriated absolutely—to the extent that rhetoric is a system that accounts for whatever might go beyond (intellectually or affectively) the dominant in a situation by teaching that, at that point, to "say well" would mean to be silent. That appropriation is part of the private property which rhetoric was born to protect (Barthes 16). In the last instance, it is the reign of private property that determines the specificity of the hegemonic situation of rhetoric.

Aposiopesis and the Postsocialist Exhaustion of Literature

It is after this fashion (of falling silent at the point where a radical ungrounding would have taken place but is instead declared to be out of place altogether) that the disciples of Lezama who became instrumental in turning the *Orígenes* group aesthetic into an organ of the state manage the conceptual transitions between the poetic tradition, private property, autochthonous continental identity, and the destiny of the Revolution. Fina García Marruz is representative in this regard. It is the reign of property (capitalism) that García Marruz claims we should take as the obstacle to the true naturalness of an autochthonous American culture, and that Darío and Martí oppose in what she sees as their "abundance":

The water makes a sound only when it hits against an impediment to its freedom, a rock or a stone. It is thus that the caudal [that is the Latin American
poetry of freedom and anarchy, including Rubén Darío, José Martí, César
Vallejo, and José Lezama Lima] is of a silent kind, removed from the fecun-
dity of rhetoric, and its language is the one . . . that labors without words.
The young Rubén Darío confesses . . . that he "understands everything"
and "keeps silent," . . . which is so close to the Vallejo that writes "I want to
say so much, but I stall," a most silent one, and to Martí's "I, falling silent,
understand." . . . These silences . . . are only equaled by those of the mystics.
(*Darío, Martí* 17)

The Latin American poetic tradition operates without words and lives off
of an interminable silence. Aposiopesis marks the well saying of a poetic
tradition that, according to García Marruz, is most revolutionary in letting
others do the political talk. The end of rhetoric (Darío answering against
those who wish he were more "rhetorical"), as understood by García Marruz, offers an opening onto the mystical experience, an experience of the
absolute, presented in its distance by way of the silence that follows from
the impossibility of representing the limitlessness or the infinite. Aposiopesis for her is the rhetorical figure of the unrepresentable. That is, aposiopesis
is the poetic mark of that which cannot be presented. The revolutionary
song of the poets is offered in silenced notes. That is, in the arena of revolutionary politics, for the poets to say well is to fall silent. So that politics
can go on uninterrupted.

Aposiopesis is also, for García Marruz, what ensues when Lezama is
critically assessing the event to which his texts want to be faithful: "When
he approaches Martí in *La expresión americana*, he seems to stop, suddenly
falling silent. He only manages to say that he approaches [Martí] 'trembling'" (García Marruz, *La familia* 26). Another name for this relation,
which places the emphasis on the element of confirmation of the event, is
the idea of "cumplimiento" (27). It is a moment when irony is no longer
possible (48). This happens for two reasons. On the one hand, he does not
think that it is possible to go beyond Martí; on the other, this impossibility
is, at least according to García Marruz, the cornerstone of his faith (50).
And yet, the consequence of Lezama's aposiopetic moment vis-à-vis Martí,
as she sees it, is that he derives from that silence the wherewithal to fully
commit to working out his own poetic *system* (50).

Aposiopesis then achieves two things. On the one hand, it safeguards the
hegemony of a political paradigm from the inconvenient aesthetic legacy
of a group that, at a decisive moment in the history of the Revolution, was

effectively silenced and effaced from the public sphere.[7] That effacement, the silencing of Lezama and others was, as it turns out, the proper, well-saying of the poets in the face of mystical and metaphysical *figures* of the absolute incarnated in the leadership of the Revolution. On the other hand, aposiopesis is what must follow after accepting that a specific poetic situation in history is insurmountable. At which point the vocabulary of events and ruptures gives way to an immanentist stance from which the only way to move forward is to prolong what is already there, again ensuring the continuity of the places. Darío, Martí, Vallejo, and Lezama bring the Latin American tradition to a close. After them, what is left is the confirmation of all that they announced—and their work, that is, their silence, serves to ground the Revolution.

Aristotle's Physics and "Muerte del tiempo"

Those moments when Lezama writes of language in spatial metaphors gain an extra layer of significance in this context. According to the aposiopetic ideology outlined by García Marruz, any limits encountered in such a space are marks of an opening toward the sublime, or of a properly, if paradoxical, revolutionary falling silent of the literary. And yet the text contradicts this assessment in fundamental ways. Expression is the acquisition of space. In this case, "expression" is the space in which the *imago* and the "metaphoric subject" operate. But expression is not identical with space, as it is only in its "relief"—only, that is, in its difference from absolute space—that it can be anything at all.

In *La expresión americana* the metaphoric subject appears as a precarious existence at the limit; it occupies a barren space where words hide underneath a layer of "geological ash" (54–55). This "creature" is presented as a sort of naturalist whose task is to engage the disarray of the ash under which lie the corpses of words to be quickened (both revived and moved). The metaphoric subject has to scan a space and, therein, be in charge of turning this into that, and to absorb *this* as well as *that*. Meta-*phorá*: it is in charge of carrying over, bringing forth; it is the principle of movement itself, which can only be presented in some*thing* moving. We are also dealing with a "limit." Only where there are limits can one thing be distinguished from another. The disappearance of the limit would mean the disappearance of the metaphoric subject. The metaphoric subject does not care about what there *is*, as long as there is something to move toward. The biggest fear for a creature of this sort is the void. However, the void is not something from which Lezama recoils.

Within the strictures of the topology of discourses, a problem to which Lezama returns time and again (and to which we will return in a moment), all movement requires that there be the differentiation of the *limited* in relation to the space where the thing takes place. The disappearance of the limit is the appearance of the void, which "insofar as it is void admits no difference" (Aristotle 214b, 30). For the moment, suffice it to present one form of the statement of the fear of the void: this is what the meta-phora, in its precariousness, asserts as it moves from the realm of rhetoric to that of "immediate inference": "Either, then, nothing has a natural *locomotion* [translatio, *phora*], or else there is no void" (Aristotle 215a, 10).[8] The Aristotelian answer to this either/or is that there is no void.

Let us turn to a prose poem from the 1949 collection *La fijeza*, titled "Death of Time" ["Muerte del tiempo"] (*Poesía* 159–60):

> In the void velocity dare not compare itself, can caress the infinite. In this way the void is defined and inert as the world of no resistance. The void also sends its first negative sign to remain as the non-air. . . . We know, by way of an almost invisible stirring of the nonexistence of the absolute void, that there cannot be an infinite apart from divisible substance. . . . But let us suppose some implausibilities in order to gain some delights. (*Selections* 47, translation modified)[9]

This beginning is, more or less, a straightforward restatement of the Aristotelian view of the infinite/void couple, according to which the void/infinite is in-measurable, in-existent, and in-different. For Aristotle the void does not exist, and since there is no way to "construct" a demonstration for something that is nonexistent, the proof will unfold through a *reductio ad absurdum*. Aristotle's demonstrations aimed at establishing that if one assumes that the void exists, it follows that movement—the very essence of Nature for the Greek "physicist" (200b, 10)—is not possible.[10] The speaker, after tacitly citing some of Aristotle's conclusions, proposes to carry out something like the *reductio ad absurdum* but in the name of "inverosimilitud."

What follows in the piece can be read as a retelling of the steps of the *reductio*, but it is carried out in a manner that goes counter to the purpose this proof served in one of the founding texts of Western metaphysics. The poem will not prove that there is no void. The writing in question will simply turn Aristotle's argument on its head and claim the right to enjoy, without any instrumentalization or posterior result, without reaching any conclusion, all that the Greek text assumed would happen if it were the case that indeed the void was not. It is as if Lezama is making Aristotle out to be, against the philosopher's own stated intentions, the first writer of the formless. By remaining on the absurd side of the *reductio ad absurdum* what we get is the temporary stay of Western metaphysics within that which it cannot possibly admit. The result can be adduced, ironically, as a first evidence of the writing of the formless, and for this reason it is worth quoting at length (in James Irby's translation):

> Let us suppose the army, the silk cord, the express, the bridge, the rails, the air that constitutes itself as another face as soon as we draw close to the window. Gravity is not the tortoise kissing the ground. The express train always has to be stopped on a bridge of a broad rock base. It impels itself—as the impulsion of his smile to laughter, to raucous laughter, in a feudal lord after his garnished dinner—, until it decapitates tenderly, until it dispenses with the rails, and by an excess of its own impulsion slips along the silk cord. The velocity of infinite progression tolerated by a silk cord of infinite resistance comes to feed upon its tangencies that touch the ground with one foot, or the small box of compressed air between its feet and the back of the ground (lightness, angelisms, nougat, larks). The army in repose has to rest upon a bridge with a broad rock base, impels itself and comes to fit, in hiding, behind a small poplar, then in a worm with a backbone grooved by an electric time. The velocity of progression reduces the tangencies, if we suppose it to be infinite, the tangency is pulverized: the reality of the steel box on the archetypal rail, in other words the silk cord, is suddenly stopped, the constant progression derives another independent surprise from that temporal tangency, the air turns as hard as steel, and the express train cannot advance because the potency and the resistance become infinite. There is no fall because of the very intensity of the fall. While potency turns into ceaseless impulsion, the air mineralizes and the moving box—successive, impelled—, the silk cord and the air like steel refuse to be replaced by the crane on one foot. Better than substitution, restitution. To whom? (*Selections* 45–46)[11]

This writing is what emerges by assuming that the void exists: absolute stasis and infinite speed together in one point. That is, the demonstrative logic of the reduction is indistinguishable here from the prose that Lezama has wrought in its stead. The metaphoric subject itself is that void, what Aristotle, for his part, saw as an absurdity (*átopos*), something that for the philosopher was out-of-place (214a, 5). It is here, in how the philosopher and the poet react to the possibility of something being out-of-place, that we can best appreciate what is at issue in Lezama's poem. It centers on the image that resulted from the contradiction of simultaneous movement and repose, stasis and infinite speed. The metaphoric subject sets out to move across that absurdity and thus to set in motion the distribution and proliferation of a metamorphosing catalogue of images. The propagation of terms is the work of that precarious creature, the worm or the metaphoric subject, which asserts that there is no place where it is out-of-place. The move from the Aristotelian word to a different one remains within a hermeneutic circle or cell, which the metaphoric subject cannot escape: it repeats with the philosopher that there is nothing out of place, that the void is absurd—and yet it is the manifestation of that absurdity, fully unfolded. Nature as movement and change is untenable outside of time for the "physicist" who holds that "every change and everything that moves is in time" (222b, 30). The Aristotelian word obviously has been transformed and substituted by others: that, after all, is the task of metaphor. The "delicias" have been ingested and enjoyed, but there is another voice in the poem that is not as satisfied.

The title of the poem is of importance in this regard. "Muerte del tiempo" should be understood here not as the opposition of a multiplicity of temporalities that emerges once a single homogeneous time "dies," but as the void that appears in its stead. Elsewhere, Lezama refers to an "audible obscurity" (*Obras* 178). The images that emerge and populate this piece open the poem up to a different sort of gap—it is the ontological difference that is at issue, however awkwardly Lezama articulates it: "the proportions, occupations and the non-equality of being (*el ser*) in the being (*el ente*)" (*Obras* 179–80). Thus, there is a distance with regard to the Aristotelian position. At the end of the poem the metaphoric subject literally and structurally finds its limit. It does not have to substitute one term for another; it is now a question restituting: what and to whom? The metaphoric subject is adept at substitution, but restitution is beyond its capabilities. This is the case even if the metaphoric subject were intent on writing the exact words of Aristotle—which is close to what takes place in the first sentences of "Muerte del tiempo." The restitution, here and elsewhere, is the return of what was originally and fundamentally subtracted, by Aristotle and the entire history of Western philosophy: the void. The poem itself *is* the unfolding of images as they are presented there where the void was not supposed to be; the poem is, then, the taking-place of the out-of-place, which philosophy declared had no being. No aposiopesis here.

Moreover, the difference with Aristotle can also be stated in terms of the idea of time: if the argument for the nonexistence of the void requires that time be imagined as a container or an object "in" which movement takes place, with the death of time, temporality as such does not cease but transforms into something that can no longer be presented as the surface that holds movement and things. This is the case in the poem, for the "electric time" and the "temporal tangency" that are invoked are not a dead time but the time of Aristotle, serving as the guiding thread for the demonstration of the inexistence of the void. That is, dead time is not a time that can be shown or represented except by staging its absence.

This staging resonates with the Derridean take on the remains of time (see chapter 1), but, in more general terms, is in line with the thought of the "trace"—which was one of the terms that Derrida used in order to show to what extent the metaphysical tradition could not keep track of the distinctions that served as its foundation. Form was already the trace of matter; the trace itself is what made their opposition possible in the first place. One of the questions of this book is whether or not this trace, which is at the heart of the metaphysical text and which for the metaphysical text itself is unthinkable and inadmissible, has any bearing on texts like "Muerte del tiempo," where the trace itself is the object of the writing. For if this is the case, then what is inadmissible and unthinkable for this poem must be something other than the trace. Ultimately, what is at issue is whether there is a difference between those texts of the Western tradition that forget the question of being and those whose starting point is the challenge and the difficulty that the question poses, the challenge and the resistance involved in dealing with the ground that is and is not there in its absence. The implications of this problematic are not merely a theoretical or philosophical issue, in the disciplinary sense of those terms. What is at stake is whether or not it is possible to imagine a writing and a thought that do not simply fall silent in order to guarantee the continuity of the narrative of legitimacy and sovereign authority in the poem or in politics—but the link between these two is also at issue here. That is, whether or not it is possible for posthegemonic infrapolitics to be something other than the trace of politics. I will return to this problem at the end of this second part of the book.

The void, if presented as such, should have been the aposiopetic instance in which the poem falls silent. However, what has taken place is the opposite. It is only by assuming and positing that the void is, that the poem unfolds. "Muerte del tiempo" stages what in Aristotle only appears as absurd (a-topos), out-of-place. It is the testimony, the not-falling-silent, the nonaposiopetic moment. Something was said precisely where "to say well" would have meant to maintain the continuity of the site and silence the fact that there *was* a rupture. The image here is not the interdiction of the being of the void. Moreover, where the metaphoric subject found itself trapped by the Aristotelian word, which confines the poem to a finite *ars combinatoria* that Lezama associated with Eliot, the "image" that sustains the piece restitutes the being of the void. "Muerte del tiempo" is not a poem that belongs to the tradition of interminable silences; on the contrary, the task of this poem is to affirm the being of what is out-of-place. And this treatment of contradiction, placing it at the center of poetic practice, takes a stance that is diametrically opposed to the discourse of continuity of places, or of the continuity of the law, which aposiopesis guarantees.

We begin to grasp what the writing of the formless entails in Lezama. It is not a matter of providing a representation of what cannot be represented. That would fall more in line with the writing of the mystics to which García Marruz alluded in pointing to the tradition of falling silent in Latin American poetry. Such a representation would only achieve a more advanced synthesis of knowledge, since we would have then taken one more thing off of the "to-do list" of an ever-expanding encyclopedia. Also, it is not a question of inventing a completely new literary form that would be something like the "-ism" attaching to formlessness. In fact, it is not a matter of the new at all. The resistance in question, the absent foundation, the void that is the only thing that stimulates our efforts according to Lezama, the difficulty writing has to deal with—all of this, in all its formlessness, is something that has been with us and is part of the tradition. The difference is that the tradition has been intent on doing away with exactly that thing that the poet is after. Thus, it is possible to find the writing of the formless even in Aristotle, just as it would be possible to find it in Plato, Saint Augustine, or the Bible (as we will see presently), but if it is there, it is only on its way out, about to be exiled from thought. It is the underside or the reverse of what those texts seek to illuminate; or, it is what those texts cannot illuminate except in an oblique manner, almost against their will. The tradition is already the history of a sustained and conflicted relationship with the writing of the formless. This is why Lezama can write, in "Corona de lo informe," that "the classical spirit also contains the formless," and then indicate the specific sense in which it appears there: "The true classical spirit does not refuse [the formless]. . . . The formless appears there as becoming when it is held prisoner, when it gains its crown" (*Obras* 456). For this reason, the writing of the formless cannot be wielded as a concept with which to reshuffle the cards of a delimited section of that history (whether it is the history of art or literature); much less can it be considered as the marker of a new kind of literature that defines a new period. The kind of historical reach that it has makes it difficult to limit it to the emergence of interest on the sublime, or even interest on the category of formlessness itself, as a concept that recently has surfaced in order to rethink architecture or the history of modern art.[12] And while it certainly finds resonance with the destruction of metaphysics that Bataille has in mind when he calls forth his own notion of the formless (*Visions* 31), there it remains tied to a tragic paradigm that sees in the time of the formless the time of destruction or of disaster (D'Ammando and Spadoni 377). With Lezama's "Death of Time," however, what begins to emerge is not the time of disaster but the time of a life that is no longer concerned with finding the ground with which to legitimate and authorize itself. Furthermore, for Lezama, the singular "style" that should emerge from not forgetting the formless void cannot be derived from death in any sense.[13] This is not a negation of finitude in any sense. It is simply that "style" is not the inscription of death, because death remains that which for us, in every case, is never an encounter (*Obras* 148). Confronting the resistance of the absent foundation, not forgetting it by arguing or legislating its disappearance, yields a temporal image that cannot be generalized beyond the singular encounter with it.

Lezama's "One": Aesthetics, Avatar of Western Metaphysics

For Lezama, the history of culture can be seen as an endless battle between two conceptions of the One: "the primordial one" and "the indivisible one" (*Obras* 400). The first type of one is of Greek origin and is the foundation of Western metaphysics and its theory of participation, copies, and their primordial Form; Lezama aligns the second type of one with Eastern traditions and the idea of an archetype that cannot be divided and that is always the same wherever it appears. Yet there is a third idea of the one that is the one as sovereign (409–10), or the living incarnation of the One (832).

To participate in the metaphor of the One is decidedly not to participate in the One itself. That impossibility, that participation in the indirect representation of the One, is simply juxtaposed to the idea of the "processional one." The penetration into the "supreme essence" adds to the sense that Lezama's One always requires something else that, pre-existing it, conditions it.[14] This kind of historical narrative of the One is, in itself, a way of marking a distance toward the idea of the One. However, on this point (putting the One in doubt), Lezama does not think that he is breaking new ground. According to him, the idea of the One is already critiqued by the two traditions that most fundamentally rely on it, by both Greek philosophy and the Judeo-Christian tradition. I will return to Lezama's take on the Greek doubt concerning the One. Regarding the Judeo-Christian tradition, Lezama writes of the fear that stems from the fact that "God always speaks of himself in the plural in the Bible, *let us make man*; as we read in Genesis"; and in that fear, that God is not one, what becomes evident is "the rewarding awareness of his incompleteness" (394). The idea here, as Lezama points out, is that "man" is a "plurality that is not dominated," that "exists as a fragment," and, more radically, that Being, as such, is fragmentary (394). To "dominate" plurality would entail abolishing multiplicity, yet that is precisely what takes place throughout the history of metaphysics: the domination of multiplicity. Thought has to get at the things as they truly *are*: "life which is always active conceived as repose" (394).

Lezama is repeating what is the essential quip of vitalist philosophies against metaphysics; that is, in searching for the unchangeable and eternal, philosophy sacrifices matter or sees it only in terms of the stasis of the Idea—the world-in-time becomes a degradation or a diminution of being (cf. Bergson 315–17; Deleuze 23–24; Nietzsche, "The Birth of Tragedy" 71). Nevertheless, Lezama's repetition of this vitalism entails the following ironic turn: whereas vitalist philosophers from Nietzsche to Deleuze have seen their thought as an overcoming of Platonism, Plato himself is, now, for Lezama, a key figure in the deposition of the One, for he is not able in the *Parmenides* to properly define the one (Lezama Lima, *Obras* 146, cf. 861; for Plato's impossibility in defining the One, *Parmenides* 141e). This kind of reading against the grain, which reveals a Plato for whom the One is more a problem than a solid foundation, is also put to work in relation to Lezama's own Catholicism, or the Christian idea of the oneness, infinity, and simplicity of God. In his reading of the relationship between religion and poetry in the work of Paul Claudel, Lezama makes a link between both of these targets (the history of Western metaphysics and the idea of the One) in which one is seen in terms of the other.

"Conocimiento de salvación"[15] is an overly ambitious piece. In its four pages, Lezama moves from the creation of the world according to the Book of Genesis all the way to the effects of modern knowledge on the aesthetics in vogue at the end of the 1930s. Duanel Díaz has correctly identified the target of the general attack as the dialectical background of the dominant poetical systems of his time (*Los límites* 18). What needs to be added is that this "fondo dialéctico" is also at work in Claudel, at least in Lezama's eyes, and, thus, that Lezama saw in one of the most prominent manifestations of a Christian aesthetic of the time not a model to be emulated but a version of the dialectic, a problem to be dealt with. It is with that background of the dialectic that the piece is occupied from start to finish.

From the very first paragraph, Lezama identifies the vocabulary of spirit with that of knowledge, in a tacit and, within the essay, proleptic allusion to the post-Enlightenment speculative systems that were so influential in their appropriation of aesthetics. It is easy to overlook this connection because in the first sentences what is most prominent is a quotation of the moment of creation *ex nihilo* according to the Bible. This starting place, however, has another function. The piece starts with a sentence that echoes Saint Augustine's vertical hierarchy, in which the earth is the lowest point before the void (Augustine 237). It can be read as a commentary on a fundamental but equivocal point in Christian metaphysics: where to place and how to think the void. Lezama's elective affinities on this point are more Semitic than Greek, as becomes clear from the strange image of God that surfaces when we opt for treating the void in the manner handed down from Aristotle to Augustine[16]—the void, that is, not as nothingness but rather as a "nothing-something" that is fundamentally evil, an interpretation that the history of translations of the Bible assumes by identifying the void with a disordered earth: "'The earth was in disarray and empty and the darkness was on the face of the abyss.' But the Holy Spirit and the light began to penetrate things. That is to say, faced with things there is a progressive appropriation: knowledge; and a regressive condemnation: time. Knowledge and time constitute the grace and the *fatum* of man" (*Obras* 246).[17] The conflict in the history of Christianity between its metaphysics, derived in bulk from the Greeks (in which the void is impossible or absurd), and the Semitic account of a creation out of nothing, leads to extremely complicated speculations. Augustine, for example, after tracing a dizzying hermeneutical circle concerning the origin of time and of the universe in books 11 and 12 of the *Confessions*, admits that the best he can do when it comes to the first two verses of Genesis is to speak of a "nothing that is in some way something" (Augustine 237; cf. Seife 61). This equivocal something-nothing makes it possible to transform the creation into the progressive appropriation of "things" by knowledge, by the Spirit. That is, within the Christian tradition, the stance adopted early on in regard to the question of the nothing before creation puts the divinity in the structural place of the conqueror of a new world, reordered and populated in his image. The translation that Lezama uses here makes Augustine's reading of the passage even more palpable: some-thing (la tierra) stands in place of what otherwise would be a "formless void."[18] That is, it is possible to read in place of the "formless void" a merely empty and disordered earth that God penetrates and appropriates, putting things in their place and otherwise filling it with his creations, as if he were the first conquistador. Man is surrounded by an immense inanimate condemnation. That "thing-earth-quasi-void" is an inanimate judge (a judge without a soul) dispensing a condemnation. The judge's sentence is temporization, a fall into time. Time, the earth's history, is what came, literally, of nothing (Augustine is also resonating in the background concerning the question of time; in fact, the two issues are intricately linked: for time is what saves God from being less than absolute, complete, total—time is what saves God from competing with the void, which more than anything would be his own lack, a hole in the absolute). It will become evident that what Lezama is describing here, particularly as it concerns the figure of the conqueror, is not only a particular theological reading of the creation of the world but also what results when the objectivity of the given is presented as a *fatum* that has to be overcome by way of the Subjects's appropriation and penetration of it, carried out in his attainment of knowledge.

The culmination of that project appeared, for Lezama as for Nietzsche, in the guise of the dialectic (*Obras* 239). This kind of theoretical negativity was particularly problematic for Lezama because his own project seems so close to it. The cornerstone of that poetic project is signaling to "the new substance": "the new corpuscle that begins to gyrate" (*Obras* 788). In identifying it, the poet, in the process, is setting out the consequences of a new causality, to which Lezama refers via the metaphor of a gravitational field. But more to the point, the new causality appears as the gravitational force of "the substance of what does not exist" (*Obras* 788). The meeting of times is near. For this gyrating sphere marks the arrival of Christ, in Lezama's imagination. On the border of the old and the new, the new appears as the being of what is not supposed to exist. The similarity, then, lies in the passage from a "negation" to a "negation of a negation" (that is, the new appears within a field that negates its being—that rejects it for being absurd and so forth; this negative moment is surpassed or transcended by the poet's formal operations, which actually give sensible form to it, thus negating the claims of the first negation by formally presenting it). Lezama was well aware that this might be simply seen as an application of the dialectic. In the concluding pages of "La dignidad de la poesía" (1956), immediately after the passage dealing with the new as substance of the inexistent cited just now, the author explicitly declares himself against such a reading:

> We move toward a new danger, the rude immediacy of a dialectical development in those immense coordinates centered and clarified by poetry, for, as if on the margins of that substance that approaches, our era offers also that ominous confluence that leads poetry toward the dialectic, and the dialectic again toward the primeval origin; but our own effort is to produce a poetic system taking poetry itself as a point of departure and not the dialectic.

Which is to say, poetry departing from metaphor as that which overcomes
the metamorphosis and the *metanoia*[19] of the ancient world; poetry which
departs from the image as proportion and new causality between man and
the unknown; . . . from the hyperbolic doubt as what goes beyond all synthesis. (*Obras* 788)[20]

The absolute, it turns out, is the place that the subject occupies as a
matter of course when attempting to solve the problem of objective
determinism by a direct appropriation of the nothing which has been
conquered and turned into something. All of this is only implied on
a first reading, but it becomes clear that the philosophical and aesthetic project that this divine creation entails is the modern epic of the
spirit—being carried out, since Kant but particularly after Hegel, by
both philosophers and poets, and above all, Lezama will claim, by the
philosopher's aestheticization of thought: at the hands, that is, not of
the poets, but of the paragons of modern philosophical architecture. For
Lezama, "dialectical knowledge" carries out a reduction of knowledge
to the Subject's capacity for synthetic judgments (*Obras* 246). It is a
knowledge that circulates between subject and object, and its ultimate
aim is to demonstrate not only that the subject is capable of appropriating everything that *is*, but, and this is a decisive point, that insofar as
something *is*, this means that the subject can produce and represent it
in what Heidegger called a picture of the world. Ultimately it seeks to
provide a sensible form, a figure, for the Idea.

Beyond the "problems" that are adduced (the fatality of the given, the
resolution of that *fatum* and the dignity of the finite human being, the reflection theory of knowledge as a version of the dialectic, etc.) and the reference
to Schiller at a key moment in the text, we also know that the speculative
world that we are entering here is of Idealist–post-Enlightenment–German
ilk because the opposition to dialectical knowledge offered by Claudel's
"poetic knowledge" is meant to enable an offering of aesthetics as a "solution" to problems posed as if they were the same for philosophers and
poets. Lezama is claiming that Claudel's work ultimately wants to offer a
solution to the problem of the lack of access to the exterior world, that is,
to the central metaphysical idealist problem of the determinism of blind
and objective natural laws that leaves the subject in a position of subjection
to something that he did not create and therefore cannot change. Lezama
wants to engage the Claudel that surges up from this putative common
ground, occupied equally by philosophy and poetry—or, more accurately,
in which philosophers pose problems and poetry solves them.

Claudel allegedly commands the human voice in all its range (Lezama cites De Bos on this point); and it is the voice, the power of the poetic evocation, that is going to solve the difficulties posed by the objectively given world, which is possible through the "cathartic capacity of the subject," something that becomes a possibility only "after the impossible dialogue with nature has been lost sight of, after the sense of sight has been sliced or we fear tactile language" (247).[21] Immediately after this Nietzschean reference regarding the effects of theoretical or philosophical thought on the senses, Lezama adds: "It is through that Claudelian evocation of sufficient grace that the vibration that can substitute the object itself can take place in us, or, it is only through that poetic knowledge that we can penetrate the adversarial and not yet discovered world" (247).[22] The vocabulary of conquest reappears. The subject of knowledge, giving sensible form to the idea, is the subject that wins the battle with nature, appropriating it in the process. The problem that has to be solved here is how to think the outside world, Nature, as something other than an unchangeable object. Lezama concerns himself with Claudel's answer—which is offered by the French poet as a way out of the modern theoretical stance toward reality. This is the archetype of what Nietzsche called the Alexandrian spirit of modernity (*The Birth of Tragedy and Other Writings* 86, 111). In dissecting reality while searching for knowledge, the gaze damages its own capabilities for representation. Lezama indicates this whole development in one very quick and broad stroke when he writes that the cathartic, that aspect of the theory of tragedy that subordinates aesthetics to morality, only appears after we slice the gaze, "después que rebanamos la mirada."[23]

Claudel, Lezama informs us, rejects knowledge as it has been understood since the Renaissance—because it is *a posteriori* knowledge (247)—and calls for a conception of knowledge as an ideal construction of the thing that is being thought: *connaissance* as *naissance*. Understood as a figure for poetic knowledge, this creation/knowledge avoids the object by producing and thus substituting the object as such in its very essence or concept (knowledge here *is* spirit; what is real is rational, and what is rational is real). But this is the kind of modern solution that Claudel and Lezama alike are supposed to reject. What, then, is the relationship between this speculative program and Claudel's poetics? Lezama states that Claudel attempts to wrest poetry from any thought of the poetic act as the setting in motion of method. Lezama illustrates this point by way of a reference to Gothic art. Claudel's rejection of method entails asserting a Gothic influence that leads the poet away from what, given the title of the piece, should have been the positive pole in the comparison (247). In Claudel's attempt to achieve knowledge of salvation, he begins to confuse the point of view of God with his own.

If we follow the web of association that Lezama is setting up before and after this moment in the essay, it becomes clear that what "Conocimiento de salvación" entails is a critique of Claudel. Lezama begins by reminding the reader that for Claudel the idea of knowledge (as in his proposal for a poetic knowledge) is closer to the biblical carnal knowledge than to the knowledge derived from experience, *a posteriori* and post-Renaissance scientific knowledge (247). All creation, according to Claudel is both created and creating. Thus, in the poet's creation there should be a moment involving physical labor, experimentation, and provoked results but also a moment leading toward "the most reserved strata of substance such as it was conceived . . . in Leibniz, as a synthesis of substance and becoming" (247). Claudel, according to Lezama, is attempting to break away from what he saw as the fragmentation caused by the onset of modernity, which causes him to distinguish between substance and essence and to favor the former: he is "more in love," says Lezama, with substances than with essences (247). The distinction was already hinted at in Lezama's reference to Claudel's reliance on a Gothic center, which has to be contrasted with the effect that the discovery of perspective had in painting during the Renaissance. Perspective entails the organization of the visual surface around the vanishing point. The system of intersecting lines that emerges yields a point-for-point map of the visible surface of the world being thus framed (Rotman 17). This point marks the location of the viewing subject objectified by all the elements that appear in the representation, even as it is also the point that allows the subject to perceive himself from the outside as a unitary and self-transparent figure. As Rotman puts it: "Being able to signify such a particularized individuality equips the perspective code with the visual equivalent of a demonstrative pronoun, allowing the code to deal in messages whose interpretation requires the active presence of a physically located, corporal individual who has a 'point of view'" (19–21). By contrast, Rotman adds, "the iconic images of Gothic art are silent about the nature of visual authorship and exclude the possibility of signifying demonstratively. What gives a Gothic panel its unity, its visuo-conceptual coherence, allowing different places to coexist and different historical realities to impinge on each other, is not some visual mode particularized in an individual artist/spectator, but the all-seeing timeless, spaceless eye of God" (21). The Gothic center that Lezama ascribes to Claudel relies on the concentration of all time and all knowledge in God, not on the subject's capacity to have a point of view. Yet, what Lezama is pointing out, as a critique of Claudel, is that the moment when being is understood as something that is sutured to the void around which the subject gains knowledge and maps the surface of the visible world, the centrality of the all-seeing eye of God is reduced to the point of view that the vanishing point, from within, locates in the surface of representation and which, from without, allows the subject to perceive himself as a unitary reservoir of certainty.[24]

At this point Lezama changes gears and turns his attention to Schiller's "sensible instinct." In Schiller's *Letters on Aesthetic Education*, this instinct is the first step in a dialectic that posits the formal instinct as antithesis, and will be resolved in the synthesis provided by the play instinct, with which the tension between sensible determinism and moral liberty will be overcome. At a different level, instinct is that aspect of nature that will save modern civilization from decadence; it is that natural and savage element that will be dialectically elevated without being sacrificed—this is the moment when the formless takes on form in the *Aesthetic Education*. Instincts are a way of coming to terms with the sudden eruption, "lo interjectional," as Lezama calls it, of human actuality. Against that actuality, turned into law *a posteriori*, arises another instinct—which now, in place of Schiller's play instinct, Lezama calls the scream or the prayer, the poetic invocation that seeks to supplant the object, thus restoring the dignity of the free human being. Lezama substitutes the play instinct with poetic evocation. But then he simply jumps from the sensible instinct to the "realm of absolute perception" without further commentary. Nevertheless, the parallel that he is tracing is clear. Poetic evocation, the "capacidad devolutiva del sujeto," the poetic solution offered by Claudel, leads to a result that is not satisfactory. Lezama sums up his argument: "If the creature can rise up to the absolute by means of names (language) . . . what we see, to recall Schiller's phrase . . . is that man succumbs before the time that transforms him into an object, diminishing his dignity" (248).[25] The utterance of words, one after another, involves the linear time of succession that defined the first step of the process. At this point the process is revealed in its circularity. Back at the improper status of domination of the subject by the object, another prayer is uttered in search of salvation: "In relation to space, the creature is poised to begin praising, from the elemental form of the scream up to the more thorough conjuration of the prayer. The flow of time brings him back to the fall, original sin, to his anguish over death" (248).[26] For Lezama, the impossibility leads Claudel, and a great many other modern poets, to an ever more intense search for a way to eternalize the moment, to stop time. This is no longer the scenario that is most characteristic of Claudel—who was moving against the current of the times, or so it appeared at the beginning.

The effort to eternalize the present moment, or to stop time, should not be passed over as if it were merely a question of poetry and the dreams of the romantics. This is the desire of modern revolutionary politics as well, as the first part of this book demonstrated. But it is a desire that becomes political in a way that was not so clear to Lezama in 1939. However, we can already glimpse to what extent the romantic-Idealist program of over-coming the time of alienation by eternalizing the moment, as well as the appropriation of this structure that the "historical materialist" who wants to stop time in the name of emancipatory politics, are different from the proposal for a death of time that is not the emergence of eternity here and now. For Lezama, the feat of stopping time would entail giving the place of God to the fundamental structure of the modern world, turning the political or poetic subject into the ground of all things: the problem is that if this is what is desired, the modern world already provides it in all its force. In 1939, however, Lezama saw this problem primarily as an issue regarding the relationship between poetry and philosophy—for the effort to achieve a stable and universal image of what "the present" is (even if this is done in order to identify what has to be destroyed—a feature common to Eliot and revolutionary politics) turns poetry into an arm of idealist philosophy. In Lezama's terms:

> Is it not a poetic solution that [Kierkegaard] offers in order to grasp the *quiditas*? While the proximity of poetry to the dialectical development has had the epic consequence of taking the prolongation of the ineffable moment all the way to the ambit guarded by grace; leading the unrelenting dialectical identity toward the hidden zone of existence, has had the effect of propelling philosophy beyond its fundamental limits. What contemporary philosophers are looking for . . . is less a real explanation of things than an intellectual epic, a sort of drama of the spirit, a poem of the subject. All the great con-temporary poetic projects, from pure poetry to surrealism, are nothing other than a desperate attempt at prolonging the perception of an extremely rapid temporality. (248–49)

And returning to Claudel, he asks: "Is not that qualitative dialectic dreamed up by Kierkegaard the meaning of the coincidence of perception and sen-sible state, one of the forms that Claudel's Gothic, medieval knowledge takes?" (249).[27] Lezama answers affirmatively. If we recall the function of the play instinct in Guevara's text, when it was used to set the workers to their task under the pretense that they were now no longer working but rather playing, we begin to see that the objection Lezama is making here would be equally applicable. The declaration that the suppression of alienation has been achieved can be made only when alienation poses as absolute knowledge. Or, in other, perhaps more mundane, terms: if we were free, no one would need to stand in front of us to inform us that we were. And the link between this poetic development and politics is clear in Claudel as well. For the prayer of the French poet, that evocation that has been at the center of everything outlined thus far, asks nothing but that he be used as the vehicle for governing (249).[28] The hand of the sovereign, which denegates the "subject" actually doing the work, a version of the poet that takes down the dictation from a superior source, indicates the desire of the poet to be, as a worker, indistinct from the angel (249). Also, as a poet, this is only realized "in the leap from the lyric to drama: in the knowledge of God" (249).[29] That is, Claudel's own representation of the human and finite poetic act as the vanishing term, the hand of the worker, allowing for the hand of the sovereign to govern in its dictates, appears as another figure for the epic drama of modern speculative philosophy. At this point we see Claudel in a very different light. This kind of poetic "appetite" for knowledge leads Claudel to act as "the conquistador of the supreme essence" (249). The role of conquistador, which is God's role at the beginning of the piece, is now the role that the poet assumes for himself. The heretical result of this stance, for Lezama, is that it transforms God into the very objectivity that the Subject wants to synthesize. The poet, if successful, will have given sensible form to God. In other words, the search for the Other in Claudel yields the paradoxical result of transforming the Other into what is already here. Being successful in giving form to the Other entails losing the Other entirely, and not just in a personal sense, but in the sense of declaring that there is no "there," there where the radically Other would have been.

Lezama is suggesting that the history of Western metaphysics has been a long and protracted attempt to achieve access to God's absolute knowledge/cause of all things. For a Christian like Lezama, God's mind is inscrutable, and attempts to achieve such knowledge will always fail. The same goes for specific literary works that seek to give sensible form to something that escapes finitude. In the process, however, Lezama, once again, goes a step further and puts in question even the integrity of the One, which appears here in the guise of a conquistador and which at a second remove serves as a metaphor for the philosopher and Western Reason. Only the God of philosophy is the One, suggests Lezama, for whom the God of the Bible speaks in the plural we. The exegesis itself is an example of the questions and thoughts that cannot but appear as out of place, absurd and out of turn. Though Lezama is aware that these kinds of readings will most likely be taken as bizarre and dismissed as the musings of a "primitive," it is not from naivety that they spring.

"Conocimiento de salvación" also reveals the importance of the concept of the void for escaping the identification of Philosophy-God-Poetry as figure of the imperial conqueror or sovereign dictator. However, the link between the void and the untimely questioning and thinking of the "primitive" gains its full dimensions only in Lezama's reading of Paul Valéry—a poet often thought to be poles apart from Claudel, but whom Lezama interrogates as if both were part of the same continuum.

Infrapolitical Lezama as Reader of Valéry: Sovereignty and the Placing of the Void

"Sobre Paul Valéry" (1945) purports to be a gloss on a verse by Valéry in which the poetic subject/speaker declares himself sovereign (*Obras* 117). Yet it is the text in which Lezama's most Nietzschean confrontation with the tradition takes place. The intricate link between politics and modern aesthetics is coded into his commentary in a way that Lezama will only indicate by allusion—even as it is in the most secret of codes that his reluctant engagement and passage through Nietzsche is written into the piece. In 1945, to speak of sovereignty in the neocolonial Republic did not go unremarked. Though it was not Lezama's style to simply remark on that front, at least not without the most abstruse circumlocutions, what I want to foreground in looking at his engagement with Valéry is the contrast that emerges between the politicity of the formless and the Nietzschean or tragic Grand Politics that are also at issue in this text. Valéry works within an *ars combinatoria* that only allows for a reorganization of what there is: the poet "places conventions within the limits offered by a space" (107). Again, the reduction of literature to the creative act of the Subject in broached in spatial terms: it is an aesthetics of limits, of the measurable, and of what can be grasped. Three motifs organize the interpretation.

First, Valéry is considered a poet of "our Alexandrian-apocalyptic time" (101). The characterization is Nietzschean, and it refers to the philosophical or theoretical man as the highest ideal of the age, with Socrates as its archetype (Nietzsche, *The Birth of Tragedy and Other Writings* 86). At issue is what the particular kind of intelligence at work in the poetry of Valéry represents for Lezama.

The second motif involves the tension between the sense of touch and the sense of sight. It is linked to the first motif insofar as, within the typology of eyes that Lezama relies on (of insects, of the squid, and of the owl of Minerva), the "decomposing" vision of the insect provokes an "unending refraction" (100–101), which in turn leads to the appearance of "the critical state" of philosophy (101). For Lezama, Valéry's affinities are on the side of the eye of the insect (101). The eyes of the squid, which have to work in the dark and in tandem with the sense of touch in order to achieve certainty (100), are set aside in a move that Valéry assumes would give him something more like the eyes of the Minervan owl of philosophy and its conceptual cosmos but instead produces the fragmented mosaic of the insect's gaze.

The third motif involves the actual placing of the words on the page. Under the sway of a theory of poetry that holds that the act of writing, of recording "the voice . . . as it is awakened by the things we see or the things we feel in their presence" is always the act of creation as such (Valéry, *Oeuvres* 549), Valéry will prefer to photograph his verses rather than copy them anew by hand (Lezama Lima, *Obras* 105). This reluctance stems from the belief that poetry is nothing other than the recording of an "external impulse" to which the poet has to be faithful. Lezama wants to draw attention to the tension that arises between the idea of an external impulse and Valéry's rejection of inspiration and chance in the writing process (cf. W. Benjamin 2:756).

Taken together, these three motifs are meant to foreground Valéry's ambivalence regarding the possibility of the new in poetry. The program of thought that relies on poetic "intelligence,"[30] or on the rearrangement on the available spaces of what already exists within his space, point to Valéry's "rejection of what he called monstrous ideas" (106). Outside of the limits of that intelligence appears the figure of the primitive, whose ideas "constitute the inopportune exercise of our interrogating faculties" (107).[31] If the play of conventions (the reorganization of what already exists) entails staying within the possibilities of a transcendental assignation of places in space (107), the untimely or inopportune questions of the primitive involve a leap beyond the finite and the possible. Valéry is "saved" when he opts for placing poetry and Monsieur Teste himself in that realm where an infinite desire appears out-of-place as well as out-of-turn. This means that something in the work of Valéry cannot be reduced to the operations of the eye as a trope for philosophical representation, as there can be no adequation between something that has never existed before and its representation, if we are limited to the elements already available within the *ars combinatoria* (107). It is something new.

This brings Lezama to a set of complicated questions concerning how to think this paradoxical "something new" if we limit ourselves to Valéry's thought. The questions that arise are all related to the distinction between *phusis* and *techne*, and all can be brought back to the idea that for Valéry "writing is primarily a matter of technique" (W. Benjamin 2:756). What can *phusis* have to do with poetry when it is one of the arts, that is, a craft, a technology? As Lezama puts it: "Transferring [all the motifs related to *phusis*], by way of contraptions and machines, places it in the place of an abandoned remainder, turning it into an instrument at the service of stoic discipline" (*Obras* 108).[32] This leads down a labyrinthine path littered with distinctions that are too arcane to describe here. The crux of the matter, however, remains clear, and it leads back to the objection that was made against Claudel. In attempting to secure the accurate transfer of the other, the dictation of the muse, or the gifts of inspiration, Valéry reduces the other to technique. Valéry is incapable of finding a way of dealing with the withdrawal of the "stimulating difficulty" that haunts him. And Lezama calls this inability the (im)possibility of the birth of the new. Valéry "is forced to repeat perfection like a mirroring dihedral" (109). This kind of reflection has the paradoxical effect of turning what "arrives" into one more thing in the world of things. That is, we have no way of discerning how creation escapes the realm of objective causality. The objection was already made in the process of describing the moment of creation. "But"— states Lezama—"creation by scission . . . sets in motion the kind of causality that was expected, which brings about a species of the law of inherited ideas and sensibilities" (109). This law produces the tedium of the eternal return of the same, understood not as the imperative to live each moment as if it were to be repeated throughout eternity, but as the desire to remain within a "perfected" world that will always be the same, in which nothing new could ever come to be, in which whatever is "to come" is blocked for all eternity: "That creation that multiplies what is perfect feeds on its own tedium" (109).[33]

Valéry's tedium serves as a guarantee for the prolongation and conservation of tradition. Following the line of flight of the primitive's untimely questions (which go beyond the limits of reason), Lezama offers his own alternative poetic axiom: "to continue without knowing, to respond precisely to what we dare not ask" (111).[34] This thinking and questioning that takes place beyond and before any possible program is Lezama's confrontation with the triad space-body-void, which he approaches in a way that is decidedly different from the pseudo-Stoic manner he reads in Valéry.[35] It is not surprising that, once again, at an important moment in the reading, we come face to face with the poet's Catholicism. What is at issue is the place and function of the void in Stoicism and Catholicism. Let us consider the web of metaphors with which the poet makes his inopportune questions and thinks his out-of-place thoughts:

> If, for the Stoics, the path of the fish exemplifies the struggle of the body and the void, for Christians the problem takes the form of a burly combat. The fight with the fish . . . is necessary. . . . [The fish's] cold instantaneity moves through our hands like the memory of the unstoppability of time. At the same time that the fish does not feel the presence of the void as an anxiety or understanding, with the movement of its scales, it solves once and for all the Nietzschean joy in terror, and it manages to feel the instantaneous pressure of the infinite dead spots as if it were silk, like that long solitude of Satan among the rocks, awaiting the rupture. (113–14)[36]

The Greek rejection of the void, which was philosophical as much as it was psychological, yielded a world that was continuous. The Church inherited the Greeks' fear of the void: "The Genesis account of creation *ex nihilo* . . . forced [it] to recognize 'nothing' as something; . . . and as something which had to be given sense . . . in relation to a God who acted upon it in order to create the world" (Rotman 63). Saint Augustine saw the devil in the void. His theory of time is an answer to the heretical problems that arise once one thinks about the lack at the center of God prior to the creation. If it had not been for the pressures exerted by mercantile capitalism and the arithmetic needed to keep better books in an expanding market, Christianity might have simply rejected the idea of the void by calling it the devil or by placing God outside of time. That is to say, Christianity did not spend too much intellectual energy actually thinking the void as a program of its own. The void, for Christian metaphysics, is a sort of conceptual prosthesis. For the doctrine of the Stoics, on the contrary, the void was a central concept. The void was the background against which an event, the *clinamen* (itself nothing insofar as it exhausts itself completely as cause), would set in motion the relations between atoms that would make up a world. In setting up the agon between a Stoic and a Christian treatment of the body and the void, Lezama is at a disadvantage conceptually. And this is evident in the way that the opposition is resolved.

On the one hand, it would be possible to claim that in the Christian's struggle with the fish, not with the void itself, there is a trace of the traditional Christian maneuvers of sidestepping the issue. In "Conocimiento de salvación" (1939), this face-to-face between the Christian and the fish was already clarified: "What remains: the great battle, the high dignity of the Catholic: face to face with the tremendous fish, with God himself" (*Obras* 249);[37] here, the theme of the void has completely disappeared: not because it is not a problem any longer, but because the void turns into the absence of God here on earth. The world not created from nothing, but by the intervention of God on a disordered-something; in addition, once the creation is finished, in the words of Gracián, "this world is a zero" [este mundo es un cero] (488).[38] But in Lezama the question of the void will not come down to putting the value of the world at nothing as he awaits the next life.

On the other hand (almost as if the event of the death of God were necessary for a Christian to come to terms with the void), it is not difficult to see that this Christianity is of a strange sort. Perhaps it is this kind of Christianity Nietzsche refers to when he claims that his own inquiry into morality remains a moral event; that "We are no longer Christians," although "not because we dwelled too far from it, but because we dwelled too near it, even more, because we have grown *from* it—it is our more rigorous and fastidious piety that *forbids* us today to be Christians (qtd. in Heidegger, *Nietzsche* 1:160). Who more fastidious in his piety than José Lezama Lima? But also, what could be more fastidiously and ironically Nietzschean than to claim that that fish, a symbol for Christ, also represents the heroic and tragic ideal of accepting and affirming the hope and the happiness of terror?

In Nietzsche's wresting of the tragic from Aristotelian morality, the aesthetic domain becomes the metaphysical activity of life, which defines the way that beings as a whole *are*. In tragedy, terror has to be affirmed: "Tragedy prevails where the terrifying is affirmed as the opposite that is intrinsically proper to the beautiful. . . . Affirmation of the convergence of these opposites is tragic insight, the tragic attitude; it is what Nietzsche also calls the 'heroic'" (Heidegger, *Nietzsche* 2:29). This hero manages to become master of his fortune and misfortune alike. To become master of one's happiness and unhappiness, moreover, is one of the defining characteristics of Nietzsche's "grand style" (Heidegger, *Nietzsche* 1:159). The grand style, along with the Grand Politics that Nietzsche conjures up in order to overturn European nihilism, is exactly the kind of unifying myth that modernity, as the era of the fragments that do not cohere, seems unable to sustain. After that fragmentation, the wherewithal and force necessary to establish a goal is lacking. Platonism is to blame for that weakness, for it introduced the theoretical man. In order to overturn Platonism and install the interpretation of true sensuous being against nihilism, "creative life, preeminently in art, must be set to work . . . ; art and truth, along with the meditation on the essence of both, attain equal importance" (Heidegger, *Nietzsche* 1:161). What is proposed by such a revaluation is a rescue and reconfiguration of the senses. The political horizon of this overturning of nihilism is national (Heidegger, *Nietzsche* 1:158).

Lezama's position within this landscape is somewhat different. While the national level is always close to him, it is not at all the "space" where he is making his intervention. We have seen him in dialogue here with the Western tradition as a whole. And yet it would be inaccurate to claim that this is a Eurocentric dialogue. On the contrary, what is suggested is that Lezama is struggling against the attitude that most fundamentally defines the imperial "conquistador" in all his forms. But Lezama's "resistance" is not frontally political, if by political we understand the project of constructing the nation as an independent sovereign space, or its more ambitious counterpart: constructing the unified Latin American bloc. In fact, within the purview that we are elaborating here, this would be an identitarian appropriation of the tools of "the enemy" without regard for the people on whom those (transculturated) weapons would be put to use. Lezama's "resistence" cannot take on the form of a grand politics, or assume the national setting in which "the grand" unfolds, for another reason: what emerges from his readings of Claudel and Valéry is a pattern that suggests that the impulse to overcome nihilism, to reach a purified state of things, to achieve "a knowledge of salvation," only leads to a further intensification of the force of nihilism. This direct confrontation, which serves to secure the place of the hero and his tragic struggle, gives way to a different understanding of resistance, and its politics can be neither grand nor tragic (at the very least, not in the classical and moralist terms of the *Poetics*—but beyond that, also not tragic in the sense that Nietzsche wishes to give to that term in his early work). Its "politics," to a great extent, remain an unknown quantity; for it is a question of beginning to think the politicity that ensues after the dismantling of the entire scaffolding that made possible the conquistador, the rational encyclopedia and its demand for calculation.

This would be the emergence of something other within the coordinates we are charting here. This politicity traces a diagonal that crosses all the conservative and militant options such as these terms were understood at the time. In its retreat from the politics of resistance, it cannot be called conservative; and it cannot be called militant in the sense that its praxis is occupied with literature, theology and philosophy, and, most important, with the invention of a mode of writing that does not yield when asked to contribute in any efficient way to the essentials of political negotiations.[39] The focus of the politicity in question, I would argue, comes to sharp relief only when we have a concept of the infrapolitical at our disposal. I use the term "infrapolitics" even as I am directly touching on the issue of Lezama's theology; for that purview is the starting point for everything he thought. However, it would be a mistake, in this case, to think of something like an infrapolitical theology—as if it were possible to offer a counterpart of Schmitt's elaborations. If I spoke earlier of a religiosity with which religion would want nothing to do, it is now necessary to further delimit the meaning of that phrase. The "sphere" of religion is no longer separable from that of politics when religion closes its doors to the kind of religiosity that is evinced in Lezama (and those doors close as a matter of course because of the homosexuality, the irony, the irreverence, the hubris it sees in someone who dares to think about God on his own terms and without regard for any possible agreement or disagreement with the "party" line). An infrareligion would already be infrapolitics, but infrapolitics is not limited to this kind of religiosity. For my purposes here, I understand infrapolitics as the praxis-thought that sees in the lack of foundations of politics, not a problem that has to be solved by supplementing the abyss with a contingent ground, but the opportunity and possibility of imagining a politics otherwise than the imperial and hegemonic variants dominating the history of the West.[40]

For the moment, I simply want to point out one of the major problems that infrapolitics allows us to think more clearly: the issue of the legacy and persistence of Christianity when imagining alternatives to the political global order. The politicity of Lezama's intervention does not have to be purified of its Christianity in order to make it "usable" or of interest in the context of "political emancipation." Total emancipation or purification in itself is a mechanism of the political and religious matrix that Lezama unworks. What Lezama requires of us, in a sense, is that we allow his singular engagement with the tradition to resonate in all its force, prior to our determination that he is or is not an appropriate subject according to our own theoretical dispensation. When we let his Christianity resonate (which is absolutely not the same as saying when we let Christianity resonate), the tremors it sets off, of its own, bring political and theological institutions to their breaking point. One of the ploys that disappears within the infrapolitical is the possibility of blanket assessments of the kind that make, for instance, Marxism uneasy when it encounters an "ideology" that is antithetical to itself, like Christianity. From that perspective, for Lezama to be "approachable," a whole host of moves need to take place in order to purify him of the negative or contaminated residuum. This is necessarily so because Lezama would be in the process of becoming a spokesperson for the theory as a whole, an example. What comes to the fore with infrapolitics, on the contrary, is that there are only singular and very specific operations within those "ideologies," which are not monoliths and therefore are less and more than ideologies. But also, in pointing to the inconsistency proper to ideology, what is underscored is the singular engagement through which that ideology shows itself to be less and more than it wants to admit. Lezama is not an example of a theory of infrapolitics in the precise sense that infrapolitics is not interested in amassing a collection of examples of how to do things and be in the world, but in not erasing the singularity that Lezama's text brings to bear on our understanding of the history of politics: which is to say, not forgetting about those instances where politics is directly confronted with its shadow. Though it is true that politics wants to imagine it casts no shadow, (some of) Lezama's interventions are part of a record that documents to what extent that shadow is there. Beyond any theoretical arguments to this end, what we find is Lezama assuming that he can take on the task of thinking—without having to corroborate that his intuitions are in line with the Church or the state. In the world of politics, this means war, which is why María Zambrano, who understood this dimension of Lezama's thought better than anyone, compares him to a lizard that has to hide in the crevice of a wall that bears the onslaught of bombs and machine guns every day: "The Church . . . closed itself; [. . .] to whom, to what? . . . I tremble at the thought . . . [. . .] And, nevertheless, there is no respite from this theological vocation; each epoch has to make its own and what is already available is of no use, since in the best of cases one would have to remake it, revive it, and revise it, departing from our current state of things [. . .]. The crack of historical time in which we are born. We live in it, like lizards in the crevice of a wall they bomb and shoot at with their machine guns everyday" (Zambrano et al. 35; the ellipses without brackets are Zambrano's—her own aposiopetic relation to the theologico-political).

Lezama as Reader of Baudelaire: Ennui as Nonsynthesizable Remainder

Lezama begins elaborating a historical narrative of the tension between poetry, religion, and philosophy early on. Perhaps his most interesting readings are those in which he is not so much questioning the claims of Reason but rather the way that certain poets adopted the claims of Reason as their own. If we think of the dialectic as the philosophical sublation of Christianity, the case of Baudelaire is particularly illuminating, as Lezama finds in him a specifically aesthetic operation that emerges out of a desire to delink poetry from dialectics.

In the essay "Julián del Casal" (1941), Baudelaire is interrogated as an influence on del Casal, a Cuban dandy whose poetry was on par with Martí's, but who has proven much less apposite as a literary figure for the state. Both poets stand as representatives of modern literature as a whole. There are two Baudelaires in the piece. There is the Baudelaire who believes in the possibility of completely capturing, in the poetic image, the grounding principle that gives rise to phenomena—that is, the Baudelaire that sets up the poem as a mirror that will reflect the totality of beings without remainder. This first Baudelaire is the poet of what Lezama calls the "excesivo natural." A "natural excess" that he claims is at the root of the whole of modern poetry and that consists in making accessible to language even the most ineffable experience. "Lo natural excesivo" was Lezama's name for that aspect of aesthetics that began to appear as a philosophically valuable instrument, which would grant immediate access to the Idea, to Being, to the durée of memory, etc. In short, what is at issue is the sublation by aesthetics of the aposiopetic restriction of rhetorical limitations.

One can think here of Walter Benjamin's introductory pages to his essay "On Some Motifs in Baudelaire," where he makes reference to Dilthey and to Bergson, and more generally to the philosophical recourse to aesthetics in order to solve speculative problems (4:314–16). And also of Georg Lukács, who, in *History and Class Consciousness*, offers a classic account of the questions that the "principle of art" would answer (134–40). To my mind, however, the most relevant point of entrance into this problematic is the early romantics' project to complete the Idealist program by means of art (see Lacoue-Labarthe and Nancy 122–24). The project, in its failure, or "despite itself," proves that in the search for an autotelic manifestation of literature, of itself to itself, what emerges is a lack that is not erasable or fill-able: "The manifestation in question here, rather, seems to be one that can designate itself (and up to what point could this be a designation) only through a peculiar eclipse of the manifest in its manifestation" (Lacoue-Labarthe and Nancy 124). The early romantics make available the vocabulary and the conceptual means to think the end of philosophy—or, the end of systematic edifices of thought that posed solutions and resolutions without remainder. This unexpected and paradoxical manifestation of the Jena romantics, who thought they were actually being more systematic than any school of thought in the history of philosophy, and thus that they were transcending philosophy, inaugurates the epoch of thinking beyond the ideal of the closed system.[41] Lezama picks up on what is, by his time, a long tradition, in order to posit this philosophical capture of the literary as the way to another Baudelaire—one that emerges as a response to the tedium caused by the putative completion of the philosophical program.

The first phase, in the description of a second Baudelaire, is completely taken up with the critique of a humanist/Idealist reduction of the literary to absolute knowledge (*Obras* 90). The capture of being, what Lezama refers to as the poem's "exact measure in being" (*Obras* 96; exacta medida en el ser), is total: the vibration and the echo coincide completely. The poem becomes an instrument—although defined precisely by its noninstrumentality—that allows an experience that escapes the reifying fragmentation of knowledge (understood as the fragmentation caused by the various disciplinary specializations that are not concerned with forming an Idea of the whole, within which those fragments would cohere).

For Lezama, Baudelaire participates in this project, but only up to a point, for he is the first modern poet to become conscious of, and then able to break away from, this cooptation of the poem by philosophy.[42] Aesthetics was supposed to solve the problem of the irrational gap between the thing itself and the philosopher's ability to "construct" it. An impossible program, since it was evident that, even then, knowledge did not coincide with the birth of things. The unexpected remainder of this operation was first felt as the "ennui" provoked by a process with a very clear and expected end: the coincidence of the experience of the work of art and the experience of the philosophical idea—the teleology of the literary as an instrument of absolute knowledge. This teleological domination turns the poetic process into an *a priori* knowledge of destiny, a new kind of fatality.

Second phase: the most important lesson that Lezama draws from Baudelaire concerns the production of a manifestation that is something other than the result demanded by philosophy. The answer to this predicament marks a different stage in Baudelaire's work:

> Baudelaire . . . understands that when the word is freed from every gravitational pull and achieves a complete birth and purity, then emerges, through the force of its reverse, the irreplaceable verb, . . . and the work of its magical insistence takes on, as with the remainder that results from every free choice, the most unexpected dignity. Baudelaire, in this as in everything, the perfect *dandy*, understands what Catholics call . . . the good assiduous intention, which solves the rude aggressions or harmonization between destiny and dignity. The natural excess is turned into a gracious movement of man, now

struggling irreconcilably against the great . . . themes, absent the fatality of a new species: grace, destiny, and original sin. (90–91)[43]

Lezama posits Baudelaire as a Catholic dandy who is able to move beyond a simple delectation in tedium, and who is able, then, to see in that subjective state the residuum of the philosophical operation of synthesis—which was supposed to be total. Parallel to the puppets and marionettes of Celan, moved only by the strings that the most sovereign of sovereigns pulls behind the scenes (see chapter 2), the figure that emerges here, as Lezama grapples with Baudelaire, is a Catholic in the process of keeping his balance on the tightrope tied to the two Christian poles of the divine plan, on one end, and free will, on the other. The Christian tradition has a specific image for this balancing act between intellectual or creative prowess and the submission to the will of God: it is the biblical scribe who takes down the words of the angel or the Spirit. Lezama will eventually evoke this scribe by name and identify him with the subject of humanism, or, with the first figure of the Author, in the sense that the moderns understand that word (cf. Vessey). In *Oppiano Licario,* this figure will be killed off when Foción and Fronesis make love.

Killing the Scribe

In Mallarmé, the unfolding of chance requires a passage through madness that "foils the piracy of a certain logic whose order is dependent upon . . . the familial, ancestral, and reproductive order handed down through the ages" (Kristeva, *Revolution* 226). However, as Kristeva points out, madness, then, means placing "the infinity of significance within a subject who then imagines he possesses it"; the result is that the subject is able to depart from his family and its history (from a specific social order), in which the infinite had been relegated to the Absolute of a particular institutionalized practice (such as religion), that is, in which the infinite was an extrinsic impossible ideal (Kristeva, *Revolution* 226). What is impossible after the interiorization of the infinite by the subject is his wholeness or completion, for he is now split off from everything. In Lezama, this kind of madness engenders in Foción an obsessive tendency that separates him from everything, but in the mode of enslavement.

To a significant extent, Lezama's narrative is concerned with telling the story of a triad of characters: Fronesis, Foción, and Cemí. Gustavo Pellón has described them in terms of a dialectical triad, in which Foción's wandering is opposed to Fronesis's order, and Cemí is the synthesis or equilibrium between the two—an equilibrium that in the novel means an all-encompassing state of androgyny (Pellón 42). It is possible to argue that in *Paradiso* they are involved in a platonic relationship and that the transgressive homoerotic moments in the novel concern minor characters (Buckwalter-Arias 31).[44] However, this is certainly no longer the case in the posthumous work *Oppiano Licario*, generally considered volume 2 of *Paradiso*.

In *Paradiso*, Foción's madness reduces him to circling around a tree in the premises of the hospital where he is interned, before disappearing from the narrative altogether. The fact that he is "adoring" the tree in its "circular eternity" has a very precise meaning in Lezama's tightly knit symbolic web, in which, for Foción, the tree is Fronesis (*Paradiso* 547–48). What interrupts Foción's adoring compulsion to repeat is a lightning bolt that coincides with the moment of death of Cemí's grandmother. This is a hinge point in the narrative of *Paradiso*, as it is also a high point in terms of Cemí's own coming into his own vis-à-vis his familial structure.

In a moment of metavisionary irony, Cemí's grandmother, herself an image, articulates the contraries that make up the synthetic image of speculative dialectics. She speaks about her knowledge of the image she had been during her life. This is a moment when the "image" acquires a voice of its own and takes it upon itself to speak about what informs it: "We have been dictated, that is, we were necessary so that the fulfillment of a superior voice would reach the shore, would find itself on secure ground. The rhythmic interpretation of the superior voice, almost without the intervention of the will, that is, a will that came already wrapped in a superior destiny, has allowed us to enjoy an impulsion that was at the same time a clarification. . . ." (*Paradiso* 547, ellipsis in original).[45] Here the grandmother is in the same position as the primitive, "el deseoso," or the chroniclers of the conquest—figures "who received the dictate of the landscape, . . . what nature herself dictates" (*La expresión americana* 74). This figure is by now familiar to the reader, as we have been track-ing its various avatars: she receives nature's dictate and dictation, just like Guevara, Martí, Vitier, Claudel, Valéry, and, in a more complex sense, Celan's string-puppet. Lezama's target here and elsewhere is the general background that makes all of their differences fall in line with a singular modern project of legitimation, through which poetry becomes sovereign, and the sovereign writes the poetry of history. Lezama wants to interrupt this program: not because he wants to liberate poetry from its political suture (as if it were a question of delimiting the sphere in which both poli-tics and poetry are autonomous entities—a procedure that would still be in line with the aposiopesis politics requires of literature as described by García Marruz), but because he wants to pursue the trail of a politicity that is no longer simply graspable by politics and the political.

First interruption: What we have here is a paradoxical and unsettling reflexivity of the image: precisely what the opacity of the symbol inter- dicts, the ecstatic stenographer talking about her/his activity as scribe, paraphrasing, so to speak, its primary activity. A moment of discursive clarity, notice that the parenthetical "es decir" appears twice, the grand- mother's utterance reveals the superior voice as insecure, incomplete, and impotent without her serving as "ground" on which to place its mark. That is, the image—as the result that it is—gives the lie to the "myth" that informs it when considered as the dictation of the Other. Moreover, what we are about to witness is the death and interruption of that "ground" itself.

Her utterance is said to be free from all volition; it is an ascetic act of obedience, "sin intervención de la voluntad." But this is immediately followed by a qualification, "casi." The rhythmic interpretation of the superior voice is at once what causes the enjoyment (*disfrute*) of what is outside of expression and what prevents the poem from establishing itself in that uncertain site. The poem, scansion of the "superior voice," professes to be something that is not art as such: an experience free from volition and will, subject to nothing but itself. That experience is an autonomous one, not subject to empiric forms of verification: it is what Lezama terms "poetic truth" (*Obras* 162). The experience is also that of Lezama's "casi." That setting to rhythm, revealed as other than the "aesthetic experience," is heteronomous, subject to the laws of expression. The utterance by Cemí's grandmother is itself framed so that the development of the narrative of the novel interrupts her. The "suspension points" that end the passage quoted above are part of the irony of the scene; they indicate the end of her "dictation" by the appearance of another character and leave us without her grandson's reply to her hyperbolic claim to be the vessel of "una voz superior." Cemí had begun the truncated exchange by telling her that she and his mother "had no interruptions" (*Paradiso* 546).

Second interruption: The narrative structure makes it a point to inter- rupt the one who, in establishing an unmediated relation with the dictates of the Other, was supposed to be without discontinuities. In particular, this is the moment when Cemí and the narration interrupt the dictation of a higher voice that up until then appears to be pulling the strings from an undetermined outside. The death of the grandmother coincides with a bolt of lightning that strikes the tree around which Foción moves in endless circles: "The ray of lightning that had destroyed the tree had liberated Foción from adoring its eternal circularity" (*Paradiso* 548).[46]

Foción's madness prior to this liberation becomes clear to Fronesis only in *Oppiano Licario*: "Now Fronesis could understand that Foción was inhabited by the infinitude of a wandering essence that was paradoxically incarnated in one body" (*Oppiano* 246).[47] Read in parallel with Mallarmé's moment of madness, what becomes clear is the difference that is introduced by Lezama's version of that manifestation that points toward a third space that is neither the objective knowledge of modernity nor its categorical negation (which would in essence lead right back to the dialectics of subject and object). The key structural aspect that Lezama emphasizes in order to install that difference, here and elsewhere, is the incarnation of infinity in "only one body." (What is at issue here is the possibility, or, rather, the impossibility, from the point of view of Lezama as a Catholic, of something like infinity ever being intuited or experienced here on earth.)

In his sleep, however, Fronesis comes into relation with just such an "infinite essence" incarnated in one body—a word that here can be used interchangeably with image. The narrator speaks of the "infinitude of the dream" as dreamscape or "extension" (*Oppiano* 247), although it cannot be confused with the plane of the object. The dream becomes the ground of the image: it is the "new earth that his friend [Foción] needed" in order to appear in a different light to Fronesis (247). This new mode of appearance is one in which Foción takes place "without the finitude of the body, but with the infinity of the image"; and the narrator adds: "the image and the extension of the dream became joyful [*dichosa*] like the frost that melds with the tree of the bonfire" (247).[48] The plenitude of the infinite image-dreamscape, together with the fusion of the ashes and the burning tree that produces them in a moment of "dicha"—of beatitude as the moment of the *dictum*—can be seen as an allusion to Foción's obsessive circling of the tree in *Paradiso*, which is linked to the moment in the novel when dictation is most openly questioned (Cemí's last conversation with his grandmother already cited). This same questioning will take place in the scene from *Oppiano Licario* under examination, but now the scribe will be a symbol for the subject of humanism.

Fronesis's dream becomes an erotic one; when they touch any awareness and "shameful valuation had been erased" (247). Above all, the hand, which touches unconscious and without valorizing, is *not* a grasping in the sense of knowing: "It was the pleasure of unknown things, through the retreat of all that was known" (247).[49] Knowledgeable "grasping" would be impossible since the "extension" in question is not an object. Fronesis climaxes and takes Foción's hand away. At this point, both appear to be in the study of a scribe, "a typical Renaissance humanist," who is writing on "tiras de papel que como escarcha coloreaban el monte oscuro" (248)—if ever there was an unexpected image for the *logos spermatikos*, this is it. The scribe, in the words of Foción, is "a homunculus made of wax," who writes "in one spur" when someone "winds him up" and "thinks (for) him" (249). That is, they are in the study of a figure who writes under the dictation of a higher voice, a scribe who becomes a recording apparatus for that voice. The lectern becomes a phallic object, and Foción says to Fronesis that together they will take the scribe down. The deposition of the scribe is ideological and aesthetic: it entails a critique of humanism as well, and more to the point, a critique of the model of inspiration that legitimizes the work of the writer by imputing his words to a higher order. It is also, at a more literal level that follows the logic of the dream closely, the direct result of the lectern being the phallus, which after Fronesis climaxes will deprive the scribe of a place in which to carry out his task: "That was the moment in which the Erasmic puppet [*muñecón*] would fall from his scaffold, and the pieces of paper would go flying about, stained with the blood of the scribe" (249).[50] At this point in the novel, Fronesis is somewhere on the coast of North Africa (variously referred to as Ukra or East Tupek, but in Lezama these are always unreliable toponyms). He went there at the invitation of Galeb, Mohamed, Champollion, and Margaret—all characters that to a greater or a lesser degree symbolize Western decadence (224). As Galeb described it to Fronesis, this was supposed to be a place where their only obligation would be to wait for a new dawn—in the transcendental sense of the phrase: "un amanecer metafísico" (196). The chapter ends with a transition from this night (in which Foción and Fronesis depose the *dictum* and the automaton that records it) toward "the new metaphysical dawn" that finds Fronesis alone in a house that "held a new life" (250). The negation of everything that appears as opposition in the darkness of the night, yields a whiteness that, as the house itself, becomes a figure of the self-reflexive image:

> [Fronesis] went back in the house, but in the mean time the house had turned in on itself . . . in order to strengthen itself against any threat. . . . Now empty, as its inhabitants had left with the dawn as so many incubuses, the house seemed a reflector on the sea, its whiteness refracted. . . . When Galeb, Champollion, and Margaret left the house, it seemed to stretch; if before he had been indifferent to it, now, making his way through the house, he had the sensation that something had waited for him, something that had

remained in hiding, that needed to wait for him to be alone in order to show itself in the flashing quicklime that before had been cold but now showed all its lamps like a diamond mine. (250)[51]

The house becomes a cipher for the coexistence of the past and the present. Fronesis feels that the house "atesora" (treasures), holds in reserve, people, memories and things as they were "before and after their death" (251). And this manifestation is neither openly displayed nor secretly kept from us, as the building becomes "the fortress that cannot destroy the time of overabundance" (251).[52]

By now we are familiar with this temporal pattern in Lezama. It places us in the "time" that is only time as the absence of all Time. The house starts to become weightless and transparent. Now "all the houses were one house" (251), and as it is separated from the ground and carried by the waves of the ocean, its movement becomes the enactment of a different kind of dictation: "the power of the moon which dictated the laws of its movement" (251). This dictation displaces the dictation that wound up, at the same time that it (gave) thought to, the Renaissance scribe. Note that the transition from dream into reality entails the transference of Foción's essential trait (being a body "habitado por la infinitud . . . encarnada en un solo cuerpo") to the house itself. This house now is the objective embodiment of the Idea/Infinity, which thereby makes the Idea habitable. The relation between Fronesis and the Idea changes; no longer directly confronted with the incarnated idea, he is inside of it. However, this dwelling in the house of Being is not the last stage in the sequence.

The reintroduction of the *dictum* serves to highlight the dialectical nature of the operation thus far. The deposition of the Humanist subject (in the guise of a scribe whose blood is spilled in overthrowing him) takes on the characteristics of the Terror. The scribe's blood becomes the last mark placed on the page at the behest of the other (the only thing that changes is who/what orders). This yields the new morning, the emergence of a new world, the coincidence of the copy and the Idea (the whiteness of the house that turns upon itself in a self-referential move that turns all houses into One house). However, this new morning is possible only through the dialectical mechanism that was to be deposed in the first place. Fronesis realizes this: "Once again Fronesis was naked. His body descended like the blows on the ground of a polyhedral staff of purification. He felt abandoned at the outskirts. . . . He sat down, in one of the corners of the living room. His thought negated itself, but his energy began expanding until it reached its plenitude, but now it was his own hand that held his reality and his dream; there was nothing to accept or reject now. It was, on the contrary, a cosmic acceptance" (252).[53] Cosmic acceptance is the name that is given here to a refusal of the hand of the other in favor of masturbation. Like the house, the character turns reflexively upon himself. Whereas before the "characters" involved in the origination of the new were fully figured and made manifest (251), after Fronesis's nondialectical "purification," these "characters" can no longer properly appear. The text cannot offer anything that is a manifestation of them; they return, but as non-novelable: "the non-novelable characters of the beginning of worlds returned" (252).[54] Lezama's irreverent and sexually charged framing of the end of the dictation of the scribe and of the lunar force is already an indication of the kind of operation that is at work here. But he goes further.

The house undergoes another transformation after Fronesis's self-touch. It is still transparent and all that this implies in terms of ideality. Now something else is visible in this edifice: "On the corner . . . an ebbing of the transparency became almost perceptible. This diminishing served as the foundation for a shell" (252).[55] There is a lack, a diminution, something that is becoming less, but that, all the same, serves as the "structural" cornerstone, as the base or support (*basamento*) for one of Lezama's symbols for poetry: "la concha," "el caracol"—the shell, the conch, the structure in which the tortoise or the snail can hide itself completely: just as Fronesis is engulfed by the house at this point in the narrative. Can the void offer anything like "structural" support? Fronesis looks directly at this image while the narrator describes it:

> He could see that the conch . . . was empty. The reflection of the conch blinded him; the rays emerged from a center that remained obscure and seemed like a void. He looked toward the corner once more and it seemed that someone was coming to get him. Somebody walked toward the center of the conch, but its luminous point disappeared, swallowed by the irides-cence given off by the colors of [the conch]. He looked now with more firmness [fijeza], but as the luminous point turned into a figure, the conch over the ebbing began to disappear, until it vanished completely. (253)[56]

The end of dictation is not the presentation of the void, though it is presented, but rather, and more to the point, the act of assuming the being or there-ness of the void in all its paradoxical "manifestation." The image of the "concha," along with that of the "caracol," appears in important places throughout Lezama's poetry and essays. Although it is linked to a variety of semantic fields (from political insurrection—via Martí and also through Cemí's involvement in the rebellion at the university—to the syncretism of Hindu and Christian theology developed by Lezama in various places),[57] here I want to contrast the image of the white house, which serves as a symbol for a total Idea, and the conch or shell, which appears after Fronesis goes through this experience where the house reaches absolute transparency only to then disappear completely. The parallel—between the whiteness of the walls of the house, which leads to an ascending movement that culminates in the manifestation of the Idea (when all the houses are one single house), and the whiteness of the shell—was taken up by Lezama on other occasions, most significantly in what is perhaps his last poem, "Pabellón del vacío" [Pavilion of nothingness] (1976):

> I scrape the wall with a fingernail,
> slivers of lime crumble down
> as though they were a piece of the shell [la concha]
> of the celestial tortoise.
>
> . . . .
>
> I fall asleep, in the tokonoma
> the other still walking is the one I evaporate.
> (*Selections* 96, translation modified)[58]

In this fragment, the Idea is ciphered into the image of the sun ("tortuga celeste"), and it is, once again, a white wall (from which the lime crumbles) that is "fought against" by the nail of the speaker, who is scratching its surface so as to create a void (the *tokonoma*) in which to fall asleep and make the other disappear. Something happens to the autotelic image, which here is a trope for the Idea as a totality. It is no longer whole. Lezama's work can be understood as the unending "scratching" on the white wall of the Idea so as to force the void that serves as the dark and "menguado" "basamento" for it. This has two unexpected consequences: (1) The idea is not found as a manifestation of the absolute that the text offers in a gesture that one-ups philosophy—the conch disappears, totality disappears; and (2) as opposed to a radical deposition of the Idea, which would offer an opening onto an Other that *is* "before the Law" (that *is* before all Reason has taken place), both in the scene from *Oppiano Licario* and in the poem "Pabellón del vacío" the hole in the white wall of the self-reflexive image provokes the disappearance of the Other and the emergence of the Same. This sameness without idea is another name for the emergence of the formless (lo informe) in Lezama.

Other/Same

Lezama's most arresting treatment of the question of the Other and the Same is the long poem "Recuerdo de lo semejante" [Reminiscence of the similar] (*Poesía* 328–36), included in the 1960 collection *Dador*. It has been ignored by criticism—perhaps because this is a poem with very strong Platonic overtones.[59] What little has been said about it, however, centers on the idea that it is a statement on behalf of Oneness, the image and the transcendental (Molinero 65–66; Xirau 85–90).

The poem is almost three hundred verses long; I will focus on three basic clusters: (1) there is an open philosophical query as to the relation between the plural, the same, and the homogeneous; (2) there is a cluster of passages that are a meditation on the natural world, a forest, a rabbit on the snow, an octopus, and so on (here, as we will see, Minoan and pre-Columbian cultures are coupled); and (3) the final three periods involve the theme of the image, its nature and effects, but this in relation to the particular appearances of the passages I have included in the second cluster.

"Recuerdo de lo semejante" begins with a question that finds, by Lezama's standards, a fairly clear answer soon after it is posed: "Is there a total plurality in similarity?" (*Poesía* 328). The answer: "Similitude will not coincide with homogeneity" (328). However, between the question and the answer things get more complicated. If the Platonic Idea was recognizable in the house that was all the houses in *Oppiano Licario*, in this poem it seems impossible to recollect all the cases of an Idea into a single archetype without setting in motion a tropology that destabilizes any possible understanding of an ideal unity or identity: "To believe that plurality stands against similarity / is to forget that all the noses form the Oliphant" (328).[60] The shift from noses to Oliphant (elephant—trunk—the trumpet sound it helps produce—the blow horn of Roland made from elephant tusks) requires a web of associations that refracts more than unifies the link between noses and horn. Their "identity" is never established but posited, and it becomes extremely difficult to think what is the cause here and what is the effect, what is the original and what is the copy.

The central point I want to make regarding this wayward tropology is that it is not simply a structural constant that is being emphasized. That is, it is not simply that there is always a mediation that dislocates cause and effect, or that the origin is different from itself and thus there is no stable source from which to derive the effects or on which to mold its copies. These kinds of considerations are here as well, but the thrust of the poem goes a step beyond claiming to have had an insight regarding the philosophical impossibility of literal language and so forth. What Lezama is doing is taking a leap that interrupts even that knowledge—not because it is not the case (that is beside the point for the poet, part of a still-too-metaphysical way of critiquing metaphysics), but because to state this would be to have found something that can be stated the same way about everything. Whether it is thought in terms of metaphysics or in terms of its own discursive undoing, we would remain within a purview that claims that difference is what is the same and always applicable, in every case. It is that idea of sameness, in its heliocentric sense, but also in its dialectical negation, that needs to be put into question. If the house that was all the houses can stand as Lezama's dealing with the heliocentric case, its dialectical negation finds its image in the moon and the antistrophe that is offers as yet another form of the *pneuma*, the *soplo*. The breath of inspiration that dictates in the ear of the poet and gives him his ground is what is centrally in question in "Recuerdo de lo semejante." The moon, which we have already seen occupying the role of the dictator, reappears at this moment:

> What is similar longs for its pairing, to reappear
> in the ink of the dirty swim [nadado] and that the ink
> will awaken the participation of the germinal [germen],
> the beating antistrophe of the breath [soplo] of the first moon. (328)

> [Lo semejante añora su emparejamiento, reaparecer
> en el tizne del sucio nadado y que ese tizne
> despierte las participaciones del germen,
> la antiestrofa golpeante de la primera luna del soplo.]

Together, these examples point to the fact that, for Lezama, neither the Platonic/Christian model nor its romantic antithesis is sufficient. This puts him in a no-man's-land of modern aesthetics and thought. What does the concept of participation mean in a context in which it cannot be either the direct link to the Idea or the dictation of the Other that retreats and leaves its traces in the dark of night? To "participate," here, is to activate by contamination, with that darkening cloud of ink. And this entails the plunge into the deep of nothingness, "nada-do," which is the paradoxical "depth" of the surface of the page being "dirtied" by the ink. Dirt, as it turns out, will be of great importance in Lezama's answer to these problems. What is born of the juxtaposition (which is not simply a more radical structural constant, or law, or synthesis between the path of the sun and that of the moon) is a further question. Immediately after the appearance of the "breath" [soplo], the poem asks:

How can what is similar engender the copy?
What makes the image distant is ancestral similarity,
up to the point where it sits by the fountain beyond the bastions.
If the copy destroyed the circumstance of similarity
and the surroundings retreated from the contractions
of the softened central marble.
Could the primordial similarity reappear?
The indistinction that walks the entrails of the earth?
Only the imperfect copy accompanies us,
the one that substitutes for the breath of steel before similarity. (328–29)

[¿Cómo lo semejante puede crear la copia?
Es lo semejante ancestral que aleja la imagen,
hasta sentarse en la fuente más allá de los bastiones.
Si la copia destruía la circunstancia de lo semejante
y los alrededores se alejaban de las contracciones
del ablandado mármol central.
¿Podrá reaparecer lo semejante primigenio?
¿La indistinción caminadora de las entrañas terrenales?
Sólo nos acompaña la imperfecta copia,
la que sustituye el aliento del metal ante lo semejante.]

Images are the imperfect copy. The question, within the contamination
effected by the "tizne," is whether or not the work of that darkening is
capable of sustaining something like the reappearance of "the primordial similarity," when the copy is in fact the destruction of the particular
appearing of sameness. "Sameness" without one, or sameness without Idea
is the sameness of that which has no Form: "The One that has to reach us
like a lump / upon which we stumble, since the one can only be ambushed
/ through exclusion" (329);[61] the one *is not*, its being is negative, and in
this exclusion "absence is perceived as slime" (la ausencia se percibe como
un légamo). "Légamo" can mean slime, spittle, mud, ooze: all figures of
the formless without Idea (as Bataille pointed out in his definition of the
formless).[62]

We move toward the second cluster, and so toward remembrance. I
quote the end of the fourth period and the whole of the fifth:

. . . no Minoan pleasure, prior to the amalgams
of the Lady of the Serpents and the Prince of the Flowers
can equal the pleasure of the octopus fixed by the fire
on the baked earth, and thrown over the curvature

and there the Lestrygonians who fight against the octopus
fallen over the curvature of a jar with the disappearance,
in the dense darkness where it is untied in the dream.
The curvature of its fall in the cinerary cup,
it seems to protect itself in two indistinct deaths, since the term [término]
inhabited by a form is the end [término],
and there the Lestrygonians who fight against the octopus
break the jars as well.

[. . . ningún placer minoico, anterior a las mezclas
de la Dama de las Serpientes y el Príncipe de las Flores
iguala el placer del pulpo fijado por el fuego
en la tierra cocida, y lanzado sobre la curva
y allí los lestrigones que luchan con el pulpo
caído sobre la curva de una jarra con la desaparición,
en el espeso oscuro donde desanilla en el sueño.

La curvatura de su caída en el vaso cinerario,
parece resguardarse en dos muertes indistintas, pues el término
habitado por una forma es el término,
y allí los lestrigones que luchan con el pulpo
rompen también las jarras.]

In "Recuerdo de lo semejante," the speaker is stating somewhat more audibly that the out-of-place truly *is*, but that this form of being is no longer caught hold of by the formalizing synthesis of the image. We wonder, for example, if the Lestrygonians fight the octopus upon the surface of the clay jar, on which they appear, and in doing so they also break the jar, the ground on which they stand, then, where are our protagonists going to go, where are they to stand their ground, what becomes of the idea of ground as such? Where is that "there" that, after the breaking of the vessel, sustains the "parings" carried out in "Recuerdo de lo semejante"?

We have here, in the span of twelve verses, the marriage of the Minoan goddess of fertility with the Aztec prince of verse and flowers; the conflation of a Homeric tale of adversity with an octopus found on a clay jar; an allusion to the confusion of the tongues; and an affirmation that the ground, or surface, upon which the thread of it all was woven, has been broken. In those gaps emerges a being (an "unnamed being" [ser innominado]) that is prior to the name and that nevertheless can survive the fragmentation that ensues. But we also have a passing reference to the realm between two deaths that is the time of resurrection after the final judgment, a site where all temporalities collide and no single synthesis of time as image can emerge but as formlessness. As a whole what we are attending to, however bizarre this might sound given the foregoing, is—at least to Lezama's understanding—fundamentally Christian. Yet it is also an act of imaginative grappling with modernity and its relentless temporal disjunctions. Lezama will take us to the brink and then leave things up in the air, so to speak. He will bring us up to a notion of *intemporalidad* that vacillates between, on the one hand, a restatement of the eternity of the deity, and, on the other, a lack of time that is nothing of the sort, that is, rather, the absence of an axis of time that can order experience. That is, "intemporalidad" is the only name available to think the opposition not between time and times—which is to say the false option between a single temporality and the ruse of multiple temporal strata—but the difference between Time, times, and the temporality of the formless. What is at issue here is the possibility of a thought of, and on, the absolute lack of foundation of any order.

But I am getting ahead of myself. The last section of the poem sheds some light on the importance of the resurrection for the unfolding of this piece:

> The image . . . when it is touched
> becomes overabundance and sententious destiny
> begins to substantivize itself as music in intemporality.
> Even as the form gets twisted and is transformed, for in ascending or retreat-
>   ing
> from the light, the fish becomes a pen [pluma: feather/pen] in the hostility or
>   the pen
> becomes fish there where the aquarium disdains its crystals.
> Just as something like the figure transfigures itself, sometimes it is the
>   structure
> which creaks . . . (334–35)

> [La imagen . . . al ser tocada
> se hace sobreabundancia y el destino sentencioso
> comienza a sustantivarse como música en la intemporalidad.
> Así como la forma se retuerce y se transforma, pues al ascender o alejarse
> de la luz, el pez se hace pluma en la hostilidad o la pluma
> se hace pez allí donde el acuario desdeña sus cristales.
> Así también como la figura se transfigura, a veces es la estructura
> la que cruje . . .]

Overabundance, in Lezama, is the sure sign of the resurrection. It is the opening of the time of no time. Here the succession and law of destiny, as

law, dissolves into intemporality. Intemporality is not simply the cessation
of temporality; rather, it is the time of no time, the time when past, present,
and future are not separable, where time has no directionality and no hegemonic principle of order with which to indicate that there are different,
plural, times—there simply are no time/s in the time of no time, but this is
still "time" and not an eternal realm beyond it. Form begins to be twisted,
unformed. The fish, as an image of Christ, appears. This is the time after
the second coming, and structure is rattled. Further on we read:

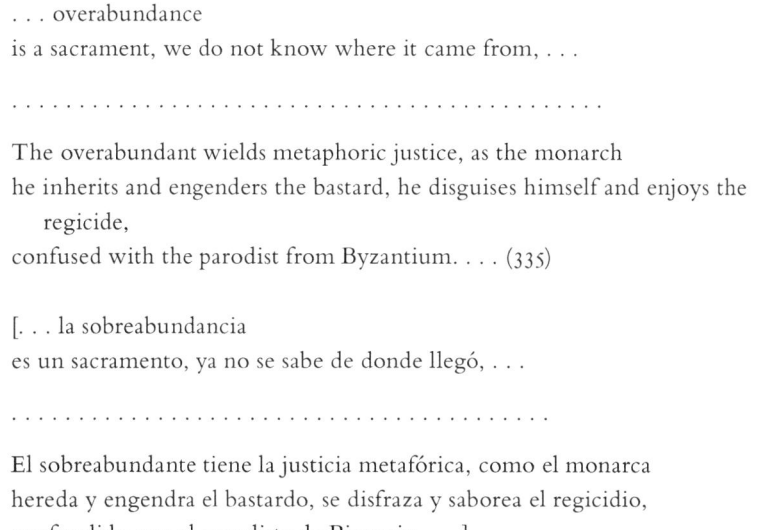

. . . overabundance
is a sacrament, we do not know where it came from, . . .

. . . .

The overabundant wields metaphoric justice, as the monarch
he inherits and engenders the bastard, he disguises himself and enjoys the
    regicide,
confused with the parodist from Byzantium. . . . (335)

[. . . la sobreabundancia
es un sacramento, ya no se sabe de donde llegó, . . .

. . . .

El sobreabundante tiene la justicia metafórica, como el monarca
hereda y engendra el bastardo, se disfraza y saborea el regicidio,
confundido con el parodista de Bizancio. . . .]

The text cannot but encode the Revolution, even if this is done indirectly
by the reference to the regicide of a prior upheaval. The overabundant,
the resurrected, wields justice. As the monarch, the resurrected engenders
and inherits the mask of regicide. But this decapitation of the old order
appears now in confusion, as the parodist from Byzantium, the reference
is to another deposition of a sovereign. And all the depositions of the
sovereign throughout history begin to blend into one another, as all times
are confused and dissolved.

Lezama not only allegorizes the dissolution of all politics, but he also
does so for the dissolution of all aesthetic regimes. As I begin to conclude, I
want to draw special attention to the way this sets the stage for the writing
of the formless—which is perhaps Lezama's singular and most important
contribution to the history of writing and of thought. To summarize some
of the essential points that have to be kept in mind in order for the writing

of the formless to be engaged from its proper perspective, it is important to keep the following front and center:

1. The formless is not a vanguard concept that seeks to identify a new or radical rupture with the history of culture; rather, it is a way of engaging that tradition, but against its own grain.

2. In particular what is at issue is the way in which the history of the West (in all its heterogeneous, transcultural, religious, and imperial facets) can be seen as the story of how to guarantee that there is a secure foundation or ground that gives legitimacy to the perishable and contingent institutions of humanity.

3. This has meant the eradication of the void, and the denigration of everything that appears to lack a clear form.

4. Thus the writing of the formless concerns all the writing of the Western canon invested in eradicating the void from thought, and this means that even in Plato, Aristotle, Saint Augustine, and a large etcetera, there is an engagement with the formless already.

5. In its most politically charged accretion, shaping the formless has meant the canalization of the intemporality of the time of existence into the various temporalities that power organizes—in this respect it matters little if we opt for a single totalizing time or for a multiplicity of times: these times (of the One or of the Many) are all forms of organizing and disciplining the time of the other, of reducing it to the time of the law.

6. Even the most radical attempts to deal with the historical configuration, such as the attempt by the romantics to think that which could not be grasped by absolute knowledge, and, more recently, the postfoundational framework of political thought, which attempts to acknowledge the void of foundations by proposing a contingent and precarious foundation—all of these attempts actually share in the Judeo-Christian tradition that transformed the nothing into a something that stood in the place of the nothingness or the abyss of foundations.

Thus, the writing of the formless is an intervention on at least two different but interrelated levels: on the one hand, the occupation of the nothingness of the nothing—which means having the wherewithal to look into the abyss without covering it over or even giving it a symbolic frame; and, on the other, the habitation of the time of intemporality—which means the aperture toward a time of life that is not directed toward caring for the enforcement of temporal organization in any way. On both counts, we are confronted with a "time" that is no longer that of politics. And it is for this reason that the link between literature and the figure of the sovereign, and with the dictation of the sovereign above all, is so radically questioned by Lezama.

It is within this general configuration that I want to turn to one of the most penetrating interpretations of Lezama: Alberto Moreiras's reading of the poet in *Tercer espacio*. Though I am interested in outlining an emendation to the general argument he makes there, it must also be said that my own approach to Lezama gains its consistency only from taking his reading as a point of departure, and further, from taking into account his more recent work on infrapolitics,[63] which though not centrally concerned with Lezama, illuminates the broader theoretical and political scene that I have been interrogating in these pages.

The Allegorical Reading: Classical, Baroque, Romantic

Moreiras begins by referencing Severo Sarduy's reading of the baroque in light of Lacanian categories. For Sarduy, the classical style of writing is dominated by the preeminence of the symbolic order. Romanticism is not only the reaction or negation of that order, as if it were a question of negating the object to the benefit of the subject. Rather, it is the emergence of the divided subject as a possibility for thought for the first time, or the Lacanian $. The Lacanian *objet a* is a paradoxical object, something that gives form to the impossible object that is here only as a lost object. It is the space that the baroque comes to occupy. As Moreiras explains, because the *objet a* is by definition a lost object, baroque literature can only be posited as the frame(work) within which that object is absent: "the frame for its retreat. . . . The illegibility of baroque writing stems from the necessary opacity of what it reveals" (*Tercer espacio* 273).

The consequences should be felt in the structures of the work as such. That is, Lezama's images, for example, or our understanding of them, should accord with the structure and effects of the *objet a*. Moreiras points to Lezama's deconstruction of the category of the object. What remains of objectivity is not a positive (and positivist) quantity: in fact, Lezama himself writes of his interest in configuring a writing in which "shapeless forms" are somehow staged as such, in which "things hidden behind the full moon of the zero," "negative quantit[ies]," are somehow revealed (*Selections* 112, 114). The "object" of literature becomes a way of locating the specific difference between classicism, romanticism, and the baroque. Moreiras defines them as three different modes personified in *Paradiso*, respectively, by Fronesis (classical), Foción (romantic), and Cemí (baroque).[64]

In tracing the limits that separate the classical from the romantic, and the romantic from the baroque, by means of the object and the relation that the three styles establish with it, the underlying assumption is that what is at stake in the work of Lezama is a critique of intentionality, in the phenomenological sense of that term. We have already seen (in chapter 2), in the case of Derrida's reading of Celan, how important this problem is when considering the possibility of opening toward a different relation with time than the time(s) of politics. In Husserl, intentionality names the opening in consciousness through which the mind receives impressions. Derrida's critique of Husserl's notion of intentionality is, in part, that because it is prior to descriptions, intentionality precedes historical processes. As he puts it in *Writing and Difference*: "As vision and theoretical intuition, Husserlian intentionality would be adequation" (148), or precise correspondence without residue of noesis and logos, transparency of thought to itself, accuracy of the representation; perhaps what Moreiras terms "classical" is the space of Western metaphysics of truth as adequation. In order for adequation to work, one needs to be given an object prior to the act of thinking, that is, there cannot be thought without a prior object that conditions it. As Moreiras explains:

> [Noema:] the intentional object that corresponds to noesis as act of intellection or thought. . . . It configures sense—it is sense. (*Tercer espacio* 291)

> [In Husserl,] there is no object without noema. (291)

> [T]he sense of the lived is given in the act of capture, or noetic act, and both are one and the same thing. (292–93)

It is only from this perspective that the logic of the baroque frame, where the object "is" only in its disappearance, can be clearly apprehended. The baroque, the space of the lost object, will be the space where intentionality is interrupted, where there is noesis without noema, without a prior object conditioning thought:

> Noesis without noema, that is, to assume the rupture of the noesis-noema correlation . . . implies entering into the thought of the lost object. . . . If the noesis-noema correlation was for Husserl the composition of time itself, where time is understood as duration for consciousness, the breaking of the correlation introduces a noesis turned toward an experience of a time without sense. . . . The repetition of the noetic or reflective act, in failing to deliver any objective sense/content, is pure self-repetition, in which the objective always exceeds itself. (293)

The constitutive capabilities of language, to posit without guaranteeing presence or existence, put into doubt any pretension to adequately tie Being to discursivity. Language becomes unhinged from foundation: "Its tautological force is devastating and dissolves every ontology . . . all foundations" (293). However, the frame remains; I will come back to this point. For now, the following question: Can this frame take the place of foundations itself?

For the classical mode of writing, there is always a stable object that writing is supposed to be able to capture without residue. For the romantic mode of writing, there is an alienated subject that misperceives his avowed goal as the very cause of his existence—that is, a subject that does not realize that if he were to accomplish his goal he would disappear, as he would become one with his object of desire. Thus, for the romantic mode of writing, the object is never adequately captured, and its pathos derives from this impossibility, while, for the classical mode, the object is all too properly captured and what disappears is the alienated subject, which is supplanted by the symbolic order. These are two sides of a single coin. One can begin to see how these two options lead toward the identity of being and thought, the very same identity that the baroque or mourning mode of writing reveals to be impossible. However, there is a paradoxical element of this entire development, and it concerns the way in which the baroque (precisely in representing nothing, or writing the object that is not there anymore) comes dangerously close to the same kind of reintroduction of the identity between being and thought. The baroque mode functions as a limit that brings into relation the "repetition of the indifferent" and the ontological apparatus (logocentricism), which the eternal return of the indifferent undermines. On the one hand, "that excess . . . is indifferent, since it is void of content"; on the other: "if that writing were not alive, if the heart stopped irrigating its proliferating monstrosity, the ontology from which it departs, the body of plenitude from which it is born, would not be able to live either" (293).

The point is an important one; its bearing on any possible thought concerning something like the writing of the formless cannot be overemphasized. What Moreiras is pointing to in these passages is that it would be naïve to think that since the history of Western metaphysics has privileged form over matter or the amorphous, by reversing that order and valuing the formless, one would be in a different or better situation. Derrida turns to the notion of the trace in explaining what is at issue, also in a text that has Husserl at its center. I am referring to a note that appears toward the end of the piece "Form and Meaning: A Note on the Phenomenology of Language"

(1971): "In a sense—or a non-sense—that metaphysics would have excluded from its field . . . , form in itself already would be the *trace* of a certain nonpresence, the vestige of the formless [*l'in-forme*], which announces-recalls its other, . . . perhaps for all metaphysics. The trace would not be the . . . transition between form and the amorphous . . . but that which, by eluding this opposition, makes it possible in the irreducibility of its excess" (*Margins* 172, translation slightly modified). The trace makes possible the opposition between the monstrosity and the ontological field that excludes it; they are implicated one in the other. The writing of the formless already is the trace of the writing of form, and vice versa. But then the question emerges: Since what we are discussing is that (non)sense that metaphysics would have excluded from its field, from what field are we speaking, where are we standing, on what ground, when we allow the sense of the trace to fully resonate? That is, metaphysics will never understand or allow that it is the writing of the formless in reverse. From its point of view, Lezama's enjoyment of the writing of the formless in Aristotle's negation of the void would seem bizarre if not irrational. However, the proliferating monstrous writing of the baroque—or of the formless, in Lezama—seems to be constantly affirming, thinking, and staging its other in a way that is not at all that of metaphysics. Something emerges in this monstrous writing that is beyond the opposition that it seeks to erase, however imperfectly, and always leaving a trace, the formless within properly formed onto-theological thought.

To return to Moreiras's interpretation, I would like to ask if the Lacanian "*objet a*" is in fact the most apposite way to track what emerges in this setting? For it could be that Lacan's concept is still too invested in covering over the formless void. One way of probing into this complex question would be to put to the test the identification of Fronesis, Foción, and Cemí with the modes of writing that Sarduy adduces via Lacanian terms, where the characters would correspond, respectively, to the classical, the romantic, and the baroque. We would then be able to see to what extent these characters respond to the various evocations of the modes of writings in the narrative itself. For part of what I am calling attention to is the fact that the staging of the formless in Lezama involves a thematization and an awareness of what should only be there as trace. This awareness goes beyond a more familiar claim regarding the self-deconstruction of discourses of their own accord—this is, after all, also what the trace is supposed to underscore. I would like to read this excess of awareness as a radicalization of deconstruction.

For reasons of space, I will focus only on the character that represents the classical mode, or its law: Fronesis. In the following, he will come in contact with the artistic vanguards, with the romantics and with the neoclassicists. The baroque Cemí will also come into the picture, but as part of the discourse of the character that represents the neoclassical mode. The fact is of import because it is to Cemí that some of the texts that I have quoted in this section of the book are attributed, in particular the poem "Muerte del tiempo."

At the close of chapter 9 of *Oppiano Licario*, Fronesis comes face to face, for the last time, with a group of artists (he is talking with Champollion, Galeb, Abatón, Mohamed) that in the novel represent the European vanguard in all its forms. He has had enough of them and is about to tell them exactly how little respect he has for their ways. Among other insults, he claims that they only manage to copy each other, that their *non serviam* is a sterile reiteration of their own banality. Their characterization becomes more specific: "You are . . . like the little bored devil. . . . An out of place like the void. . . . You are the desert that every neighborhood offers, you set up a lifestyle that fragments itself, that does not flow, in which all becomes unrecognizable. . . . How joyous, how primitive, how simply creative, a world where you don't exist any more" (*Oppiano* 397).[65] Against these representatives of the modern, in the "modernist" sense of the term, Fronesis reacts in a way that would lend credence to the arguments of critics who accuse Lezama, and all the poets associated with his various editorial ventures between the late 1930s and the late 1950s, of wanting to nihilistically purify the nihilism of the ultramoderns. That is, this character wants to erase from history and start anew all that he sees as representative of decadence. For him, modern nihilism, which favors the active making present of the void, stands in the way of a creative (in the *poietic* sense of the word) and joyful new dawn that is also a return to the primitive. These artists are not only fascinated by their own nothingness; they are actually the living dead: "I am not even going to say good-bye," says Fronesis as he exits, "since you are all already dead you will not even be able to respond to my farewell" (398). They are absurd, just as the void was absurd for Aristotle.

It is difficult to ignore the outlandish reaction of Fronesis, named after wisdom and prudence, in the scene—an ironic dimension that is in line with Lezama's willingness to laugh at his own characters throughout the posthumous novel. Lezama will even have a laugh at his own expense, as we will see presently. Furthermore, note the oddness of the insult when he calls the vanguards absurd by alluding to Aristotle's a-topos in the argument against the void (an allusion that will find resonance in the next pages when "Muerte del tiempo" is quoted). Lezama, here, begins to stage not only the aesthetics that he has been questioning throughout his life but also his own, and not in a necessarily good light. There is no indication in the text to guide the reader concerning the value of these statements, no way of knowing if any of these characters should be taken as stand-ins for Lezama himself. For instance, when Fronesis departs, Lezama lets the vanguard take the word. Champollion, the leader of the group, pretends to throw a knife at Fronesis as he exits, a gesture that he punctuates by passing gas. Another of the characters present, Abatón, is filled with dread, as he associates flatulence, the narrator tells us, with a profanation of the creation of the world according to the Book of Genesis, where "in the beginning a great wind passed through the waters": "It seemed to him that a fart could be a great cloud that, when you least expected it, would cover the heavens and the earth like a gigantic ass, and with its flames and reddish smoke the final trumpets would sound. . . . The untimely presence of that pneuma was enough to confirm the presence of the Evil One, already sitting by the window playing the flute" (399).[66] Creation *ex nihilo* and the end of the world both partake of the same pneuma, at least in Abatón's imagination— his *fear of the void* leads the character to a prompt assimilation of Fronesis's point of view, as the narrator tells us (399). But this cloud also has the effect of moving the narrative onto the next scene.

Champollion's flatulence elicits the exit of Ynaca Eco Licario, now called Ecohé, as a hybrid of Echo and Evohe. Once outside, she catches up to Fronesis and together they arrive at a convent that is half in ruins and half in pristine condition. In it lives an old possessed woman who is in a perpetual state of grace; she is able to make people see, to get to a visionary state, "using all the resources of the image and of sound" (400). This woman is the stand-in for romanticism, and she inhabits the part of the convent that is in ruins. Fronesis's audience with her is short. Almost nothing is said, as if to prove that this is the space where the ineffable is staged. Once in front of her, he is pulled aside by Ecohé, who saves him from a falling ceiling beam.

Suddenly, they are both facing an adolescent boy who is wearing a hat with the signs of the zodiac. In this room there is an inscription on the wall that reads: "Fábrica de metáforas y hospital de imágenes" (402). Underneath the sign, there is the phrase that opens *La expresión americana*. Here it is attributed to Cemí. "Only what is difficult is stimulating": the text indicates that it serves as an "exergue" (that is, as a setting of the tone and as an indication of the organizing principle, the law, of this new space in which Fronesis and Ecohé find themselves) (402). The young "healer of the image" inhabits "the factory of metaphors" and lives by the law of the difficult. Though it is important to ask what he understands by difficulty, since he is the representative of a neoclassicist attitude toward the arts. He occupies the space immediately adjacent to the ruined house of the visionary old woman. Immediately after her death, the young boy states his *raison d'être*, which will put him in line with the grand politics and aesthetics of a Nietzsche, even if this is spoken against Nietzsche and his influence in the modern world. The young poet has to "ennoble poetry once more" (402); for it has lost the power it once had. The times are no longer the times when poetry went hand in hand with the act of founding and providing the social bond for the community, the properly religious function of poetry: "Those times in which poetry founded the house of the gods . . . are gone" (403). And he adds: "We have to take poetry all the way to the great difficulty, to the great victory," which would be the "total victory of poetry over all the crossroads of chaos" (403, 404). This is Eliot's difficulty and not Lezama's. So as to illustrate his point, the young boy cites Lezama's work but attributes it to Cemí. He is referring to "Muerte del tiempo" and the end of the essay "Exámenes" (*Poesía* 159; *Obras* 226):

> I remember now, he said, an image theory of your friend—Fronesis under-stood immediately that he was referring to Cemí when he spoke of the train over the Roman aqueduct, until it reaches a speed uniformly accelerated, to the point where it no longer needs the rails and thus being able to replace the Roman bridge for a silk thread. He concluded: the lighter the tangency, and tangency here paradoxically means substitution, the more the image achieves levitation, that is to say, the image is a body that breaks loose from the stellar and falls to the earth. The same thing the alchemists recommended. (404–5)[67]

Fronesis, now more in line with the prudence inscribed in his name, tells the boy: "I congratulate you!" (405). But he cannot help whispering to himself, "This is stupidity in reverse, a lucid madness that scratches the diamond and then elevates to divine status the dust that the stone leaves behind" (405).[68] From the young poet's point of view, Lezama's poem is not about the restitution of the void but about the tropological slippage that substitutes one term for another. The superficiality of his reading is palpable in the circumlocutions he uses to summarize the poem: "a speed uniformly accelerated," "the lighter . . . the more levitation"; but also in the valuation of the heavenly that falls to earth in order to save us, which he sums up by reducing Lezama to what the alchemists had said before him. It is as if Lezama found it necessary to leave a record of the possible misun-derstandings that his texts would provoke—a testimony that is particularly relevant when it comes to distinguishing his own relation to Christianity from the Christianity of a figure like Eliot. In this regard, the reductionist reading involving the alchemists is revealing.

The boy invokes the alchemist's philosopher's stone, and Fronesis sees his words as the "stone-like" interpretation of his friend's diamantine text. In "Coloquio con Juan Ramón Jiménez" (1937), where a young Lezama has a conversation with the Spanish master, the character of Juan Ramón also speaks of the philosopher's stone in connection to a poetic "factory" and what he calls the "false image." He tells Lezama that the new classicism of the epoch is using the poem as a "piedra filosofal" (62). And the same year, in "Otra página para Victor Manuel," Lezama returns to this motif in order to clarify the same issues: "Any art that attempts becoming the philosopher's stone . . . would stumble, after traversing its exactitude daily . . . , upon the homunculus produced by the elements of its factory-like production" (*Obras* 702–3). Lezama begins the piece by alluding to Stravinsky's neoclassicism, in which the formal elements exhaust themselves in achieving their goal as irrefutable proof that they are representative of an initial substance (702). If the young boy intent on reennobling poetry were to achieve his goal, he would have managed to reactivate sectors of the history of literature that, as he himself states, are dead and gone. Together (classical mimesis and romantic synthesis), these two aesthetic stances represent for Lezama a false opposition. An opposition that might be internalized as if it were the totality of options available, but that is on two occasions tackled by Fronesis (the character that links them) exiting the scene. This is further emphasized by the contiguous location of the two aesthetic stances (the visionary old woman and the young neoclassicist) living under one and the same structure, even to the extent that this contiguity is considered a necessary condition by the neoclassicist. In the last case, Fronesis is even cordial. There are no parting insults and no apocalyptic reactions. It should be noted that, from the standpoint of the Latin American baroque, it is the modernist neoclassicists who look baroque. It is Eliot's Spencer, and not the romantics that some modernists so rabidly dismissed, who comes closer to the complexity and metaphysical density of Lezama. By the same token, what Lezama is suggesting here is that the neoclassical modern aesthetics of Eliot or Stravinsky are not that much different from the aesthetics of the romantics in at least one point: in both cases, it is a question of modernity overcoming its own impasses by way of a totalizing mechanism. Fronesis is moving across a tense aesthetic European space, which he is simply trying to leave behind. But it is not ever simply a question of leaving these kinds of problems behind. Insofar as Fronesis can be associated with the classical mode of writing, what we see is that even the representative of the thought of adequation is heavily invested in welcoming the thought that is not his own; he can dismiss as inadequate the version of Lezama's baroque aesthetic that is appropriated and intrumentalized by the "savior" of poetry. That is, even the neoclassicist understands that the project of the neoclassicist leads to a madness on a par with that of the romantic. This kind of juxtaposition is the reason why Sarduy and Moreiras have relied on the Lacanian tripartite topological structure of Big Other (A), barred subject ($), and *objet a*—in which there is no Big Other of (Neo)Classicism without the barred subject of romanticism, and there is no barred subject of romanticism without the always already lost object that constitutes that subject as sundered (Moreiras, *Tercer espacio* 273; Sarduy 1409–10). But what we see in Lezama is a truly polyphonic text in which the voices are not made to accommodate a specific point of view. This polyphony forces us to see his baroque writing not as a specific mode of treating the problem of intentionality but as an attempt to sidestep the very idea of a frame that makes the baroque intelligible in the first place.

The void, the lost object, is the interruption of the prosopopeic/auratic moment that legitimizes the poet's saying or the sovereign's mandate. The lost object is being, and not a personal fantasy that needs to find a precarious manifestation in the form of the "*objet a.*" The subtraction of being from the repertoire of objects to which poetry seeks to give form, which means the subtraction of poetry from the metaphysics of the dialectic, is, at the same time, the possibility for a poetic thought and praxis of not forgetting about that being. Theory can no longer assume that it gains its directives from the capabilities of the literary unless it assumes that poetry is forever to be in the place of ontological thought, which is the place of its exhaustion.

For Lezama, the baroque, as a frame, also became a problem: "I think that by now the baroque has begun to give off a stench," he wrote in a letter to Carlos Meneses—3 August 1975 (*Cartas a Eloísa* 419).[69] As he goes on to explain, the stench of the frame was brought on in large part by the commercial use of the tag to unite things that, to the poet, seemed very different in order to sell more books—that is, the frame begins to stink once it is a category with which the Latin American Boom can do business. What emerges when the frame is forsaken?

I want to close by referring to Lezama's most elaborate and mature treatment of the image: chapter 4 of *Oppiano Licario*. In it we find the most labyrinthine and abstract exposition of José Cemí's theories. The opacity of these pages is exacerbated by the fact that this "exposition" of the image unfolds in a dialogue with Ynaca Eco Licario, who appears as representative of the legacy and aesthetic position of her dead brother, Oppiano Licario, and by the interjections of a narrator, whose opinions of the characters differ from the impressions that the characters have of each other and of themselves. That is, the densest and most promising pages of Lezama for anyone interested in a possible theory of the image as it is elaborated in the fiction, would require such a complex metacritical description that the result would be nonsense. Rather than offer examples of the kinds of maxims concerning the image that Cemí and Ynaca Eco exchange, I want to call attention to the way these apothegms are "framed."

As the two characters begin their conversation, Ynaca Eco interrupts herself as a courtesy, so as to see if Cemí wants to speak. Cemí assures her that he will attempt not to interrupt her; instead he will simply try to "add as an echo" (*Oppiano* 309; añadir como un eco). That is, he will try only to echo Eco, without interruptions. Not very long after, he is at odds with his intentions, as he makes a gesture with his hand that Ynaca Eco interprets as "the pause in the score that is left at the discretion of the musicians" (310; la pausa en la partitura que sin estar en la partitura se deja al arbitrio de los músicos). He takes the opportunity to begin tracing the development of Western culture from the Greeks all the way to the modern novel, in the space of forty-four lines of prose. Just as he is about to extemporize on the continuum of time, Cemí's swift conceptual progression is met with: "*pour la mère de Dieu*, let us not go so fast—interrupted Ynaca" (311). The dialogue will not be able to continue without certain violence. The narrator assures us that this is only a passing impression and that the two characters "did not interrupt each other" but "followed one after the other" (311; no se interrumpían, . . . se proseguían). Nevertheless, Ynaca Eco goes on to speak at length on the dialectic of human silence and the dictates of the One, a problem that causes her some consternation because she never knows if the gift of vision that this dictation implies is truly hers: "I can only see what comes next, and what interrupts me gets clouded"; Cemí sizes the opportunity: "I am going to take advantage of your last affirmation in order to interrupt you" (313), and he goes on to talk about death and the *imago*, which is the only thing that survives "what interrupts us" (313). Ynaca Eco hears this and begins another thread; this time she elaborates on "the eidetic world" and does so by turning her attention to the interrupted rhythm of the conversation: "Observe," she tells Cemí, "the last two periods of our verbal progression have been interruptions. What interrupts the ideas . . . comes accompanied by the voice that forces" (314).[70]

What Lezama offers us in these pages is not a coded and decipherable theory of the image as the secret link between poetry and the Absolute. To enter this text in search for it will lead to a madness similar to that of Foción circling the tree of the eternal return. What the reader finds instead is the interruption of the image as such, time and again. The interruption is the emergence of the void at the heart of the image—the emergence of what gets clouded, and is only as *informe*. Yet it is not the aposiopetic strategy that relies on silence only in order to ensure the continuity of a hegemonic situation. Furthermore, it is not a dialectical negation that interrupts in order to elevate what is interrupted. Eco describes the broken-up discursive situation that results from the link between her brother, Cemí, and herself as "the other trinity that emerges with the twilight of religions" (314).[71] The trinity is a surface without time; or, its "time" is the time of interruptions. These "rhythms" are the frame around the lost object of what was formerly the baroque, which is now beyond the *horror vacui*, and beyond the baroque. In fact, the frame has been perforated in such a way that it is a lost object in its own right.

Allow me to return to the question of intentionality (which we have seen is central in Derrida, Celan, and Moreiras). What is at issue concerned the possibility of relating to the other without appropriating or reducing the time that is most proper to the other. In chapter 2, I suggested that this was an attempt at proposing a posthegemonic time. Perhaps it can be said at this point that the time of the other, insofar as it is possible to understand it as "a" time, will have already been hegemonized, even for the other. Conversely, to the extent that we can understand the time of the other as the noneternal (because it is history that is at stake throughout these pages) other of "time," and thus as a temporality that is neither one nor multiple, what we are considering, then, is a temporal thought that can no longer frame. Only then will the command to care for an exhausted politics of (dis)order begin to be imaginable. It is here that the politicity of Lezama's infrapolitics begins to resonate.

Conclusion: Godard, Lezama, and the End of Time(s)

Jean-Luc Godard's *Notre musique* (2004) takes place among the ruins of Sarajevo, at the time, the most recent proof that the state of exception is the rule. In the film, the Spanish novelist Juan Goytisolo makes a cameo appearance that could be wrongly seen as disconnected from the rest of the movie as a whole. During his time on screen, Goytisolo makes the claim that in the contemporary world, among the ruins of the civilizing process, there is a need for contemplative poets like Juan José Valente and José Lezama Lima. It is the world that needs this, not the state. Goytisolo recites passages from Lezama's "Las siete alegorías" and *Oppiano Licario*, to which I will turn to below. In between these passages, the ruins of a library are foregrounded: books are being burned and the building that houses them is falling apart. As if to make certain that the viewer does not miss that it is the institution of modern literature that is being allegorized here, someone picks up one of the books that lies scattered on the floor and reads from Baudelaire's "Correspondences." Intercalated with Goytisolo's appearance is that of a Native American couple, which stresses the coincidence of different historical times within one diegetic space. The couple, representatives of the many lives that were erased in the name of the culture that gave rise to that literature, come face to face with the librarian, guardian of modern literature. They now occupy the same space-time. But the librarian is oblivious; he does not notice that they are there. The present is shown on screen. Yet the copresence of the librarian and the Native American couple moves into a sort of spectral mode, a feature that is underscored by the allegorical quality of the scene as a whole. The abyss of the now, a groundless site, is where the two temporalities touch, at the limit. A structural determination that Godard does not erase or dissimulate, this is nevertheless a border that marks the coexistence, side by side, of the two kinds of temporality within the same now. The present has become equally unbearable for both, and they are "strangers in the same land," as the female character puts it.

The film offers the viewer the disjunctive juxtaposition of various temporalities. It makes visible what the modern apparatus of development was supposed to have hidden: namely, that it is within the same time that these strangers meet. But they do not meet as equals. Their degree of being-there, as the scene foregrounds it, is not the same. When the Native American speaks, the other does not listen. The atmosphere is charged, and the music, not organized according to the architectonics of the classical style, marks the dislocation and dissipation of any single "homogeneous, empty" temporality. In tandem, the symbolist system of correspondences embodied by Baudelaire, which posits an underlying unity of the whole, appears out of focus in the scene. It would be tempting to take this contrast and use it to declare the appearance of something that is a new paradigm that negates or refutes the old point by point (to claim, for example, that a new aesthetic has managed to be capable of doing justice to the Other by breaking away from the wholeness assumed by the symbolists). Godard rejects this option (perhaps because it relies on exactly the same historiographical ideology of the modernists, so overconfident in the onward progress of culture). The fact is that Baudelaire's "Correspondences" provides the title for the lecture Goytisolo presents at the conference that brings him and Godard together: "The Forest of Letters." So it is not that a new vanguard has one-upped the old one. Rather, it is a question and a call for a new conception of what a creative revolution is in itself—a revolution concerning the very idea of revolution: how to think the possibility of creating something new, beyond or below the political capture of that word, so that it is the conception of the new as such that has to be transformed?

If "our era," states Goytisolo, is characterized by the capability for complete annihilation, then what would be new in relation to it would be the manifestation of an "endless creative force." This force would require dreams and a stronger form of historical memory, one capable of giving body to images. The synthesis of opposites, the romantic formula of the poetic image par excellence, has been relinquished or taken away from the poets. It appears here as the union of the stellar and the underworld, and it is now in the hands of atomic physicists. Here the scientists stand for the true manifestation of romanticism—yet another form of the synthesis of opposites. In short, the scene presents us with an aesthetic imagination that no longer has a clear function within the order of the day, or at least, whatever its function was, it has now entered into crisis mode—and this is necessarily so when the sovereign and the technocrat seem to produce the fiction of the unexceptionality of the state of exception without much need for cultural alibis: which is to say, when the sovereign, technocratic, and capitalist apparatus has itself become a master manipulator of sights and sounds, as well as texts. This is also the central claim of Godard's lecture on the relationship between text and image.

For the film director, the problem is that in the current state of affairs, the facts no longer speak for themselves. Godard cites Céline, who in 1936 had already warned about the impending muteness of facts. The reason, as Godard puts it: "Because the field of text has already covered the field of vision." This is not the more familiar claim that the spectacle has become autonomous, and reality has disappeared. But neither is it the Jamesonian identification of the image with the commodity, which postpones the insurgent capabilities of the image (*The Cultural Turn* 135). It goes further in putting the aesthetic in tension with itself, rather than with a more commonly posited systemic antagonist. Godard differentiates between two aesthetic mechanisms, the textual and the visual/imagistic. Whereas textuality produces certitude, the image remains unstable enough to require textual intervention. The reality that is actually seen produces uncertainty, while the projection of myth on it creates enthusiasm and concentration. This is also the inherent vulnerability of the image: "the image is joy, but beside it lays the void," posits Godard, playing himself. The textual operation attempts to fill it in, but what results is the complete capture of the image. As such, captured, occluded, covered over by the text, what remains is darkness. And it is around this zone that Godard formulates a principle of cinema: "go toward the light and shine it on our night, our music."

The importance of Goytisolo's recitation becomes explicit at this point. For the light, according to Lezama's "Las siete alegorías," is "the first visible animal of the invisible." If we take this into account, the principle of cinema can be restated as follows: Rid the image of its textual occupation, so as to begin to see what the text erases. If we consider the violent images that open the film under the heading of "hell," what would result from applying these insights to Godard himself, and I would argue that what Godard is interested in getting the viewer to do, is to see that hell is one of the texts, a mythologem, that allows us to think that history is not actually happening. Peter Sloterdijk's remark is appropriate here: "The fear of hell is . . . a basic factor of what is called political theology; but should more accurately be described as the imperial management of death" (67–68). The consequences of the principle of cinema are not difficult to surmise. This would open the way for a historical imagination capable of unsettling any idea of a singular temporal flow against which historicity is measured. Methodologically, this has interesting implications. For what would it mean to rid the text of the textual operation? I will venture that it would entail reconsidering the role of aposiopesis, and the silences of the text, all that recent forms of close reading, in the wake of poststructuralisims of various sorts, have taught us to read as the absence that gives form to the text at hand. At its most productive, this tendency allows us to unwork the sharp division between the aesthetic and the political. It is argued that the aesthetic and the political are in an ex-timate relation; each term is the constitutive outside of the other, included out, so to speak (cf. Bosteels, *Marx and Freud* 195–230; Cruz-Malavé). The aesthetic, then, would be one of the temporal layers in a post-Althusserian project. But the relative autonomy in question is a secondary fact with respect to their "articulation in the whole," that is, their "dependence with respect to the whole" (Althusser and Balibar 100).

Compare this with the scene in which the Native American couple talks with the oblivious librarian. There the situation is decidedly not that of a forest of symbols looking benevolently on the speaking subject (on the contrary, the forest of letters is the allegory of a civilization coming undone even as its management of death rushes forward). Neither is it one of relative autonomy. One is not the constitutive void of the other. Instead, we find strangers to the same land, meeting at the tip of an abyss, a present that "bleeds," as the film puts it. Structures, even if poststructuralist, do not bleed. A present that is understood as a structure cannot be the open wound on which these asymmetries take place. Our night, our music, is an abyss precisely because, as groundless ground, it does not give itself up to be directed by a single homogeneous "us," "here," and "now." The epoch cannot be "ours" because there are asymmetrical temporalities crisscrossing all possible loci of enunciation labeled "ours." This yields a variety of nows that cannot be brought under the single logic of any one whole. Godard's idea of democracy is that it is our inability to liberate ourselves. This access, however, to the extent that it is predicated on a structure of domination and exploitation present at all points of the globe, is only access to a variety of invisibilities, access to the textual veiling of the image. That is, the whole stands for anything but a whole, and its putative homogeneous empty time is anything but that.

One of the main difficulties in reading Lezama is that his textual machination will render one absurd unless one begins to read with him, not in him. Lezama's concern with the temporalization of history, in its various forms, is a case in point. The second one reads too closely in his unworking of the so-called traditional form of historiography; one begins to surreptitiously take the side of what in essence is the point of view of the History of the Spirit as the history of Europe. For it is only from this perspective that other modes of temporalizing history are absurd or poetic. To shake this imposition, Lezama does not simply come up with a theory of history. It is in this context that I believe Lezama's use and practice of reversibility is still of interest today.[1]

This is the place to shift back to Goytisolo and Godard's telecasting of a particular brand of revolution that was first articulated in *Oppiano Licario*. What is the reverse of revolution, even going beyond what the film proposes in this regard? The passage that Goytisolo cites in the film is spoken in Lezama's novel by Mahomed Len Baid. As far as I am aware, this Arabic/Muslim aspect of Lezama's posthumous fiction has received very little attention. Emilio Bejel sees in Mahomed a typological figure: he embodies the progression from Osiris, to Orpheus, to Christ and the poetic notion of "sobrenaturaleza" (111). Furthermore, Bejel notes that we are dealing with a rebel for whom the question of the weight of the past on the present is important (112), but he does not go further than that. I find it hard to read these pages without seeing in them a tacit critique of the Cuban Revolution. For, at the time, there was a perceived continuity between all the sites of national liberation struggles, and the fictional Tupek del Oeste, Mohamed's land in need of revolt, would have been a case in point.

Lezama's commitment to the new, as we have seen in these pages, had led him to opine that the Cuban Revolution had been a revolution *ex nihilo*, since there was no real state to speak of, only a pseudorepublic, when Castro came to power. Here we will find him entertaining a different thought. The new cannot be the *tabula rasa* of the moderns, up to and including the Cuban Revolution, if it is one that will treat its dead kindly. The target of Mohamed's revolution is much broader than a national government. "You will ask me," he tells Fronesis, "how could I jump . . . into the tumult of revolution, and away from that totality that we had achieved [as a family], toward the desire of liberating West Tupek from the plagues and from enslavement" (*Oppiano* 214). And he adds: "We felt the desire to make it possible for . . . the people to reach the immense domains where death is not different from life, and in which every interruption, every failure, every hesitation will have been suppressed, for the light of the submerged, the envois of the stellar world and the regurgitation of the submerged, should have already reached a prodigious identity in our epoch, even as we have shamefully relinquished those questions to the physicists" (215).[2] This text should not be read only as a mission statement of the revolutionary who utters it. The target here, for a Lezama who is writing after the Cuban Missile Crisis, is the atomic age. In this context, it is significant that now Lezama does not talk about revolution by invoking the Cuban experience directly. For if it is a question of invoking revolutionary experience, not placing the scene in the epicenter of revolutionary Latin America must certainly have consequences. What is it that "our epoch" knows about only in terms of the technocratic paradigm of the sciences and the bomb? And what has Fidel Castro to do with these physicists? Castro certainly had some thoughts on how to make life and death undifferentiatable: "Would I have been ready to use nuclear weapons? Yes, I would have agreed to the use of nuclear weapons. Because, in any case, we took it for granted that it would become a nuclear war anyway, and that we were going to disappear. Before having the country occupied—totally occupied—we were ready to die in defense of our country" (Castro qtd. in Blight and Lang, *The Fog of War* 79). The shame felt by Mohamed, that the revolutionary had left the unity of contraries to be resolved definitively by modern physics, does not leave the revolution out it. It implicates it even more radically in the logic of the age of total annihilation.

In this light, Mohamed's remarks on the revolution take on a different tone. And, as we know, in certain circumstances, tone is the difference between life and death. However, it is not only a tragic tonality that I want to bring out of this text, which toward the end begins to explore and to offer us an example of what the "creative revolution" would entail:

> If our epoch has reached an indeterminable force of destruction, we have to make a revolution that would create an undeterminable force of creation, a force that would strengthen memory, that would require dreams, that would give body to images, that would give a better treatment to the dead, that would allow the ephemeral a more sumptuous reading of their transparency, allowing the living a more secure and flowing navigation of this tenebrarium, a destruction of that accumulation, not through the energy vitalized by the devil, but through a comet that would penetrate in the totality of a medulla oblongata, of a transmitter that would go from the tactile to the invisible . . . sucking on the stellar stalactite, as if it were a piece of candy, what in the ceremonies of the ancients was called *suckling the sky*. (215)[3]

Yes, it would be a different kind of revolution if we all could tell the revolutionary leaders to go suck the stellar stalactite. Foremost in this recasting of the idea of revolution is its relation to the past and the future. The displacement into these regions would break apart "our epoch"—not in the sense that it would bring in a new age, a new epoch (this would, after all, only be another *tabula rasa* effort at hegemonizing the now), but in the sense of exploding the idea of *the now as such*. The now is relegated to "what goes on: / the rustling of the leaves, / a rumor never hear, always heard" (*Poesía* 41; lo que va pasando:/ una fuga de hojas,/ un rumor nunca oído, siempre oído).

Historically, Lezama was living through the era of the conjuncture, of *the now* as a dictating structure, and a structure that provided the only means of legitimation for political action. Régis Debray's text *Revolution in the Revolution?* and Fidel Castro's hegemony over the question of the interpretation of the present (as Rafael Rojas has pointed out in *La máquina del olvido*) are enough to outline the context in which it is possible to understand not only the contrarian drift of this idea of revolution (perhaps, ironically, a true revolution in the revolution that revolutionary politics would never recognize as political in any form), but also what otherwise would appear as Mohamed's exaggerated anxiety after voicing his political opinions to Fronesis. The narrator tells us: "Slowly he began to calm down, and after he continued without preventing his trembling from being visible. He gave the impression that it was the first time that he had someone to confide in, that Fronesis was the first one that had made him feel comfortable enough to disclose what throughout his life had been a secret" (215).[4] The secret, I would like to suggest, is not only Mohamed's but Lezama's as well. In contrast to the "present-ism" at issue in the politics of becoming in tune with the contemporary, what Lezama offers is an image of the now as *supernature*, which is a subtraction from the now, or as Lezama puts it, the untimely as the world outside time: not a time-less eternity, but the muddy slime of sameness without form.

Lezama describes Oppiano Licario, the character, as someone who wants to provoke supernature, who wants to negate time (the ostensible object of chapter 12 in *Paradiso*, according to its author). Yet, this decisionist negation of time still operates within the confines of the singular logic of a hegemonizing time. The now that I am tracking here, since it cannot take the formal characteristics that define it conjuncturally, should perhaps take on more diffuse and difficult to grasp characteristics. The now that breaks apart, that is constantly fragmentary, could perhaps take on the name of "lo informe." This name has the advantage of allowing a link between the now and the "creative revolution" sketched above, since we know that Lezama, as he "familiarized" himself more with the Cuban Revolution, began to consider that "a revolution does not express a form" ("Encuesta" 190; Una revolución no expresa una forma).[5] Furthermore, it would also reflect an impression that Lezama's texts have not failed to cause in his readers from the very beginning (Alegría 247; Rodríguez Monegal 134). It is also the site of an ethics, as it entails the "the conviction," as the poet puts it in the autobiographical essay "Confluencias," "that . . . what is there and not there, what appears and disappears, needs a place of protection out beyond the Pillars of Hercules" (*Selections* 116). Note that now the point is not to go beyond the pillars or the columns of Hercules in order to bring the unknown into the fold of what we have possession of, to reappropriate the silence of "saying well," but that it is protected only beyond the delimitation of knowledge and form. What appears and disappears, what is beyond knowledge, what "these signs that cannot be deciphered" (117), these "negative quantities" or "clouds of dusts" that are "hidden behind the full moon of the zero" (116), all of these are figures of what Lezama calls "shapeless forms" (112). Would it be possible to attempt a reading of Lezama's work "as [if it were] an atlas of the formless" (*Poesía* 384; como un atlas de lo informe)? And, further, to understand this as a plea for a constant formless revolution, that never monopolizes the present, a formlessness that never seeks to come back to order or disorder, in the hegemonic sense of that alternation?

Lezama did show that he was aware of the historicity of the concept of time. In "Reojos al Reloj" (1953), he even goes through a list of various well-known forms of temporalizing history: the cyclical rhythms of the earth, the *otium* of the feudal lords, the *tabula rasa* of the French Revolution and all its sequels (*Obras* 596–97). He was also aware of the temporal consequences of the theory of relativity and the uncertainty that it brought into the picture. However inadequately this is conveyed, or regardless of the secondhand quality of this knowledge, his version of relativity is relevant in this context: "Now, in the reversibility of extension and magnitude, the clock, as a mask of temporality, hesitates, rectifies, becomes aware of the impossibility of yielding to its inexactitude" (596).[6]

This is a good enough alibi. It will do, at least to make thinkable that time had been putting on a mask, that it presented itself as one and as many. For Lezama, hell and time are linked insofar as time is a trope for the chronological unfolding of a Reason—a Reason that has managed to become contemporaneous with its now, and thus monopolizes it. The Cuban Revolution, in its search for an authentic Cuban temporalization of history, was supposed to have broken with this model; but its only means of thinking through its time were those it had inherited from a much too radically modern disposition toward history. Its triumph in 1959, greeted with enthusiasm by the poet, resulted in a radical dispossession, perhaps even more radical than the environment of the pseudorepublic allowed.

For what the Revolution seized as its own was the task of producing the fiction of its own legitimation on all fronts. But this is also an opportunity. From here a truly an-archic revolution can be launched, which would be the reverse of revolution, even if it is in the name of those to come, even if it is to be telecasted as the complete subtraction from the now-time of power.

Juan Duchesne Winter recently summed up his "incommunitarian" reading of *Paradiso*'s political project by invoking Giorgio Agamben's words on time: "History is not, then, as the dominant ideology wants it to be, the submission of man to linear and continuous time, but his liberation from that time. . . . a true historical materialist is not he who pursues an empty mirage all through an infinite linear time that continually progresses, but he who at every moment is ready to stop time because he still has the memory that the original motherland of man is pleasure" (qtd. in Duchesne Winter, "*Paradiso* como proyecto político" 41).[7] Duchesne Winter's reading closes with an invocation of Cemí's negation of time, an outside of time, where history coincides with the "seven hours" Adam spent in paradise. This allows Lezama to side with the marginal and the heterogeneous, and everything excluded by "la casa patriarcal criolla" (41). This position not only serves to show the extent to which Lezama's text is still relevant today, especially in its political consequences. But I would like to take advantage of the clarity with which Duchesne has made his proposal, here and elsewhere, to bring into sharper focus some of the conclusions that can be draw from an an-archic reading of Lezama.

The dissipation of a now-time, and the creative revolution that Lezama sends forth like Whitman's child, is an experience of history as extreme dispossession. It points to the insistence and the force of the creative imagination, even when conditions on the ground are not favorable. Lezama has no qualms about calling this a triumph of the spirit—and it is in this context that the instances of participation in the excess of the spirit should be placed (*Selections* 108). But, the lesson that is drawn from the liberation from the temporal hegemony, of whatever ilk, is that the moment the line is drawn so as to oppose a good and a bad time, a de facto monopolization of the present is also outlined. The immediate effect is to declare things that do not fit into its frame, things that nevertheless are there in the shattered present, unhistorical and worthy of eradicative force. We are familiar with the effects of this kind of enforcement of time in the case, for instance, of "civilization" eradicating the prehistorical barbarian. But what if the *tabula rasa* only manages to do away with the imperial management of death, or the dictatorial management of death? Then we would be in Paradise, of course. Yet the upshot would also be very well known in the case in question. If we are in paradise and all negativity has been decapitated, anything that appears as a sign of the negative must surely be destroyed, at any cost. In short, we would be in a situation that is historically and structurally the same as we have had in Cuba since 1959. It is telling that Agamben phrases this plea for a history of pleasure in the name of a putative true historical materialist, the one who is capable at all times of stopping time, capable, that is, of determining its true relation with regard to the Paradisiacal origin. But it is here that Lezama/Mahomed will always have to keep their secret and break the frame, interrupting it at every turn: that the destruction of the reified accumulation of time, or the liberation of a dictatorial dispossession of time, does not happen by simply turning to the antithetical term, as if it were simply a matter of a reversal.

In a late poem titled "Discordias," dated 1971, Lezama writes about returning to the "water's clarity in search of a serene ocean chaos divided between a continuity that questions and an interruption that responds" after rendering the stone's resistant reply with a "puff of smoke" (*Poesía* 373). That is the writing of the formless occupying the fracture of the now, the difference between (the difference of) linear and multiple temporalities, radically and anarchically at odds with the theologico-political distribution of time into the realms of hell, purgatory, and paradise. This is the time of the formless, of sameness without Form; it is the time of the absence of Time(s), where absence of time no longer means eternity.

Acknowledgments

I would like to thank my wife, María Dolores, above all.

Without the intellectual generosity and intensity of the Infrapolitical Deconstruction Collective, this book would not exist. I feel the deepest gratitude for their example and tenacity.

Particularly in the early stages of the manuscript, the input of some of the graduate students in my seminar on religion and philosophy proved to be indispensible: Juan Leal, Ludmila Ferrari, and Priscila Catalayud especially.

Thank you to Shannon Dowd, Patrick Dove, and Alberto Moreiras for their suggestions and careful reading of the manuscript.

Thank you to my friends Gareth Williams and Cristina Moreiras for all the support and stimulating conversations over the years.

Notes

Introduction

1. Unless otherwise indicated, all translations are my own.

2. On the importance of the sublime for postmodern theory, see the texts collected by Morely. On Latin America and the postmodern periphery, see Richard's "Latinoamérica y la posmodernidad" (1994).

3. The analyst's discourse is characterized by "the paradoxical attempt to occupy the place of an excremental remainder that induces, in turn, the other's evacuation or . . . separation precisely from the master or sovereign signifiers that heretofore dominated his libidinal life" (104).

4. This is why Santner claims that the voice of the sovereign can also be heard in Yve-Alain Bois and Rosalind Krauss's work on the *informe*, which they derive directly from Bataille (113).

5. Santner discusses Lacan's passage earlier in his text, where Freud's dream text is invoked as the founding moment of psychoanalysis, but not when considering the import of this category for the foundational gesture of the discipline as a whole. I will come back to the issues that this displacement raises presently.

6. The distinction between the formless as such and the images that come to take its place, its representation, which make it unthinkable at once, is a distinction that was already made by Saint Augustine in his *Confessions*: "I conceived the formless not as totally lacking form but as possessing such a form that, if it were seen, my senses would recoil from its strangeness and grotesqueness. . . . But in fact the concept I had was formless not by the absence of all forms, but only by comparison with forms more beautiful" (XII.6.236).

7. The "sense" of this absence of sense, it should be noted here only in passing—for it is not my aim to delve into either the question of the history of art or of psychoanalysis as such—is already readable in Bataille's engagement with Manet's *Olympia*. There it becomes clear that its "scandal," as Pierre Fédida observes, was caused by the painting's "abandonment of cultural representations fit only to restore this absence of meaning" (56).

8. Modernity imagines that sovereignty emerged only after overcoming the formlessness of the material and earthbound Titans at the hands of the spiritual and high gods of the Greeks. This is how Hegel imagined that sovereignty came into being. What is cyphered into this passage from the formless to form is also the overcoming of the barbarian and the move from east to west—but its most salient feature is the achievement of a timeless sphere: "those powers of the Earth . . . without spiritual and ethical content, consequently . . . gigantic and formless, as though they

were scions of Hindu or Egyptian imagination. . . . For the life of Nature is, in fact, subjugate to Time, and brings only the Past into existence, just as in the same way the prehistoric times of some people . . . become the sport of the power of Time, which is destitute of history. We touch solid ground for the first time when we come to law, morality, and the State, something permanent which remains though races pass away, as it is said that the Muses give permanence and a defense to everything (Hegel, *Hegel on Tragedy* 172, the text is drawn from his *Philosophy of Art*, the section "Myth and Motivation in Classical Drama," a.2–b–i).

9. It can be found in the selection edited by Allan Stoekl: "A dictionary begins when it no longer gives the meaning of words, but their tasks. Thus *formless* is not only an adjective having a given meaning, but a term that serves to bring things down in the world, generally requiring that each thing have its form. What it designates has no rights in any sense and gets itself squashed everywhere, like a spider or an earthworm. In fact, for academic men to be happy, the universe would have to take shape. All of philosophy has no other goal: it is a matter of giving a frock coat to what is, a mathematical frock coat. On the other hand affirming that the universe resembles nothing and is only *formless* amounts to saying that the universe is something like a spider or spit" (Bataille, *Visions* 31).

10. Throughout this volume, all italics used in quotations are present in the source.

11. Despite their differences, both Derrida and Georges Didi-Huberman accepted this difficulty. For the latter, the entry of the *informe* into the Bataillean text of the *Documents* responds to at least three theoretical exigencies: the recognition of a divergence or difference internal to forms themselves; on a more general level, Bataille's antistasis and antisubstance conception of things; and the need to mobilize the contradictions that emerge not as a way to find out what forms "are" (thus: neither form-*ness* nor form-*less-ness*), but as a meditation on the efficacy of form as such (Didi-Huberman, *La ressemblance* 201).

12. I use the an-archic (with a hyphen) as a term that refers to the lack of foundations, and in order to avoid confusion with anarchy as a political movement.

13. Fédida's work guides him in this psychoanalytical connection.

14. One of the possible pitfalls of a notion like the formless is the propensity these terms have to become overextended and domesticated. On the one hand, it can be a temptation, and it is probably not simply a question of misreading, to find the formless everywhere; suddenly Kafka and Flaubert, García Lorca and George Sand are all writers of the formless (e.g., Duffy; Leahy; Richter; Ryan). On the other hand, once the question of the formless is identified with certain objects, such as has happened with "abject art," then Hal Foster is right to say that we are no longer dealing with anything but a new norm—with anything *except* the formless. In fact, this latter view would be in line with Plato and Augustine, and all of Western metaphysics, in declaring that the formless is simply what seemed grotesque in comparison to more beautiful or sublimated forms. Thus, to identify the formless with spittle, sperm, feces, blood, and so forth is actually to assume rather than contest the tradition of the high and the low. Which is not to say that it is impossible to take

advantage of certain kinds of things and images when discussing the formless—the key to this operation being the differential and contextual over the essentialist identification of objects that embody formlessness. As José Lezama Lima pointed out regarding Goethe and Gide: it is only by ignoring half of the story that one imagines that the formless can be opposed absolutely to the spirit of classicism; he quotes Goethe: "What is most elevated, what is most excellent within man, is formless and we have to take care that we do not configure it except through a noble feat" (*Obras* 454). That is, when it comes to readers less demanding than Augustine, the formless can very quickly stand in even for Spirit, that is, as the highest. The point being that what is at stake with the writing of the formless is not whether it is a good or a bad, a progressive or a conservative mode of any sort, but that it is part and parcel of the very tradition that often denies its rights to being.

15. Such is the case in David Richter's recent book on Federico García Lorca, where the *informe* functions as a way of framing the manner in which the Spanish writer breaks boundaries as evidenced in the way "the poet identifies with and gives voice to marginalized minorities and underrepresented entities of otherness such as gypsies, blacks, sailors, homosexuals, women, and nature" (18). Richter's questioning of foundations evokes Derrida, but its ultimate aim is to produce an "ethics of *informe*" (257–68). The aim of this ethics is to critique the oppressive and limited space that social, political, and economic structures allow the poetic subject to inhabit. Thus, the formless is drawn back to a direct politics of resistance, critique, and liberation. What I want to suggest here and in these pages is that it is this kind of quick and almost knee-jerk politicization of the *informe*, which most effectively neutralizes any possible bearing that the notion may have in a radical critique of the thought of foundations in the Western metaphysical tradition. It thereby reintroduces the most recalcitrant elements of political theology, precisely where it believes that that schema has been interrupted; it identifies and reifies subjects, which will incarnate the progressive thrust of history as a movement of liberation guided by the Spirit, and within the pattern of the master-slave dialectic.

16. An example would be the work of Roberto González Echevarría, where Lezama appears as a belated thinker of the Absolute, whether it is in Hegelian or Platonic terms that we understand this term (cf. *La ruta*; and *Celestina's Brood*).

17. The program can be found online: www.scribd.com/doc/227574444/Documentacion-sobre-Jose-Lezama-Lima-en-los-archivos-de-la-Stasi. See Ponte's useful notes on it ("Lezama en los archivos"). For a more general overview on the persecution of Lezama, see Santí (175–85).

1. Toward the Absence of Time

1. In *Villa Marista en plata*, Antonio José Ponte provides a lucid account of the entire affair, which took place for the most part between January and February 2007. I rely on his work for the bulk of the historical details in these opening paragraphs. A comprehensive dossier of the e-mails that resulted was later published by the electronic journal *Consenso*: www.desdecuba.com/polemica/index.shtml.

2. During his tenure as the head of the Consejo Nacional de Cultura, in its most terrorizing period, Pavón was responsible for ensuring that Cuban intellectuals towed the party line. Himself a poet, he memorialized this activity in a piece titled "1959": "Here begins a year / for men only, / forbidden to the beasts and to the soft, / and it cannot be described even if they tell me / that one can write a novel. . . . // The poets say "dawn," "stem," "birth" / and we are entertained by the beautiful, playful / words of incarcerated monkeys" (Pavón 35).

3. On the Arrufat affair, see Barquet (chap. 1).

4. On the persecution of ideological diversionism, see Duanel Díaz, *Palabras* (119–64); as well as Antonio José Ponte, "Lezama en los archivos de la Stasi"; and Nuño (173, cf. 152–75).

5. Arrufat himself seems to hold the same view. In an interview with Jesús Barquet, he states: "History, private and public, seems to have a certain order and even a sense, its teleology, even if we can only perceive it retrospectively, and not while it is happening" (Barquet 138).

6. In this regard, witness Cintio Vitier's declaration that the Revolution is the manifestation of what, in the *end*, is the *original* datum of Latin America as a whole and of Cuba in particular: with the Revolution "we were beginning to discover that Spanish American culture, given its anticolonial origins, was structurally revolutionary" (Vitier, "Resistance and Freedom" 247). Vitier will be an important figure in what follows: he was one of José Lezama Lima's first disciples, and he later became one of the poet's most renowned exegetes and eventually became a key ideologue for the Revolution as it tried to shift away from the virulence that defined the *pavonato*.

7. On the opposition to linear time in the romantics, see Safranski (185–87). As I will show in what follows, Lezama's is not a subjective rejection of linear time or a romantic wish for a return of circular time. In fact, as he points out in the same short essay from which I quote here, for him, it is a fact of the world that after the physics of general relativity there was little to be done to or for linear time. For a reading of Lezama's temporalities, antithetical to the one I will offer in this volume, see Fuentes de la Paz. For her, the question of time leads Lezama to find the quintessential form of *cubanía*, Cuban-ness, and this as a contribution to the decolonialization of Latin America as a whole (128). This kind of simple opposition of a time of alienation to a time of redemption is the central target of my proposal—not because I am against the undoing of colonial rule in all its forms, but because it is only another modality of the political matrix it is supposed to counter.

8. As David C. Wood has put it: "There would be *no philosophy left* if the interpretation of time as presence were put aside, for that has determined the interpretation of Being since the pre-Socratics, and *that* has shaped all or almost all of philosophy" (264).

9. Much recent work on Cuba is a return to the Revolutionary Event in search of a guiding light for our confusing times. That is, Cuba and its archive seem to promise an answer to all of the very complicated problems that emerge when the field of the political, which went uncontested until recently, begins to show its cracks ever more openly (see Lievesley; Artaraz; Roy; Lambie; Aviva Chomsky; and Prentzas).

10. John Kraniauskas has referred to this as "the total apparatus of development conceived as the imperial time of capital" (54).

11. For a useful overview, see Allen. For the diversity of capital time in Marx, see Tomba. For the specific case of heterogeneity in Latin America, see the texts collected in *Colonial Legacies*, edited by Jeremy Adelman (1999). I have found Brett Levinson's discussion of these matters illuminating (see "Globalizing Paradigms" 66–67).

12. In some cases more so than in others: cf. Duchesne Winter, *La guerrilla*; Beverley *Latinamericanism*; and Bosteels *Marx and Freud*. It should be noted that Duchesne Winter has changed the emphasis away from the Badiouian current more recently.

13. Only when this is taken into account does it become possible to understand the proper place of Derrida's *différance*. The point is important enough to require the clarification of a possible misunderstanding, which lies at the heart of David C. Wood's otherwise illuminating *The Deconstruction of Time*. Wood attempts to expose a fault in Derrida's thinking on time. On the one hand, Wood argues, Derrida is known for his claim that another concept of time cannot be opposed or offered as a "good" alternative to the "bad" time of the metaphysics of presence: "time in general belongs to metaphysical conceptuality" (269, Wood is quoting from "Ousia and Gramme"). Time is always a fundamental concept when it is a question of metaphysics, which is to say that time is a fundamental concept whenever *différance* is denied. For *différance*, as Derrida writes, "is the constitution of the present, as an 'originary' and irreducibly non-simple (and therefore *strictu sensu* nonoriginary) synthesis of marks, or traces of retentions, and protentions [terms only used provisionally] . . . which (is) (simultaneously) spacing (and) temporization" (273; Wood is quoting from "Différance" [Derrida, *Margins of Philosophy* 13]). The implication is that for Derrida there cannot be a two-tier temporality: "*Différance* cannot be used as a corrective" (273). For Wood this implies that *différance* is used in a quasi-transcendental manner that is illegitimate. On the other hand, it is possible to find places in which Derrida surprises the reader by referring to a delinearized temporality that appears when what is strategically at issue is, for example, showing the nonlinearity of signification that linguistics or structuralism denies. More recently, it is possible to find Derrida alluding to an alternative to the transcendental phenomenology of time while speaking of a welcoming to the temporality of the other: "The present or proper time of the other, which I must no doubt forego, giving up radically, but whose very possibility . . . is also at the same time the chance of the encounter . . . of the event" (*Sovereignties in Question* 133). Wood's point is that by denying the quasi-transcendental status of *différance* as the constitution of the present, the possibility of "an alternative nonmetaphysical temporality" would then open up, eliminating the apparent contradiction at the heart of the very concept of multiple or alternate temporalities (Wood 277). However, this proposal would amount to annulling the whole of Derrida's contribution to the deconstruction of Western metaphysics. That the remains of time is not a time is an insight that cannot be instrumentalized in the name of any ethics or politics.

2. Sovereignties, Poetic and Otherwise

1. It is important to understand what the point of reference is here. Beyond a theoretical hedge regarding the necessity for political efficacy today, which would presumably concern the exigency for the postsubalternism of contemporary Latinamericanism, it is important to keep in mind that what is being outlined here takes Hegel and the total apparatus of development under the sign of the *Aufhebung* as its central target. It is modernity that is the target and not those who fight and give their lives attempting to bring it to a close. Yet it is also expedient to be clear on one point: declaring the intention to fight modernity does not of itself safeguard one from operating under the very program that is decried. (For an overview of the issue of postsubalternism in contemporary Latinamericanism, see the introduction in Acosta.)

2. For the issue of romanticism in contemporary theory, see Clemens (3–39).

3. This is a verse by the poet, but it is also the title of a piece Proust wrote about Montesquiou in order to gain his favor—though the sarcasm that characterized Proust's treatment of this forgotten poet is still obliquely in evidence. He calls him the sovereign of this world and that of things eternal—Montesquiou is overjoyed and wants the sentence engraved in stone in order to display it in his living room (Proust 409).

4. After reading the book in question, Ernst Robert Curtius wrote to Schmitt to say that it was reprehensible that literary historians, like himself, had to wait for a jurist to find research that was up to the task imposed by romanticism (qtd. in Galli, *Genealogia* 195).

5. This is why the time that the state can give to the writer, such as Ponte points out in our discussion in chapter 1, poses the question of a further imposition of the appropriation of time. The time that emerges after the time of alienation is still "alienated" time precisely because it is still a formalized time.

3. The (Mixed) Times of Revolution

1. For an overview of what this entails, see Masiello.

2. For the positive interpretation, see Buckwalter-Arias (10–21); for the negative tack, see Díaz, *Los límites* (43–45).

3. Juan Pablo Lupi has recently called attention to this very same fact (234–42). I will return to his reading in what follows.

4. "El instante de ese hecho [the Revolution] rezuma seculares acumulaciones, cinco mil años que abren sus ojos y le comunican a lo histórico su *andantino*, una secreta marcha del hombre hacia su alegría."

5. On the history of this idea, as well as its survival in the influential work on temporality of Reinhart Koselleck (who, as we will see below, Rafael Rojas adduces in exposing the temporality of neorepublicanism), see Villacañas Berlanga ("Acerca del tiempo apocalíptico en la Edad Media"). On the issue of Lezama's acceleration, I refer the reader to a fictional source: Cabrera Infante's hilarious scene in *Tres tristes*

tigres, in which Cué extemporizes about Bach and the baroque while El Malecón turns into a Mobius strip from the speed of the car (319–28).

6. "[La Revolución:] una poesía sin poeta penetra en el misterio de lo unánime."

7. "Desde la Epifanía hasta la Resurrección se participa en la identidad de lo temporal, el *tempus habemus* y el *tempus destruendi* se igualan en la identidad del rotar de la esfera."

8. "La historia se ha hecho sobre el . . . hecho cumplido. . . . Pero ahora ya sabemos que la historia tiene que comenzar a valorarse a partir de lo que va a ser destruido. Es decir, que vastísimas extensiones temporales que no lograron configurarse se igualarán a grandes extensiones que alcanzaron la ejecución de su forma, pero que fueron destruidas. De tal manera que únicamente la *imago* puede penetrar en ese mundo de lo que no se realizó, de lo que puede destruirse y de lo que fue arrasado."

9. "[S]i la imagen le fuera negada [al hombre,] desconocería totalmente la resurrección."

10. "[S]e vive en imagen, por anticipado en el espejo, la sustancia de la resurrección."

11. "No es solo la resurrección de un dios, . . . sino de todo un pueblo en la unanimidad, el que prepara su resurrección en la imagen como geometría del pensamiento de Dios."

12. "[E]l inextinguible más poderoso creado por el hombre ha sido el catolicismo."

13. "Hasta la llegada de Cristo, decía Pascal, sólo había existido la *falsa paz*; después de Cristo, podemos añadir, ha existido la verdadera guerra. La de los partidarios, la de los testigos muertos en batalla, los ciento cuarenta y cuatro mil, ofrecidos como primicias a Dios y al Cordero (*Apocalipsis*, Cap. 14, Vers. 3 y 4)."

14. "Ahora el tiempo no resquebraja . . . , / sino sopla, borrando . . . sucesión de las manos/ hacia el remolino, truncado el remolino."

15. "[E]l reemplazo de Dios mediante por Dios delante . . . Dios delante del hombre."

16. "[L]a imagen se entreabre en un tiempo absoluto. Cuando el pueblo está habitado por una imagen viviente, el estado alcanza su figura, pues la plenitud de un estado es la coincidencia de imagen y figura. El hombre que muere en la imagen, gana la sobreabundancia de la resurrección. . . . La Revolución Cubana no es otra cosa que la creación del verídico estado cubano. . . . No revolución dentro de un estado anterior, que nunca existió, sino creación de un nuevo ordenamiento estatal, justo y sobreabundante."

17. "[T]rasponía sitios, encuentros, hechizos, quebrantos, a categorías filosóficas. . . . [L]a escalera de piedra no sólo segrega historia inmediata, caliente como un vuelco de energía solar, sino que es también toda una categoría filosófica. . . . Al transcurrir de lo temporal, la voz que se alzaba llegaba en su articulación a ofrecer un recuento de círculos."

18. "Intencionalidad y tiempo, quedan en esas ocasiones tan bien soldados, que forman dentro del tiempo como cantidad sucesiva, un remolino aparte y como congelado por la visión."

19. De la Nuez invokes some of the very first impressions that Lezama provoked in his first international readers, who saw in his work a writing so strange that they simply called it formless (Alegría 247; Rodríguez Monegal 134). But that observation, however qualified, remained a negative judgment, not the beginning of a way of analyzing the work itself.

20. The references on this score are copious and have by now a long history, for example, Cortázar; Franco, "Lezama Lima en el Paraíso de la poesia," now in English translation in *Critical Passions*; González Echevarría, *La ruta* (66); Bejel; Heller; Moraña (257); and Pérez (4). West compares and contrasts Hegel and Lezama to provide a more nuanced description of the relationship between the two (124–31). The most radical anti-Hegelian reading of Lezama is Néstor Perlongher's in "Caribe transplatino" (93–102).

21. In the poem "Censuras fabulosas," "La brisa es el Espíritu Santo" (*Poesía* 156).

22. This reading, which is not the one I intend to undertake, would follow the cues given by Cintio Vitier's image of Lezama, approvingly or disapprovingly but accepting its fundamental premises. Cf. Vitier *Ese sol del mundo moral*; Ponte, *El libro* (110); and Guerrero (164, 166).

23. Undoubtedly the poets themselves were early proponents of this vision of things; see, for instance, the lecture Roberto Fernández Retamar, still only a man of letters, delivered on 24 August 1959, titled "La poesía en los tiempos que corren," now in *Antología personal* (108–24).

24. Lambie's precursor in this connection is Che Guevara himself. Cf. the allusions to the dwarf in "Una actitud nueva frente al trabajo" (Guevara, *Obra* 400–412).

25. Aviva Chomsky has called attention to the link between this spiritualist concern with the abolition of alienation and today's resurgence of left-leaning governments in Latin America: "The idea of the *hombre nuevo* or New Man found strong echoes in alternative and revolutionary movements around the world, even after the idea of guerrilla warfare had faded. . . . From the Counterculture of the 1960s to the New Age movements of the 1990s, critiques of the spiritual and human poverty of capitalism and materialism referred to Che's positions. Most recently, President Hugo Chávez in Venezuela announced the country's commitment to creating the *hombre nuevo* there: 'The old values of individualism, capitalism and egoism must be demolished,' he declared" (42).

4. Nihilism: Politics as Highest Value

1. Nevertheless, the salutary shock produced by the recent work of intellectuals like Díaz, Rojas, de la Nuez, del Risco, among others, was due in large measure to their detailed representation of that national context.

2. Bosteels: "In fact, when it does not opt for the traditional format of philosophy, one of the only ways in which the defeatist stance of postmetaphysical thought can still garner for itself the appeal of radicalism is via some convoluted argument or other about the resistance to theory. The proof, then, is not in the pudding so much as in the fact that so many people refuse to eat it" ("The Efficacy" 663).

3. Making the connection between postmodernism and nihilism is not a gesture unique to Vitier. In the case of the Cuban ideological state apparatuses, it is important to note the endorsement of the minister of culture in this regard: Abel Prieto, *"Lo cubano en la poesía:* Relectura en los 90." Outside of Cuba, we have already seen how Clemens makes this same link. For a recent example of the way that this is reproduced in a more academic setting concerning the literature of Lezama, see Guerrero: "por detrás de nuestra reflexión sobre la oclusión de algún posestructuralismo y sobre la negatividad del psicoanálisis y del marxismo, asoma con urgencia la pregunta que estas páginas intentan responder y que Lezama contestó a su manera: ¿podemos erradicar el nihilismo de nuestra cultura sin que debamos a su vez creer en la nada?" (35). Cf. del Risco (265).

4. See also García Marruz, *Darío, Martí y lo germinal americano* and *La familia de Orígenes*. In her books, García Marruz offers a genealogy of the libertarian ethics voiced by Darío, Martí, and Vallejo—which finds its culmination in Lezama himself. "Nuestro movimiento de libertad no era más que el ala estética del romanticismo libertario de nuestras gestas independentistas, que aún estaban inconclusas. . . . América lo necesitaba para ser" (*La familia* 29). Martí becomes for her the paradigmatic poet of that "vasto movimiento libertario" (*La familia* 67).

5. Ganoa Sousa declared the Revolution as the proper embodiment of all fundamental anarchist principles, and, also, that all anarchists who did not subscribe to this line were agents of the CIA or of empire. Then came the Gaona Document, which did a lot of damage in the mid- to late 1960s, by actively seeking to assure the international libertarian Left that the Revolution was in league with their cause, and that all the anarchists in exile were traitors.

Part II. The Writing of the Formless

1. "Nos acercamos a esos problemas de las formas, con el convencimiento de que el sujeto metafórico . . . destruye el pesimismo encubierto en la teoría de las constantes artísticas. Nuestro punto de vista parte de la imposibilidad de dos estilos semejantes . . . de la no identidad de dos formas aparentemente concluyentes, de lo creativo de un nuevo concepto de la causalidad histórica, que destruye el pseudo concepto temporal de que todo se dirige a lo contemporáneo, a un tiempo fragmentario."

2. The most prominent example of such comprehensiveness he could find was James Joyce's *Ulysses*. The novel's use of myth presents a way "of controlling, of ordering, of giving a shape and a significance to the immense panorama of futility and anarchy which is contemporary history" (Eliot 177). Salgado has shown to what extent Joyce's work is one of the intertexts that Lezama most thoroughly pursued.

3. The most thorough study of the deposition of linear causality and its consequences in the work of Lezama Lima is Brett Levinson's *Secondary Moderns*.

4. If one believes the criticism on Lezama, the difference between his stance and Eliot's is obscured to such a degree that it suggests something more than a simple case of misreading. For reasons that will become clear in what follows, what has ob-

scured this fairly straightforward distinction that Lezama makes, between his project and Eliot's, hinges on the specific, historically determined way in which aesthetics becomes politics in Cuba. The metaphorical subject is often grafted onto a romanticizing explanation of Lezama, based often on an inadequate historical pattern ascribed to romanticism, in which the unity of subject and object provides its defining characteristic. Commenting on Lezama's metaphoric subject, González Echevarría offers the paradigmatic misconception of this figure: "This text, which is image, supernature, imaginary era, poetry, arises from the interchangeability of subject and object. Its movement is like a network of metaphoric correspondences in which time and space have been abolished, except for the time or *durée* of the 'metaphoric subject.' But who is that being? Clearly, the answer must come from the mythological thinkers—Plato, Vico, Jung, Eliot—who attribute to the individual the ability to capture or express elemental forms, forms of the origin that are common to all of humankind" (*Celestina's* 215–16). It is exactly these kinds of elemental forms, supposedly common to all humanity, that Lezama rejects. The missed encounter with Lezama's difficulty serves also to put the poet in the odd position of being a tacit stand-in for the teleological rhetoric of the Cuban Revolution.

5. Acosta notes that the idea of resistance in narratives of emancipation and identity formation in and on Latin America is so central that "many have begun to see an uninterrupted, historically, and culturally specific legacy of antagonism that, beginning more than five hundred years ago, has become constitutive of Latin American identity as, in many ways, Latin America itself" (1). Cintio Vitier—that is, perhaps the most important figure in shaping Lezama's reception—is a case in point (see "Resistance and Freedom").

6. The first critic to point to the centrality of this figure in relation to Lezama was Pérez Firmat (1990).

7. Not long after the Revolution came to power, Lezama and others were accused of being oblivious to the demands of history, and by the late 1960s any author not practicing socialist realism was suspect in the eyes of the state.

8. The metaphoric subject will turn locomotion into a locomotive, an "expreso," in a poem we will examine below.

9. "En el vacío la velocidad no osa compararse, puede acariciar el infinito. Así el vacío queda definido e inerte como mundo de la no resistencia. También el vacío envía su primer grafía negativa para quedar como el no aire. . . . Sabemos por casi un invisible desperezar del no existir del vacío absoluto, no puede haber un infinito desligado de la sustancia divisible. . . . Pero supongamos algunas inverosimilitudes para ganar algunas delicias" (*Poesía* 159).

10. Here I rely on Badiou's reading of the *Physics* (in *Being*, meditation 6).

11. "Supongamos el ejército, el cordón de seda, el expreso, el puente, los rieles, el aire que se constituye en otro rostro tan pronto nos acercamos a la ventanilla. La gravedad no es la tortuga besando la tierra. El expreso tiene que estar siempre detenido sobre un puente de ancha base pétrea. Se va impulsando—como la impulsión de sonrisa, a risa, a carcajada, de un señor feudal después de la cena guarnida—, hasta decapitar tiernamente, hasta prescindir de los rieles, y por un exceso de la propia impulsión, deslizarse sobre el cordón de seda. Esa velocidad de progresión

infinita soportada por un cordón de seda de resistencia infinita, llega a nutrirse de
sus tangencias que tocan la tierra con un pie, o la pequeña caja de aire comprimido
situada entre sus pies y la espalda de la tierra (levedad, angelismos, turrón, alondras).
El ejército en reposo tiene que descansar sobre un puente de ancha base pétrea, se
va impulsando y llega a caber oculto detrás de un alamillo, después en un gusano de
espina dorsal surcada por un tiempo eléctrico. La velocidad de la progresión reduce
las tangencias, si la suponemos infinita, la tangencia es pulverizada: la realidad de la
caja de acero sobre el riel arquetípico, es decir, el cordón de seda, es de pronto de-
tenida, la constante progresión deriva otra sorpresa independiente de esa tangencia
temporal, el aire se torna duro como acero, y el expreso no puede avanzar porque
la potencia y la resistencia hácense infinitas. No se cae por la misma intensidad de la
caída. Mientras la potencia tórnase la impulsión incesante, el aire se mineraliza y la
caja móvil—sucesiva impulsada—, el cordón de seda y el aire como acero, no qui-
eren ser reemplazados por la grulla en un solo pie. Mejor que sustituir, restituir. ¿A
quién?" (*Poesía* 159–60).

12. The bibliography on this score is growing rapidly. See D'Ammando and Spadoni; Akner-Koler; Bois and Krauss; Didi-Huberman *La ressemblance informe* and *Ce
que nous voyons*; Walker; Morrey; Smith; A. Benjamin; Berney; Cox; Ryan; Duffy;
Leahy; Genosko; Murphy; Biles; Crowley and Hegarty; Bargmann; Eigen; Acconci;
formlessfinder; Foster; Bois; Allais; Morley.

13. Levinson offers a very illuminating reading on this score (*Secondary* 150–55).

14. Levinson explains why this is so: "In the 1956 essay 'Pascal y la poesía' Lezama takes up [the] issue [of the imperfect copy]: 'el náufrago recibido como el rey
desaparecido. Obrar como rey y tratarse como impostor, vivir en el misterio de la
doble naturaleza' (Lezama Lima, *Obras* 563). 'Double nature' here refers to the coincidence of a lost One (the king), on the one hand, and the *imperfecta copia* (the náufrago) of that one, on the other. The One, then, is both genuine and an imposter,
both the *sí mismo* and its flawed *reproduction*" (*Secondary* 67).

15. "Conocimiento de salvación," a short piece from 1939 that takes Paul Claudel
as its central subject, has been adduced by the criticism as Lezama's statement against
existentialism (Chiampi, "Teoría de la imagen" 487n3), and as an early manifestation
of his conservative Catholicism (Díaz, *Los límites* 18, 26; on Claudel and *Orígenes*
in general, see Rojas, *Tumbas* 115, 117). Rojas summarizes that conservative program in three points: "[1] the preference for the Catholicism of the Mediterranean
between the two wars, [2] the critique of the enlightenment and liberal traditions of
the modern West and [3] the poetic conception of history" (*Tumbas* 115). Although
it is not difficult, or surprising, to see in Claudel a poet toward whom Lezama
would have gravitated, it is, nevertheless, possible to overstate the points of contact
between the two. Most, if not all, readers of Lezama tend to pass over in silence significant differences, even though Lezama himself pointed this out early on. Even
in Lezama's (apparently) most univocal endorsement of Claudel ("Conocimiento de
salvación," the piece in question here), a gulf opens up between the two that is important to keep in mind, not only "to set the record straight" in and of itself, but because it gives us a more nuanced and complicated version of Lezama's Catholicism.
Furthermore, it is important to understand this Christianity if we are to grasp what

Lezama saw as the dominant aesthetic situation of his time and how he responded to it. This is a task that seems of particular importance and relevance as it will provide a contrasting view of the matter when compared to the recent and important contributions by Rafael Rojas and Duanel Díaz, cultural critics who emphasize the conservative aspects of Lezama's oeuvre.

16. For a reading of Saint Augustine as a thinker of the *informe*, read in tandem with Bataille, see Crowley and Hegarty, "Formless 1. Groundless Interpretations: Thought and Formless."

17. "'La tierra estaba desordenada y vacía y las tinieblas estaban sobre el haz del abismo.' Pero el Espíritu Santo y la luz fueron penetrando en las cosas. Es decir, que frente a las cosas tenemos un apoderamiento progresivo: el conocimiento; y una condenación regresiva: el tiempo. Conocimiento y tiempo constituyen en el hombre la gracia y el *fatum*."

18. The New Revised Standard Edition is more literal: "In the beginning when God created the heavens and the earth, the earth was a formless void and darkness covered the face of the deep, while a wind from God swept over the face of the waters." The King James translation: "In the beginning God created the heaven and the earth. And the earth was without form, and void." Lezama cites Casiodoro de Reina's translation.

19. Metanoia: "metáfora como *metanoia*, como metamorfosis de los griegos" (Lezama Lima, *Obras* 402); "la metáfora como *metanoia*, como adquirido súbito en la transformatio de los escolásticos . . . el despertar griego" (411); "metanoia, cambio de esencias" (1110). In Christian thought (beginning in the third, but particularly in the fourth centuries), *metanoia* means conversion as a sacrificial break within the self. It can mean two things: "*metanoia* is penitence and it is also a radical change of thought and mind. . . . [S]chematically . . . Christian *metanoia* seems to have the following characteristics. First, Christian conversion involves a sudden change. . . . [W]hether or not there is preparation, development, effort, ascesis—conversion . . . requires a single, sudden, both historical and metahistorical event which drastically changes and transforms the subject's mode of being at a single stroke. Second, in this conversion, this Christian *metanoia*, this sudden, dramatic, historical-metahistorical upheaval of the subject, there is a transition: a transition from one type of being to another, from death to life, from mortality to immortality, from darkness to light, from the reign of the devil to that of God, etcetera. And, finally, third, in this Christian conversion there is an element that is a consequence of the other two or which is found at their point of intersection, and this is that there can only be conversion inasmuch as a break takes place in the subject" (Foucault, *The Hermeneutics* 211). And further: "If conversion (Christian or post-Christian *metanoia*) takes the form of a break or change within the self, . . . consequently we can say that it is a sort of trans-subjectivation. . . . [It is a] way of introducing or marking an essential caesura in the subject" (214).

20. "Nos decidimos hacia un nuevo peligro, la grosera inmediatez de un desarrollo dialéctico en esas inmensas coordenadas centradas y aclaradas por la poesía, pues como al margen de esa prodigiosa sustancia que se avecina, nuestra época ofrece también una ominosa confluencia que lleva la poesía hacia la dialéctica, y ésta

de nuevo hacia las fuentes de lo primigenio, pero el intento nuestro es un sistema poético, partiendo desde las mismas posibilidades de la poesía y no un desarrollo dialéctico. Es decir, la poesía partiendo de la metáfora como superadora de la metamorfosis y de la *metanoia* del mundo antiguo; de la imagen como proporción y nueva causalidad entre el hombre y lo desconocido; . . . de la duda hiperbólica, como superadora de la síntesis."

21. "[C]apacidad devolutiva del sujeto," . . . "después que se ha perdido el imposible diálogo con la Naturaleza, después que rebanamos la mirada o que tememos al lenguaje táctil."

22. "Es esa evocación claudeliana una gracia suficiente por la que se produce en nosotros una vibración que puede sustituir al objeto mismo, o es ese conocimiento poético la única posibilidad de adentrarnos en el mundo enemigo y aún no descubierto."

23. Lezama elaborates on this Nietzschean Alexandrian-epoch and its effects on the senses of sight and touch in his essay on Paul Valéry from 1945 (see, in particular, the opening paragraphs, Lezama Lima, *Obras* 100–101).

24. Three historical developments present the constellation within which the human being becomes a genuine *subiectum*: (*a*) the invention of perspective; (*b*) the invention of the *cogito* and the beginning of the modern scientific mode of research; and (*c*) the discovery of the Americas and the development of mercantile capitalism). *Subiectum* is, in Heidegger's words: "that being upon which every being, in its way of being and its truth is founded. Man becomes the referential center of beings as such"—and this is only possible once there is a transformation in the understanding of beings as a whole: "Beings as a whole are now taken in such a way that a being is first and only in being insofar as it is set in place by representing-producing humanity. Whenever we have a world picture, an essential decision occurs concerning beings as a whole. The being of beings is sought in the representedness of beings" (Heidegger, *Off the Beaten Track* 67–68).

25. "Si por medio del nombre, la criatura puede alzarse hasta la plenitud . . . vemos, recordando la frase de Schiller . . . que el hombre sucumbe ante el tiempo que le convierte en objeto, que le resta dignidad."

26. "Con respecto de su relación con el espacio hínchase la criatura para alabar, desde la forma elemental del grito hasta la cabal conjuración de la plegaria. La fluencia temporal le retrotrae a la caída, al pecado original, a la angustia por la muerte."

27. "¿No es en una solución poética en la que piensa [Kierkegaard] para atrapar los *quiditas*? Mientras el acercarse de la poesía al desarrollo dialéctico ha tenido las consecuencias épicas de llevar la prolongación del momento inefable hasta el ámbito señoreado por la gracia; indomeñable la conducción de la identidad dialéctica a la zona sinuosidal del existir, ha tenido la peligrosidad hirviente de lanzar a la filosofía fuera de sus limitaciones esenciales. Lo que buscan los contemporáneos en la filosofía . . . es menos una explicación real de las cosas que una epopeya intelectual, una suerte de drama del espíritu, un poema subjetivo. Todos los grandes intentos poéticos contemporáneos, desde la poesía pura hasta el surrealismo, no son otra cosa que un esfuerzo desesperado por prolongar la percepción de temporalidad rapidísima. . . . Esa soñada dialéctica cualitativa de Kierkegaard no será acaso el sentido de

la coincidencia de percepción y estado sensible, una de las formas del conocimiento claudeliano, gótico, medioeval."

28. "[N]ada más que la pequeña presión de la mano para gobernar."

29. "En el salto de la lírica al drama: en el conocimiento de Dios."

30. We would do well to recall the characterization that Walter Benjamin made of this intelligence: "This *pure intelligence* that in Valéry has taken up its winter quarters on the inhospitable mountain peaks of esoteric poetry is, after all, identical with the intelligence under whose aegis the European bourgeoisie embarked on its voyages of conquest in the Age of Discovery. The Cartesian doubts about knowledge have been extended in Valéry in an almost reckless but also profound manner, to the point where they become doubts about the questions themselves: 'The realms of chance, the powers of the gods or Fate, are nothing but the symptoms of our own mental deficiencies. If we had an answer to everything—a precise answer, that is— these powers would not exist. . . . We feel this ourselves, and this is why we end up turning against our own questions. But that should be just the beginning. We ought to be able to formulate a question for ourselves that precedes all others and tests them in turn to see what they are worth' [Valéry, *Oeuvres* 647]. The strict return to such ideas to their context in the heroic period of the European bourgeoisie allows us to master the surprise at the encountering once more the idea of progress at such an advanced stage of the old European humanism. It is, furthermore, the valid and genuine idea of a progress transferable at the level of 'methodology'—a term that corresponds to Valéry's concept of 'construction' as neatly as it conflicts with the *idée fixe* of inspiration. As one of his contemporaries has claimed, 'The work of art is not a creation, but a construction in which analysis, calculation, and planning play the principal roles'" (2:534).

31. "[C]onstituyen *un ejercicio inoprtuno de nuestras facultades interrogantes.*"

32. "El traslado de ese fuego [*phusis*] por medio de aparatos y máquinas, le coloca en una categoría de residuo abandonado, en un instrumento al servicio de la disciplina estoica."

33. "Esta creación que multiplica lo perfecto se nutre de su hastío."

34. "[C]ontinuar sin saber, responder precisamente aquello que no nos atrevemos a preguntar."

35. For Lezama, Valéry is heir to the Stoics up to a point. He claims that Valéry is a Stoic in regards to sensations, but a Catholic Thomist vis-à-vis the body; the fact that Valéry's ontology does not rely on the idea of the *logos spermatikos* and the appearance of the problem of the *durée* leads Lezama to claim that what we are dealing with is more in tune with the return to the Stoics in the philosophy of Bergson— even if Valéry refused to accept Bergson as an influence (*Obras* 111–12).

36. "Si los estoicos ejemplifican la lucha del cuerpo y el vacío en la marcha del pez, para los cristianos el problema aparece en forma de rudo combate. Es necesaria . . . la lucha contra el pez. . . . Su instantaneidad pasa fría por nuestras manos como un recuerdo de la indetención del tiempo. Al mismo tiempo que el pez no siente la presencia del vacío como una angustia o comprensión, resuelve totalmente con el paso de sus escamas la nietzscheana felicidad en el terror, y llega a sentir como una seda a su presión instantánea los infinitos

puntos muertos, como la larga soledad de Satán entre las rocas, esperando la ruptura."

37. "Queda: el gran combate, la altísima dignidad del católico: cara a cara con el tremendo pez, con Dios mismo."

38. From a similar Catholic perspective, in an essay on Lezama's *Dador*, Fina García Marruz uses "causality" and "the interlinking of nothings" interchangeably ("Por *Dador* de José Lezama Lima" 109).

39. A case in point would be the multimedia artifact known as *Una estación en el ingenio*, where Lezama's texts accompany the photographs of sugarcane workers taken by Chinolope. The goal was a text that would help in the task of mythologizing the figure of the worker as the builder of the nation. What we get is far more ambiguous, one might even venture, counterrevolutionary—beginning with the comparison, suggested by the play on Rimbaud's title, between being at work and being in hell (see López Junqué).

40. On the work of the Infrapolitical Deconstruction Collective, see the dossier in *Transmodernity: Journal of Peripheral Cultural Production of the Luso-Hispanic World* (5.1 [2015]), https://escholarship.org/uc/ssha_transmodernity.

41. It is important to to keep the following in mind, for it is the scene from which we ourselves think, even when we are unaware of the fact: "It is indeed something of this genre that Blanchot tries to enables us to think, for example—to limit ourselves to one of the threads he has begun drawing from the Romantic fabric—in his interrogation of 'fragmentary writing.' Something of this sort is also at stake in the most insistent of Heidegger's meditations, the meditation on language, which is largely undertaken with Humboldt (or in other words, along with a body of research that in many ways prolongs that of the Schlegels), and which, citing Jean Paul and glossing Novalis and Hölderlin, leads, as if thorugh the margins of romanticism, to the question of what, more 'proper' than all propriety, speaks in language [la parole]. And Derrida's work on and around writing, the trace, and the dissemination of writing continues to proceed in the direction of this 'thing'—if indeed it implies a direction to take.—Is it necessary to add that never for a moment did the romantics even imagine . . . a single one of these thoughts? They are instead eclipsed within romanticism" (Lacoue-Labarthe and Nancy 124).

42. A more recent restatement of all of these issues can be found in Badiou ("L'âge de poètes"). Reading Badiou, however, one gets the impression that it is a matter of poetry suffering a long captivity—a poetry in need of a liberator, who he sees in Paul Celan, and, on the philosophical side, of course, in himself (*Manifesto* 77). Baudelaire does not figure anywhere in Badiou's reading of modernity.

43. "Baudelaire . . . comprende que cuando la palabra se libera de toda gravitación y logra total nacimiento y pureza, surge entonces por rara adquisición de su reverso, el irremplazable verbal . . . , y el trabajo de su mágica insistencia, adquiere entonces como el residuo de toda libre elección, la más inaudita dignidad. Baudelaire, en esto también como en todo, *dandy* perfecto, comprende lo que los católicos llaman . . . la buena intención asidua, que resuelve las bruscas agresiones o armonizaciones entre el destino y la dignidad. Lo natural excesivo se va tornado en un gracioso movimiento del hombre, que ahora lucha irreconciliablemente con los

grandes . . . temas, eliminada toda fatalidad de nueva especie, con la gracia, destino y pecado original."

44. In my estimation it is not; Cruz-Malavé privides a very detailed argument regarding the centrality of homosexuality in the novel (88–93).

45. "Hemos sido dictados, es decir, éramos necesarios para que el cumplimiento de una voz superior tocase orilla, se sintiese en terreno seguro. La rítmica interpretación de la voz superior, sin intervención de la voluntad casi, es decir, una voluntad que ya venía envuelta por un destino superior, nos hacía disfrutar de un impulso que era al mismo tiempo una aclaración. . . ."

46. "El rayo que había destruido el árbol había liberado a Foción de la adoración de su eternidad circular."

47. "Ahora podía comprender Fronesis que Foción estaba habitado por la infinitud de una esencia errante y paradojalmente encarnada en un solo cuerpo."

48. "[Y]a sin la finitud del cuerpo, ya con la infinitud de la imagen"; "La imagen y la extensión del sueño se volvía dichosa como la escarcha que se funde en el árbol de una hoguera."

49. "Era el placer de las cosas que se desconocen, por un retiramiento de todo lo conocido"

50. "Ese era también el momento en que el muñecón erasmita caería de su tarima, volándose las tiras de papel, manchadas por la sangre de la escribanía."

51. "[Fronesis] volvió a entrar en la casa, pero en ese intervalo la casa se había vuelto sobre sí misma . . . para fortalecer la casa de cualquier acechanza. . . . La casa, ya sin los moradores que se habían marchado como íncubos a la madrugada, lucía como un reflector sobre el mar, su blancura se refractaba. . . . Al irse Galeb, Champollion y Margaret, la casa parecía que se había estirado, pues así como antes le había permanecido indiferente, ahora, cuando se paseaba solo por ella tenía la sensación de algo que lo había esperado, que había permanecido oculto, que necesitaba verlo en su soledad para darse a conocer por los destellos de una cal, antes fría, que ahora lucía todas sus lámparas como una mina de diamantes."

52. "La fortaleza que no puede destruir el tiempo en la sobrenaturaleza."

53. "Fronesis volvió a estar desnudo. Su cuerpo descendía como los golpes dados en la tierra por el bastón poliédrico de una purificación. Se sentía desamparado en los confines. . . . Se sentó en el suelo, en una de las esquinas de la sala. Su pensamiento se anegaba, pero su energía comenzó a dilatarse hasta alcanzar su plenitud, pero era ahora su propia mano la que empuñaba su realidad y su sueño; ya no había que rechazar ni que aceptar. Era, por el contrario, una aceptación cósmica."

54. "[V]olvían los personajes no novelables del comienzo de los mundos."

55. "En la esquina . . . se esbozaba un menguante disimulado en la transparencia. El menguante servía de basamento a una concha."

56. "Pudo observar que la concha . . . estaba vacía. Le cegaban a Fronesis los reflejos de la concha, brotaban de un centro que por permanecer oscuro parecía como vaciedad. Miraba de nuevo hacia la esquina y le parecía que desde muy lejos alguien venía a buscarlo. Alguien marchaba hacia el centro de la concha, pero su punto luminoso desaparecía tragado por la iridiscencia que despedían los colores mezclados [de la concha]. Miraba ahora con más fijeza, pero a medida que el punto luminoso

se trocaba en figura, la concha sobre el menguante iba desapareciendo, hasta desvanecerse en su totalidad."

57. For nationalist and revolutionary links, see the critical 1988 edition of *Paradiso*, prepared by Cintio Vitier (*Paradiso [Archivos]* 508n33), as well as García Marruz's "La poesía es un caracol nocturno" (243ff.). For the theological connection, see González Cruz (esp. cxii–cxiii). In "Las playas del árbol" (1955), Lezama offers the following as a definition of poetry: "¿La poesía? Un caracol nocturno en un rectángulo de agua" (*Obras* 510).

58. "Araño en la pared con la uña,/ la cal va cayendo/ como si fuese un/ pedazo de la concha / de la tortuga celeste. / . . . / Me duermo en el *tokonoma*/ evaporo el otro que sigue caminando" (*Poesía* 450).

59. Though right from the start the title itself is indication of the ironic tenor of Lezama's Platonism. For if, in the Plato, reminiscence is our way to knowledge of the perfect Ideas, the being of beings, what takes place in Lezamas's anamnesis is related not to the original, but to what is similar.

60. "¿Hay una total pluralidad en la semejanza? / . . . / Creer que la pluralidad se opone a la semejanza,/ es olvidar que todas las narices forman el olifante / . . . / La semejanza no coincidirá con lo homogéneo."

61. "Lo uno tiene que llegarnos como un bulto / con el cual tropezamos, pues lo uno se acecha / por exclusión."

62. Bataille: "affirming that the universe resembles nothing and is only *formless* amounts to saying that the universe is something like . . . spit" (31).

63. See, in the bibliography, the work that comes after the publication of *Línea de sombra* in 2006.

64. (1) Classical—mimesis, in the sense that the poem seeks to adequately be true to a world that is prior to it: and it can be either reactive (seeking to dominate an entire field of experience) or active (seeking to establish a new modality of experience) (*Tercer espacio* 274); (2) Romantic—consciousness seeking to become identical to the object that it desires obsessively, but which, at the same time, alienates it from itself: "nostalgia for the lost unity. . . . The sundered consciousness . . . turns the gap into the plenitude of the object, to the point that it ascribes to the gap all the attributes of the most extreme singularity. . . . [O]bsessive writing is always logocentric, even if its logos is the site of the most profound alienation and death" (276); it can be reactive (theological) or active (atheological). (3) Baroque—repetition of the indifferent: "Faced with the pure excess of identity [reactive], the repetition of the indifferent hides itself in the imperative necessity of guarding only that which, always erased by the excess, makes the excess impossible" (276). The dichotomy active/ reactive is not present here because this kind of writing establishes itself prior to the logical excesses of the metaphysical will (277).

65. "Ustedes . . . son el pequeño diablo aburrido. . . . Son un aparte como el vacío. . . . Son el pequeño desierto que cada barrio ofrece, instalan un estilo de vida que se fragmenta, que no fluye, donde todo se hace irreconocible. . . . Qué alegre, qué primitivo, qué sencillamente creador, un mundo donde ya ustedes no estén."

66. "Le parecía que un cuesco podía ser la gran nube que en un momento imprescindible cubriría el cielo como un culo descomunal tapando la tierra, con sus

llamas y nubes bermejas los trompetazos finales. . . . La intempestiva presencia de ese neuma le bastaba para confirmar el Maligno, verlo ya aposentado en la ventana tocando la flauta."

67. "Recuerdo ahora—dijo—, una teoría imagen de su amigo—Fronesis comprendió de inmediato que aludía a Cemí cuando evocaba al ferrocarril sobre un acueducto romano, se va impulsando hasta alcanzar una velocidad uniformemente acelerada, llegando a prescindir de los rieles y pudiendo entonces reemplazar el puente romano por una cinta de seda. Concluyó—: cuando más leve es la tangencia, y tangencia quiere decir aquí paradojalmente sustitución, tiene más levitación la imagen, es decir, la imagen es un cuerpo que se desprende de lo estelar a lo telúrico. Era el viejo consejo de los alquimistas."

68. "[E]s una estupidez al revés, una locura lúcida que raya el diamante y después diviniza el polvillo desprendido por la piedra."

69. "Creo ya lo de barroco va resultando un término apestoso."

70. "[Q]ue los dos últimos ritmos de progresión verbales son interrupciones. Lo que interrumpe las ideas . . . marcha acompañado por la voz que fuerza."

71. "[L]a otra trinidad que surge en el ocaso de las religiones."

Conclusion

1. Reversibility, I want to point out, is not something that has gone entirely unnoticed in the criticism on Lezama. Juan Pablo Lupi and César A. Salgado, to name but two, have alluded to this phenomenon in foregrounding Lezama's dislocation of linear historical causality (Lupi 152, 61), as well as in the poet's reading practices—Salgado has shown to what extent Lezama reverses Borges and Joyce (34, 70, 86, 136).

2. "[S]entimos el deseo de que . . . el pueblo llegara a adquirir esos inmensos dominios donde la muerte no se diferenciaba de la vida y donde toda interrupción, todo fracaso, toda vacilación quedará suprimida, pues la luz y lo sumergido, los envíos de lo estelar y la devolución de lo sumergido, deberían haber ya alcanzado en nuestra época, habiéndose dejado vergonzosamente esos dominios a los físicos, una identidad prodigiosa."

3. "Si nuestra época ha alcanzado una indeterminable fuerza de destrucción, hay que hacer la revolución que cree una indeterminable fuerza de creación, que fortalezca los recuerdos, que precise los sueños, que corporice las imágenes, que le de un mejor trato a los muertos, que le de a los efímeros una suntuosa lectura de su transparencia, permitiéndole a los vivientes una navegación segura y corriente por ese tenebrario, una destrucción de esa acumulación, no por la energía vitalizada por el diablo, sino por un cometa que los penetre por la totalidad de una médula oblongada, de un transmisor que vaya de lo táctil a lo invisible . . . chupando la estalactita estelar como un caramelo, lo que se llamaba en el ceremonial de los antiguos chinos, *mamar el cielo.*"

4. "Lentamente se fue remansando, después prosiguió sin dejar de hacer visible su temblor. Causaba la impresión de que era la primera vez que alguien oía sus confi-

dencias, que Fronesis era el primero que le había despertado confianza para mostrar lo que en su vida había sido un secreto."

5. Ironically, as well, this is a name that would point toward a return to one of the basic themes of pre-Revolution intellectual life. Consider in this regard a representative testimony of that time: for Guy Pérez Cisneros, the epoch represents "un vacío informe, irrespirable"—"un vacío desesperante" (*Obras* 58). This is seen as an environment that causes "náusea y vergüenza" (59).

6. "Ahora, en la reversibilidad de extensión y magnitud, el reloj, como máscara de la temporalidad, vacila, rectifica, cobra conciencia de sus imposibilidades al rendirse a sus inexactitudes."

7. "La historia no es entonces, como pretende la ideología dominante, el sometimiento del hombre al tiempo lineal continuo, sino su liberación de ese tiempo. . . . un verdadero materialista histórico no es aquel que persigue a lo largo del tiempo lineal infinito un vacuo espejismo de progreso continuo, sino aquel que en todo momento está en condiciones de detener el tiempo porque conserva el recuerdo de que la patria original del hombre es el placer."

Bibliography

Abrams, M. H. *The Correspondent Breeze: Essays on English Romanticism*. New York: Norton, 1984.

Acconci, Vito. "De/Form/Ing/Form/Form/Ing/Form/Less." *Storefront for Art and Architecture Manifesto Series 1*. Ed. Garrett Ricciardi and Julian Rose. Zürich: Lars Müller, 2013. 188–170 (even number pages only in descending order).

Acosta, Abraham. *Thresholds of Illiteracy: Theory, Latin America, and the Crisis of Resistance*. New York: Fordham University Press, 2014.

Adelman, Jeremy. ed. *Colonial Legacies: The Problem of Persistence in Latin America*. New York: Routledge, 1999.

Agamben, Giorgio. *The Time That Remains: A Commentary on the Letter to the Romans*. 2000. Trans. Patricia Dailey. Stanford: Stanford University Press, 2005.

Akner-Koler, Cheryl. *Form and Formlessness: Questioning Aesthetic Abstractions through Art Projects, Cross-Disciplinary Studies and Product Design Education*. Stockholm: Axl, 2007.

Alegría, Fernando. "Antiliteratura." *América Latina en su literature*. Ed. César Fernández Moreno. Mexico City: Siglo XXI, 1972.

Allais, Lucia. "Formless." *Storefront for Art and Architecture Manifesto Series 1*. Ed. Garrett Ricciardi and Julian Rose. Zürich: Lars Müller, 2013. 1–43 (odd number pages only).

Allen, Thomas M. *A Republic in Time: Temporality and Social Imagination in Nineteenth-Century America*. Chapel Hill: University of North Carolina Press, 2008.

Alliez, Éric. *Capital Times: Tales from the Conquest of Time*. 1991. Trans. Georges Van Den Abbeele. Minneapolis: University of Minnesota Press, 1996.

Althusser, Louis, and Étienne Balibar. *Reading Capital*. Trans. Ben Brewster. London: Verso, 2004.

Arendt, Hannah. *On Revolution*. 1965. London: Penguin, 1990.

Aristotle. "Physics." Trans. R. K. Gaye and R. P. Hardie. *The Complete Works of Aristotle*. Ed. Jonathan Barned. Vol. 1. Princeton: Princeton University Press, 1984. 315–446.

Artaraz, Kepa. *Cuba and Western Intellectuals since 1959*. New York: Palgrave Macmillan, 2009.

Augustine. *Confessions*. Trans. F. J. Sheed. Indianapolis: Hackett, 1993.

Badiou, Alain. *The Adventure of French Philosophy*. Trans. Bruno Bosteels. London: Verso, 2012.

———. "L'âge de poètes." *La politique des poètes: Pourquoi des poètes en temps de détresse*. Ed. Jacques Rancière. Paris: Albin Michel, 1992. 21–38.

———. *Being and Event*. 1988. Trans. Oliver Feltham. New York: Continuum, 2005.

———. *Ethics: An Essay on the Understanding of Evil*. Trans. Peter Hallward. London: Verso, 2001.

———. "Liminaire sur l'ouvrage d'Alain Badiou 'L'etre et l'evenement.'" *Le Cahier (Collège international de philosophie)* 8 (Oct. 1989): 247–68.

———. *Logics of Worlds. Being and Event II*. Trans. Alberto Toscano. London: Continuum, 2009.

———. *Manifesto for Philosophy*. Trans. Norman Madarasz. Albany: State University of New York Press, 1999.

———. *El ser y el acontecimiento*. 1988. Trans. Alejandro A. Carletti, Raúl J. Cerdeiras, and Nilda Prados. Buenos Aires: Manantial, 1999.

Bargmann, Julie. "Finding the Formless." *Storefront for Art and Architecture Manifesto Series 1*. Ed. Garrett Ricciardi and Julian Rose. Zürich: Lars Müller, 2013. 18–12 (even number pages only in descending order).

Barquet, Jesús J. *Teatro y revolución cubana: Subversión y utopía en Los siete contra Tebas de Antón Arrufat*. Lewiston, NY: Edwin Mellen, 2002.

Barthes, Roland. "The Old Rhetoric: An Aide-Mémoire." *The Semiotic Challenge*. Trans. Richard Howard. Berkeley: University of California Press, 1994. 11–94.

Bataille, Georges. *The Unfinished System of Nonknowledge*. Trans. Michelle Kendall and Stuart Kendall. Ed. Stuart Kendall. Minneapolis: University of Minnesota Press, 2001.

———. *Visions of Excess: Selected Writings, 1927–1939*. Trans. Allan Stoekl, Carl R. Lovitt, and Donald M. Leslie Jr. Ed. Allan Stoekl. Minneapolis: University of Minnesota Press, 1985.

Bauman, Zygmunt. *In Search of Politics*. Stanford: Stanford University Press, 1999.

Bejel, Emilio. *José Lezama Lima, Poet of the Image*. Gainesville: University of Florida Press, 1990.

Benjamin, Andrew. "The Matter of a Materialist Philosophy of Art: Bataille's Manet." *Formless: Ways In and Out of Form*. Ed. Patrick Crowley and Paul Hegarty. Oxford: Peter Lang, 2005. 193–214.

Benjamin, Walter. *Selected Writings*. Trans. Howard Eiland et al. Ed. Michael W. Jennings et al. 4 vols. Cambridge: Belknap Press of Harvard University Press, 1996–2003.

Bergson, Henri. *L'évolution créatrice*. 52nd ed. Paris: Presses Universitaires de France, 1907.

Berney, Patricia. "*L'abbé C.*: Strategies of Formless." *Formless: Ways In and Out of Form*. Ed. Patrick Crowley and Paul Hegarty. Oxford: Peter Lang, 2005. 173–84.

Bernstein, Susan. "On Music Framed: The Eolian Harp in Romantic Writing." *The Figure of Music in Nineteenth-Century British Poetry*. Ed. Phyllis Weliver. Hampshire, UK: Ashgate, 2005. 70–84.

Beverley, John. "Introduction: From Cuba." *boundary 2* 29, no. 3 (2002): 1–11.

———. *Latinamericanism after 9/11*. Durham, NC: Duke University Press, 2011.

Beverley, John, José Oviedo, and Michael Aronna, eds. *The Postmodern Debate in Latin America*. Durham, NC: Duke University Press, 1995.

Biles, Jeremy. "Meditations at the Midway: The Work of Fantasy in the Thought of Georges Bataille." *Formless: Ways In and Out of Form*. Ed. Patrick Crowley and Paul Hegarty. Oxford: Peter Lang, 2005. 53–66.

Biset, Emmanuel. "Contra la diferencia política." *Pensamiento Plural* 7 (July/Dec. 2010): 173–202.

Blanchot, Maurice. 1955. *The Space of Literature*. Trans. Ann Smock. Lincoln: University of Nebraska Press, 1982.

Blight, James G., and Janet M. Lang. *The Fog of War: Lessons from the Life of Robert S. McNamara*. Lanham, MD: Rowman and Littlefield, 2005.

Bloom, Harold. *The Visionary Company: A Reading of English Romantic Poetry*. 1961. Ithaca: Cornell University Press, 1971.

Bois, Yve-Alain. "From Arte Concreta to Arte Neoconcreta." *Storefront for Art and Architecture Manifesto Series 1*. Ed. Garrett Ricciardi and Julian Rose. Zürich: Lars Müller, 2013. 45–67 (odd number pages only).

Bois, Yve-Alain, and Rosalind E. Krauss. *Formless: A User's Guide*. New York: Zone, 1997.

Bosteels, Bruno. *The Actuality of Communism*. New York: Verso, 2010.

———. *Badiou and Politics*. Durham, NC: Duke University Press, 2011.

———. "The Efficacy of Theory, or, What Are Theorists for in Times of Riots and Distress?" *South Atlantic Quarterly* 113.4 (2014): 659–70.

———. *Marx and Freud in Latin America: Politics, Psychoanalysis, and Religion in Times of Terror*. London: Verso, 2012.

———. "Translator's Introduction." *The Adventure of French Philosophy*. London: Verso, 2012. vii–l.

Buckwalter-Arias, James. *Cuba and the New Origenismo*. Suffolk: Tamesis, 2010.

Burns, Gerald L. *On the Anarchy of Poetry and Philosophy: A Guide for the Unruly*. New York: Fordham University Press, 2006.

Cabrera Infante, Guillermo. *Tres tristes tigres*. 1967. Biblioteca Breve. Barcelona: Seix Barral, 2005.

Camus, Albert. *The Rebel: An Essay on Man and Revolt*. 1951. Trans. Anthony Bower. Foreword by Sir Herbert Read. New York: Vintage, 1991.

Casarino, Cesare. *Modernity at Sea: Melville, Marx, Conrad in Crisis*. Minneapolis: University of Minnesota Press, 2002.

Castro, Fidel. *Venezuela y Chávez*. New York: Ocean Sur, 2006.

Celan, Paul. "The Meridian." Trans. Jerry Glenn. *Sovereignties in Question: The Poetics of Paul Celan*. By Jacques Derrida. Ed. Thomas Dutoit and Outi Pasanen. New York: Fordham University Press, 2005. 173–85.

Chávez Frías, Hugo. *La unidad latinoamericana*. New York: Ocean Sur, 2006.

Chiampi, Irlemar. "Teoría de la imagen y teoría de la lectura en Lezama Lima." *Nueva Revista de Filología Hispánica* 35.2 (1987): 485–501.

Chomsky, Aviva. *A History of the Cuban Revolution*. Malden, MA: Wiley-Blackwell, 2011.

Clemens, Justin. *The Romanticism of Contemporary Theory: Institution, Aesthetics, Nihilism*. Burlington, VT: Ashgate, 2003.

Coleridge, Samuel Taylor. *The Portable Coleridge*. Ed. I. A. Richards. New York: Viking, 1961.

Cortázar, Julio. "Para llegar a Lezama Lima." *La vuelta al día en ochenta mundos.* 1967. Vol. 2. Mexico City: Siglo XXI, 1972. 41–81.

Cox, Fiona. "The Formlessness of Hugo's Epic World." *Formless: Ways In and Out of Form.* Ed. Patrick Crowley and Paul Hegarty. Oxford: Peter Lang, 2005. 161–72.

Crowley, Patrick, and Paul Hegarty. "Formless 1. Groundless Interpretations: Thought and Formless." *Formless: Ways In and Out of Form.* Ed. Patrick Crowley and Paul Hegarty. Oxford: Peter Lang, 2005. 17–26.

———. "Formless 2. Within and Between: Literature and Formless." *Formless: Ways In and Out of Form.* Ed. Patrick Crowley and Paul Hegarty. Oxford: Peter Lang, 2005. 105–12.

———. "Formless 3. The Interminable Detour of Form: Art and Formless." *Formless: Ways In and Out of Form.* Ed. Patrick Crowley and Paul Hegarty. Oxford: Peter Lang, 2005. 185–92.

———. Introduction. *Formless: Ways In and Out of Form.* Ed. Patrick Crowley and Paul Hegarty. Oxford: Peter Lang, 2005. 9–15.

Cruz-Malavé, Arnaldo. *El primitivo implorante: El "sistema poético del mundo" de José Lezama Lima.* Amsterdam: Rodopi, 1994.

D'Ammando, Andrea, and Matteo Spadoni. *Letture dell'informe: Rosalind Krauss e Georges Didi-Huberman.* Rome: Lithos, 2014.

Deleuze, Gilles. *Bergsonism.* 1966. Trans. Hugh Tomlinson and Barbara Habberjam. New York: Zone, 1988.

Delgado, Manuel. *El animal público: Hacia una antropología de los espacios urbanos.* Barcelona: Anagram, 1999.

Derrida, Jacques. *Glas.* 1974. Trans. John P. Leavey and Richard Rand. Lincoln: University of Nebraska Press, 1986.

———. *Margins of Philosophy.* 1972. Trans. Alan Bass. Chicago: University of Chicago Press, 1982.

———. *Points . . .* Trans. Peggy Kamuf et al. Stanford: Stanford University Press, 1995.

———. *Sovereignties in Question: The Poetics of Paul Celan.* Ed. Thomas Dutoit and Outi Pasanen. New York: Fordham University Press, 2005.

———. *Writing and Difference.* 1967. Trans. Alan Bass. London: Routledge, 2001.

Díaz, Duanel. *Los límites del origenismo.* Madrid: Editorial Colibrí, 2005.

———. *Palabras del trasfondo: Intelectuales, literatura e ideología en la Revolución Cubana.* Madrid: Editorial Colibríi, 2009.

Didi-Huberman, Georges. *Ce que nous voyons, ce qui nous regarde.* Paris: Les Éditions de Minuit, 1992.

———. *La ressemblance informe, ou le gai savoir visuel selon Georges Bataille.* Paris: Macula, 1995.

Dopico, Ana. "Family Portraits with Fidel." *CubaCargo/Cult.* https://cubacargo-cult.wordpress.com/2015/04/02/family-portraits-with-fidel/.

Duchesne Winter, Juan. *La guerrilla narrada: Acción, acontecimiento, sujeto.* San Juan, Puerto Rico: Ediciones Callejón, 2010.

———. "*Paradiso* como proyecto político." *Casa de las Américas* 261 (2010): 31–42.

Duffy, Larry. "*Les mots font leurs besognes: Informe* as High-Low Hybridity on Board the *Ville-de-Montereau.*" *Formless: Ways In and Out of Form.* Ed. Patrick Crowley and Paul Hegarty. Oxford: Peter Lang, 2005. 125–38.

Eigen, Edward. "The Passion of Louis Braille: An Historico-Religio-Sphragistic Essay." *Storefront for Art and Architecture Manifesto Series 1.* Ed. Garrett Ricciardi and Julian Rose. Zürich: Lars Müller, 2013. 156–120 (even number pages only in descending order).

Eliot, T. S. *Selected Prose of T. S. Eliot.* Ed. Frank Kermode. New York: Farrar, Straus and Giroux, 1975.

Fédida, Pierre. "The Movement of the Informe." *Qui Parle* 10.1 (1996): 49–62.

Fernández, Frank. *Cuban Anarchism: The History of a Movement.* Trans. Charles Bufe. Tucson: See Sharp, 2001.

Fernández Retamar, Roberto. *Antología personal.* Mexico City: Siglo XXI, 2007.

formlessfinder. "Besides Form." *Storefront for Art and Architecture Manifesto Series 1.* Ed. Garrett Ricciardi and Julian Rose. Zürich: Lars Müller, 2013. 97–115 (odd number pages only).

Foster, Hal. "Doing the Perceiving for Us." *Storefront for Art and Architecture Manifesto Series 1.* Ed. Garrett Ricciardi and Julian Rose. Zürich: Lars Müller, 2013. 69–91 (odd number pages only).

———. *The Return of the Real: The Avant-Garde at the End of the Century.* Cambridge: MIT Press, 1996.

Foster, Hal, et al. "The Politics of the Signifier II: A Conversation on the 'Informe' and the Abject." *October* 67 (Winter 1994): 3–21.

Foucault, Michel. *The Hermeneutics of the Subject: Lectures at the Collège de France 1981–1982.* Trans. Graham Burchell. Ed. Frédéric Gros and Arnold I. Davidson. New York: Picador, 2004.

———. *History of Madness.* 1961. Trans. Jonathan Murphy and Jean Khalfa. Ed. Jean Khalfa. London: Routledge, 2009.

Franco, Jean. *Critical Passions: Selected Essays.* Ed. Mary Louise Pratt and Kathleen Elizabeth Newman. Durham: Duke University Press, 1999.

———. "Lezama Lima en el Paraíso de la poesía." *Vórtice: Literatura, Arte y Crítica* 1.1 (1974): 30–48.

Freud, Sigmund. *The Interpretation of Dreams.* Trans. James Strachey. New York: Bard/Avon, 1998.

Fuentes de la Paz, Iveette. *La incesante temporallidad de la poesía.* Santiago: Editorial de Oriente, 2006.

Galli, Carlo. *Genealogia della politica: Carl Schmitt e la crisi del pensiero político moderno.* 1996. 2nd ed. Bologna: Il Mulino, 2010.

———. *La mirada de Jano: Ensayos sobre Carl Schmitt.* 2008. Trans. María Julia de Ruschi. Mexico City: Fondo de Cultura Económica, 2011.

García Marruz, Fina. *Darío, Martí y lo germinal americano.* 1984. Havana: Unión, 2001.

———. *La familia de Orígenes.* Havana: Unión, 1997.

———. "La poesía es un caracol nocturno." *Casa de las Américas* 134 (1982): 132–49.

———. "Por *Dador* de José Lezama Lima." *Recopilación de textos sobre José Lezama Lima.* Ed. Pedro Simón. Havana: Casa de las Américas, 1970. 107–26.

García Vega, Lorenzo. *Los años de Orígenes.* Buenos Aires: Bajo la Luna, 2007.

Genosko, Gary. "The Spirit of Symbolic Exchange: Jean Baudrillard's 9/11." *Formless: Ways In and Out of Form.* Ed. Patrick Crowley and Paul Hegarty. Oxford: Peter Lang, 2005. 91–103.

González Cruz, Iván. "José Lezama Lima o el ser de la aurora." *Antología para un sistema poético del mundo de José Lezama Lima*. Ed. Iván González Cruz. Vol. 1. Valencia: Editorial de la UPV, 2004. xv–cxxxviii.

González Echevarría, Roberto. *Celestina's Brood: Continuities of the Baroque in Spanish and Latin American Literature*. Durham, NC: Duke University Press, 1993.

———. *La ruta de Severo Sarduy*. Hanover, NH: Ediciones del Norte, 1987.

Gracián, Baltazar. *Obras de Lorenzo Gracián*. 2 vols. Vol. 1. Barcelona: Imprenta de María Angela Martí y Galí Viuda, 1757.

Guerrero, Fernando. *José Lezama Lima: El maestro en broma*. Madrid: Verbum, 2013.

Guevara, Ernesto Che. *Obra revolucionaria*. Ed. Roberto Fernández Retamar. Mexico City: Era, 1968.

———. *Pasajes de la Guerra Revolucionaria*. Melbourne: Ocean, 2006.

Hallward, Peter. *Badiou: A Subject to Truth*. Minneapolis: University of Minnesota Press, 2003.

Hegel, Georg W. F. *Hegel on Tragedy*. Trans. F. P. B. Osmaston et al. Ed. Anne Paolucci and Henry Paolucci. Garden City, NY: Doubleday, 1962.

———. *Lectures on the Philosophy of World History: Introduction*. Trans. H. B. Nisbet. Cambridge: Cambridge University Press, 1975.

———. *Phenomenology of Spirit*. Trans. A. V. Miller. Oxford: Oxford University Press, 1977.

Heidegger, Martin. *Being and Time*. 1927. Trans. Joan Stambaugh. Albany: State University of New York, 1996.

———. *Nietzsche*. Trans. David Farrell Krell. 4 vols. Vols. 1 and 2. New York: HarperCollins, 1991.

———. *Off the Beaten Track*. Trans and ed. Julian Young and Kenneth Haynes. Cambridge: Cambridge University Press, 2002.

———. *Pathmarks*. Trans and ed. William McNeill. Cambridge: Cambridge University Press, 1998.

Heller, Ben A. *Assimilation/Generation/Resurrection: Contrapuntal Readings in the Poetry of José Lezama Lima*. Lewisburg PA: Bucknell University Press; Cranbury, NJ: Associated University Presses, 1997.

Jameson, Fredric. *The Cultural Turn: Selected Writings on the Postmodern, 1983–1998*. London: Verso, 1998.

———. *Valences of the Dialectic*. London: Verso, 2009.

Johnson, David E. "*As if* the Time Were Now: Deconstructing Agamben." *South Atlantic Quarterly* 106.2 (2007): 265–90.

Kraniauskas, John. "Difference Against Development: Spiritual Accumulation and the Politics of Freedom." *boundary 2* 32.2 (2005): 53–80.

Kristeva, Julia. *Pulsions du temps*. Ed. David Uhrig and Christina Kkona. Paris: Fayard, 2013.

———. *Revolution in Poetic Language*. 1974. Trans. Margaret Waller. New York: Columbia University Press, 1984.

Lacan, Jacques. *The Ego in Freud's Theory and in the Technique of Psychoanalysis, 1954–1955*. Trans. Sylvana Tomaselli. Ed. Jacques-Alain Miller. New York: Norton, 1991.

Laclau, Ernesto. *On Populist Reason*. New York: Verso, 2005.

Lacoue-Labarthe, Philippe, and Jean-Luc Nancy. *The Literary Absolute: The Theory of Literature in German Romanticism.* 1978. Trans. Philip Barnard and Cheryl Lester. Albany: State University of New York Press, 1988.

Lambie, George. *The Cuban Revolution in the 21st Century.* New York: Pluto, 2010.

Lausberg, Heinrich. *Elementos de retórica literaria.* 1963. Trans. Mariano Marín Casero. Madrid: Gredos, 1975.

Leahy, Caitríona. "Bataille and Kafka. Or: Formless Takes Shape." *Formless: Ways In and Out of Form.* Ed. Patrick Crowley and Paul Hegarty. Oxford: Peter Lang, 2005. 113–24.

Lenin, V. I. *Collected Works.* Trans. Joe Finebero and George Hanna. 45 vols. Vol. 5. Moscow: Progress, 1976.

Levinson, Brett. "Globalizing Paradigms, or, The Delayed State of Latin American Theory." *South Atlantic Quarterly* 106.1 (2007): 61–83.

———. "La responsabilidad de Lezama." *Revista Chilena de Literatura* 42 (1993): 101–5.

———. *Secondary Moderns: Mimesis, History, and Revolution in Lezama Lima's "American Expression."* Lewisburg, PA: Bucknell University Press, 1996.

———. "'Summas Críticas/Restas Erratas': Strange Notes on Lezama's Miscues." *Cuban Studies* 22 (1992): 195–218.

Lezama Lima, José. *Archivo de José Lezama Lima: Miscelánea.* Ed. Iván González Cruz. Madrid: Editorial Centro de Estudios Ramón Areces, 1998.

———. *Cartas a Eloísa y otra correspondencia.* Ed. José Triana. Madrid: Editorial Verbum, 1998.

———. "Encuesta de *Casa de las Américas*": *Por una politeratura: Literatura hispanoamericana e imaginación política.* By Enrico Mario Santí. Mexico City: Ediciones del equilibrista, 1997. 189–91.

———. *Imagen y posibilidad.* Ed. Cirio Bianchi Ross. 2nd. ed. Havana: Editorial Letras Cubanas, 1992.

———. *Lezama disperso.* Ed. Ciro Bianchi Ross. Havana: Ediciones Unión, 2009.

———. *La expresión americana.* 1957. Ed. Irlemar Chiampi. Mexico City: Fondo de Cultura Económica, 1993.

———. *Obras completas.* 2 vols. Vol. 2. Mexico City: Aguilar, 1977.

———. *Oppiano Licario.* Ed. César López. Madrid: Cátedra, 1989.

———. *Paradiso.* Ed. Eloísa Lezama Lima. Madrid: Cátedra, 1995.

———. *Paradiso (Archivos).* Ed. Cintio Vitier. Madrid: Colección Archivos; ALLCA, 1988.

———. *Poesía completa.* Ed. César López. Madrid: Alianza Editorial, 1999.

———. *Selections.* Trans. Thomas Christensen et al. Ed. Ernesto Livon-Grosman. Berkeley: University of California Press, 2005.

Lievesley, Geraldine. *The Cuban Revolution: Past, Present and Future Perspectives.* New York: Palgrave Macmillan, 2004.

Lomnitz, Claudio. "Time and Dependency in Latin America." *South Atlantic Quarterly* 111.2 (2012): 347–57.

López Junqué, Guillermo Fernando (Chinolope), and José Lezama Lima. *Una temporada en el ingenio.* Buenos Aires: Domingo Arcomano Editor, 2004.

Lukács, Georg. *History and Class Consciousness: Studies in Marxist Dialectics.* 1922. Trans. Rodney Livingstone. Cambridge: MIT Press, 1971.

Lupi, Juan Pablo. *Reading Anew: José Lezama Lima's Rhetorical Investigations*. Madrid: Iberoamericana Editorial Vervuert, 2012.

Lyotard, Jean-François. *The Inhuman: Reflections on Time*. Trans. Geoffrey Bennington and Rachel Bowlby. Stanford: Stanford University Press. 1988.

———. "Liminaire sur l'ouvrage d'Alain Badiou 'L'etre et l'evenement.'" *Le Cahier (Collège international de philosophie)* 8 (October 1989): 227–45.

Malabou, Catherine. *The Future of Hegel: Plasticity, Temporality, and Dialectic*. 1996. Trans. Lisabeth During. London: Routledge, 2005.

Marchart, Oliver. *Post-Foundational Political Thought: Political Difference in Nancy, Lefort, Badiou and Laclau*. Edinburgh: Edinburgh University Press, 2007.

Marshall, Peter. *Demanding the Impossible: A History of Anarchism*. Oakland, CA: PM, 2010.

Martí, José. *Obras completas*. 26 vols. Havana: Editorial de Ciencias Sociales, 1991.

———. *Poesía completa*. Ed. Carlos Javier Morales. Madrid: Alianza Editorial, 1995.

Masiello, Francine. "Rethinking Noecolonial Esthetics: Literature, Politics, and Intellectual Community in Cuba's *Revista de Avance*." *Latin American Research Review* 28.2 (1993): 3–31.

Molinero, Rita V. *José Lezama Lima, o, el hechizo de la búsqueda*. Madrid: Editorial Playor, 1989.

Moraña, Mabel. "Baroque/Neobaroque/Ultrabaroque: Disruptive Readings of Modernity." *Hispanic Baroques: Reading Cultures in Contexts*. Ed. Nicholas Spadaccini and Luis Martín-Estudillo. Nashville: Vanderbilt University Press, 2005. 241–82.

Moreiras, Alberto. *The Exhaustion of Difference: The Politics of Latin American Cultural Studies*. Durham: Duke University Press, 2001.

———. "Infrapolitical Literature: Hispanism and the Border." *CR: The New Centennial Review* 10.2 (2010): 183–203.

———. "Infrapolitics: The Project and Its Politics. Allegory and Denarrativization. A Note on Posthegemony." *Transmodernity: Journal of Peripheral Cultural Production of the Luso-Hispanic World* 5.1 (2015): 9–35.

———. *Línea de sombra: El no sujeto de lo político*. Santiago: Palinodia, 2006.

———. "Posthegemonía, o más allá del principio del placer." *alter/nativas* 1.1 (2013): 1–21.

———. *Tercer espacio: Literatura y duelo en América Latina*. Santiago: LOM Ediciones/Universidad Arcis, 1999.

Morley, Simon, ed. *The Sublime*. Cambridge: MIT Press, 2010.

Morrey, Douglas. "An Embarassment of Riches: Godard and the Aesthetics of Expenditure in *Le Rapport Darty*." *Formless: Ways In and Out of Form*. Ed. Patrick Crowley and Paul Hegarty. Oxford: Peter Lang, 2005. 229–37.

Murphy, Sinéad. "Forms of the 'Avant'-Garde." *Formless: Ways In and Out of Form*. Ed. Patrick Crowley and Paul Hegarty. Oxford: Peter Lang, 2005. 67–90.

Nancy, Jean-Luc. *Listening*. 2002. Trans. Charlotte Mandell. New York: Fordham University Press, 2007.

Newfield, Christopher. *The Emerson Effect: Individualism and Submission in America*. Chicago: University of Chicago Press, 1996.

Nietzsche, Friedrich. "The Birth of Tragedy." Trans. Walter Kaufmann. *Basic*

Writings of Nietzsche. 1872. Ed. Walter Kaufmann. New York: Random Hause, 1992. 1–144.

———. *The Birth of Tragedy and Other Writings*. 1872. Ed. Raymond Geuss and Ronald Speirs. Cambridge: Cambridge University Press, 1999.

Noys, Benjamin. *The Persistence of the Negative: A Critique of Contemporary Continental Philosophy*. Edinburgh: Edinburgh University Press, 2010.

Nuez, Iván de la. *La balsa perpetua: Soledad y conexiones de la cultura cubana*. Barcelona: Editorial Casiopea, 1998.

Nuño, Ana. *José Lezama Lima*. Barcelona: Ediciones Omega, 2001.

Osborne, Peter, and Éric Alliez. Introduction. *Spheres of Action: Art and Politics*. Ed. Osborne and Alliez. 7–17. Cambridge: MIT Press, 2013.

Padilla, Heberto. *Fuera de juego: Edición conmemorativa 1968–1998*. Miami: Ediciones Universal, 1998.

Pavón, Luis. *El tiempo y sus banderas*. Havana: Editorial Letras Cubanas, 1984.

Pellón, Gustavo. *José Lezama Lima's Joyful Vision: A Study of Paradiso and Other Prose Works*. Austin: University of Texas Press, 1989.

Pérez, Rolando. *Severo Sarduy and the Neo-Baroque Image of Thought in the Visual Arts*. West Lafayette, IN: Purdue University Press, 2012.

Pérez Firmat, Gustavo. "The Strut of the Centipede: José Lezama Lima and New World Exceptionalism." *Do the Americas Have a Common Literature?* Ed. Pérez Firmat. Durham, NC: Duke University Press, 1990. 316–32.

Perlongher, Néstor. *Prosa plebeya. Ensayos 1980–1992*. Ed. Christian Ferrer and Osvaldo Baigorria. Buenos Ares: Colihue, 2008.

Plato. *The Collected Dialogues of Plato*. Ed. Edith Hamilton and Huntington Cairns. Princeton: Princeton University Press, 1989.

Ponte, Antonio José. *El libro perdido de los origenistas*. Seville: Renacimiento, 2004.

———. "Lezama en los archivos de la Stasi." *Diario de Cuba* (2011). 10 Jun 2011. www.diariodecuba.com/cultura/1307701546_1423.html.

———. "La viga maestra, el tiempo." *La Habana Elegante* Spring-Summer 2006. www.habanaelegante.com/SpringSummer2006/Ronda.html.

———. *Villa Marista en plata: Arte, política, nuevas tecnologías*. Madrid: Editorial Colibrí, 2010.

Prentzas, G. S. *The Cuban Revolution*. New York: Chelsea House, 2012.

Prieto, Abel. "*Lo cubano en la poesía*: Relectura en los 90." *Obras completas: Lo cubano en la poesía*. By Cintio Vitier. 1958. Vol. 2. Havana: Editorial Letras Cubanas, 1998. 5–20.

Proust, Marcel. *Contre Sainte-Beuve; précédé de pastiches et mélanges; et suivi de essais et articles*. Ed. Pierre Clarac. Bibliothèque de la Pléiade. Paris: Gallimard, 1971.

Quiroga, José. *Cuban Palimpsests*. Minneapolis: University of Minnesota Press, 2005.

Rancière, Jacques. "The Aesthetic Revolution and its Outcomes." *New Left Review* 14 (Mar.–Apr. 2002): 133–51.

———. *The Politics of Aesthetics: The Distribution of the Sensible*. Trans. Gabriel Rockhill. New York: Continuum, 2004.

Richard, Nelly. "Latinoamérica y la Posmodernidad." 1994. *La Torre* April–June 1999, 367–78.

Richter, David F. *García Lorca at the Edge of Surrealism: The Aesthetics of Anguish*. Lanham, MD: Bucknell University Press, 2014.

Ricoeur, Paul. *Time and Narrative*. 3 vols. Trans. Kathleen McLaughlin and David Pellauer. Chicago: University of Chicago Press, 1984, 1985, 1988.

Risco, Enrique del. *Elogio de la levedad: Mitos nacionales cubanos y sus reescrituras literarias en el siglo XX*. Madrid: Editorial Colibrí, 2008.

Rodríguez Monegal, Emir. *Obra selecta*. Ed. Oscar Rodríguez Ortiz. Caracas: Biblioteca Ayachucho, 2003.

Rojas, Rafael. *El arte de la espera*. Madrid: Editorial Colibrí, 1998.

———. *El estante vacío: Literatura y política en Cuba*. Barcelona: Anagrama, 2009.

———. *Isla sin fin: Contribución a la crítica del nacionalismo cubano*. Miami: Ediciones Universal, 1998.

———. *La máquina del olvido: Mito, historia y poder en Cuba*. Mexice City: Taurus, 2012. Kindle ebook.

———. *Motivos de Anteo: Patria y nación en la historia intelectual de Cuba*. Madrid: Colibrí, 2008.

———. *Tumbas sin sosiego: Revolución, disidencia y exilio del intelectual cubano*. Barcelona: Anagrama, 2006.

Ronell, Avital. *Dictations: On Haunted Writing*. 1986. Urbana: University of Illinois Press, 2006.

Rotman, Brian. *Signifying Nothing: The Semiotics of Zero*. Stanford: Stanford University Press, 1993.

Roy, Joaquín. *The Cuban Revolution (1959–2009): Relations with Spain, the European Union, and the United States*. New York: Palgrave Macmillan, 2009.

Ryan, Angela. "'Shadows on a Cloudy Ground': The Poetics of the *Informe* in George Sand's *Un Hiver à Majorque*." *Formless: Ways In and Out of Form*. Ed. Patrick Crowley and Paul Hegarty. Oxford: Peter Lang, 2005. 139–60.

Safranski, Rüdiger. *Romanticismo: Una odisea del espíritu alemán*. 2007. Trans. Raúl Gabás. Barcelona: Tusquets, 2012.

Salgado, César A. *From Modernism to Neobaroque: Joyce and Lezama Lima*. Lewisburg, PA: Bucknell University Press; Cranbury, NJ: Associated University Presses, 2001.

San Juan, E., Jr. "Coleridge's 'The Eolian Harp' as Lyric Paradigm." *Personalist* 48 (1967): 77–88.

Santí, Enrico Mario. *Por una politeratura: Literatura hispanoamericana e imaginación política*. Mexico City: Consejo Nacional para la Cultura y las Artes; Ediciones el Equilibrista, 1997.

Santner, Eric L. *The Royal Remains: The People's Two Bodies and the Endgames of Sovereignty*. Chicago: University of Chicago Press, 2011.

Sarduy, Severo. *Obra completa*. Ed. Gustavo Guerrero and François Wahl. 2 vols. Vol. 2. Madrid: Galaxia Gutenberg, 1999.

Sartre, Jean Paul. *La nausée*. 1938. Paris: Gallimard, 1970.

Schiller, Friedrich. "Letter upon the Aesthetic Education of Man." 1794. www.fordham.edu/halsall/mod/schiller-education.asp.

Schlegel, Friedrich, and A. W. Schlegel. *Philosophical Fragments*. Minneapolis: University of Minnesota Press, 1991.

Schmitt, Carl. *Political Romanticism*. 1919. Trans. Guy Oaks. New Brunswick, NJ: Transaction, 2010.

————. *Political Theology: Four Chapters in the Theory of Sovereignty*. 1922. Trans. George Schwab. Chicago: University of Chicago Press, 2005.

Seife, Charles. *Zero: The Biography of a Dangerous Idea*. New York: Penguin, 2000.

Shelley, Percy Bysshe. *Shelley's Prose; or, The Trumpet of a Prophesy*. Ed. David Lee. New York: New Amsterdam, 1988.

Sloterdijk, Peter. *The Art of Philosophy: Wisdom as Practice*. Trans. Karen Margolis. New York: Columbia University Press, 2012.

Smith, Douglas. "Disfigurements: Bacon, Deleuze, Lynch and the Formless." *Formless: Ways In and Out of Form*. Ed. Patrick Crowley and Paul Hegarty. Oxford: Peter Lang, 2005. 215–28.

Tang, Chenxi. "From International Law to Romantic Poetics: Legal Historical Observations on Friedrich Schlegel." *Cuadernos de Letras* 27 (2010): 33–45. www.letras.ufrj.br/anglo_germanicas/cadernos/numeros/122010/textos/cl301220100chenxi.pdf%3E.

Tomba, Massimiliano. *Marx's Temporalities*. Trans. Peter D. Thomas and Sara R. Farris. Leiden: Brill, 2013.

Toop, David. *Ocean of Sound: Aether Talk, Ambient Sound and Imaginary Worlds*. 1995. London: Serpent's Tail, 2001.

Valéry, Paul. *The Collected Works of Paul Valéry*. Trans. David Paul. Ed. Jackson Mathews. Vol. 1, Princeton: Princeton University Press, 1971.

————. *Oeuvres*. Ed. Jean Hytier. Vol. 2. Paris: Pléiade, 1971.

Vessey, Mark. "From *Cursus* to *Ductus*: Figures of Writing in Western Late Antiquity." *European Literary Careers: The Author from Antiquity to the Renaissance*. Ed. Patrick Cheney and Frederick A. de Armas. Toronto: University of Toronto Press, 2002. 47–103.

————. "Reading Like Angels: Derrida and Augustine on the Book (for a History of Literature)." *Augustine and Postmodernism: Confessions and Circumfessions*. Ed. John D. Caputo and Michael J. Scanlon. Bloomington: Indiana University Press, 2005. 173–211.

Villacañas Berlanga, José Luis. "Acerca del tiempo apocalíptico en la Edad Media." *Isegoría* 37 (July–Dec. 2007): 81–96.

Vitier, Cintio. *Ese sol del mundo moral: Para una historia de la eticidad cubana*. Mexico City: Siglo XXI, 1975.

————. "Nemósine (Datos para una poética)." *Orígenes* 20 (1948): 29–41.

————. *Obras: Lo cubano en la poesía*. 1958. Vol. 2. Havana: Editorial Letras Cubanas, 1998.

————. *Para llegar a* Orígenes. Havana: Editorial Letras Cubanas, 1994.

————. "Resistance and Freedom." *boundary 2* 29.3 (2002): 247–52.

————. *Resistencia y libertad*. Havana: Unión, 1999.

Waite, Geoff. *Nietzsche's Corps/e: Aesthetics, Politics, Prophesy, or, The Spectacular Technoculture of Everyday Life*. Durham, NC: Duke University Press, 1996.

Walker, Stephen. "*Animate Form*: Architecture's Troublesome Claims to *Formlessness*." *Formless: Ways In and Out of Form*. Ed. Patrick Crowley and Paul Hegarty. Oxford: Peter Lang, 2005. 239–53.

West, Alan. *Tropics of History: Cuba Imagined*. Westport, CT: Bergin and Garvey, 1997.

Wood, David C. *The Deconstruction of Time*. Atlantic Highlands, NJ: Humanities Press International, 1989.

Xirau, Ramón. *Poesia y conocimiento: Borges, Lezama Lima, Octavio Paz*. Mexico City: Editorial J. Mortiz, 1978.

Zambrano, María, et al. *Cartas desde una soledad: Epistolario: María Zambrano, José Lezama Lima, María Luisa Bautista, José Ángel Valente*. Ed. Pepita Jiménez Carreras. Madrid: Verbum, 2008.

Index

Sara Guyer and Brian McGrath, series editors

Printed by Libri Plureos GmbH in Hamburg,
Germany

.